Lecture Notes
in Business Information Processing   105

Charles Møller
Sohail Chaudhry (Eds.)

Re-conceptualizing Enterprise Information Systems

5th IFIP WG 8.9 Working Conference, CONFENIS 2011
Aalborg, Denmark, October 16-18, 2011
Revised Selected Papers

 Springer

Volume Editors

Charles Møller
Aalborg University
Department of Business and Management
Aalborg, Denmark
E-mail: charles@production.aau.dk

Sohail Chaudhry
Villanova University
Department of Management and
Operations/International Business
Villanova, PA, USA
E-mail: sohail.chaudhry@villanova.edu

ISSN 1865-1348   e-ISSN 1865-1356
ISBN 978-3-642-28826-5   e-ISBN 978-3-642-28827-2
DOI 10.1007/978-3-642-28827-2
Springer Heidelberg Dordrecht London New York

Library of Congress Control Number: 2012933230

ACM Computing Classification (1998): J.1, H.4, H.3.5

Typesetting: Camera-ready by author, data conversion by Scientific Publishing Services, Chennai, India

Printed on acid-free paper

Springer is part of Springer Science+Business Media (www.springer.com)

Preface

In October, 2011, the 5th International Conference on Research and Practical Issues of Enterprise Information Systems (CONFENIS 2011) was held in Aalborg, Denmark. CONFENIS is a primary international event which provides an opportunity for enterprise information systems academicians and practitioners from around the world to gather, exchange ideas, and present original research and case studies in their fields.

CONFENIS 2011 was a joint effort of the Center for Industrial Production, Aalborg University, and the IFIP Working Group on Enterprise Information Systems (WG 8.9). IFIP WG 8.9 was inaugurated in 2006 and since then the field of EIS has matured and developed. The time has now come for a more rigid conceptualization and theorizing on EIS. Consequently the aim of the CONFENIS 2011 event was to re-conceptualize enterprise information systems (EIS) from a design perspective. Thus the conference had a particular interest in papers challenging the established concepts of enterprise information systems and focused on the design perspective.

Scientists and practitioners were invited to address the current topics in the area or the research frontier at this unique international forum. The conference attracted 103 submissions and from those submissions about 50 papers were presented at the conference.

At the conference around 80 researchers, practitioners and students from around the world gathered to discuss and to scrutinize the presented papers. A doctoral consortium on Design Science Research in Enterprise Information Systems was also held prior to the conference.

The papers represented a multitude of different perspectives and research methodologies. We selected 12 full papers, two keynotes, and one workshop paper for this volume that provide the reader with challenging ideas: (1) keynotes and workshops on EIS; (2) conceptualizing EIS; (3) emerging topics in EIS; (4) EIS as a service; and (5) new perspectives on EIS. Together these papers point toward the EIS of the future, which is the theme for the next CONFENIS: evolving toward more performance through transparency and agility.

We wish to recognize the entire organization behind the conference. The sponsors of the event and all the diligent work of the program committee, the track chairs, the organization committee and all of the authors for making this event possible.

Further we wish to convey our thanks to Ms. Pia Lund who before, during and after the conference managed to get everything together and working.

Enjoy reading the papers!

January 2012

Charles Møller
Sohail Chaudhry

Table of Contents

EIS as a Service

New Perspectives on EIS

Design of Enterprise Information Systems: Roots, Nature and New Approaches

Jens Ove Riis

Center for Industrial Production, Aalborg University, Fibigerstraede 16,
DK-9220 Aalborg, Denmark

Abstract. As a scientific and professional discipline, the design of enterprise systems has undergone an impressive development. Today, it has achieved a well-established practice with clearly defined phases, tasks and methods. However, enterprises are challenged by increased complexity in their operations, externally imposed uncertainties and even unforeseeable events. Dynamic global operations call for speedy and effective responses to change. As a consequence, enterprises are challenged to adopt new approaches.

In view of this call for probing new roads, it seems useful to examine the roots of design in an effort to re-interpret many of the original ideas. In this paper, we shall briefly study significant contributions to decision-making, systems theory, project management, behavioral science and organization theory, as well as business aspects.

To further understand the nature of design, we shall discuss key features, such as purposeful intent based on a stakeholder approach, situational approach, integration of subsystems, perspectives and time horizons, the design process, and modeling.

Recent developments, e.g. in design science, design thinking, managing as designing, participatory design, and agile project management, have provided a number of new approaches that in many ways represent answers to the challenges of increased uncertainty and complexity. This has led to the development of seven propositions:

- *Understanding mutual interplay of actors* – unveiling self-sustaining informal learning processes

- *Involving stakeholders* – clarifying who wants to see the design succeed

- *Accepting diversity* – working with several perspectives in parallel

- *Experimenting with new ideas* - establishing a playful and creative mood among participants

- *Enacting key features of new systems design* – involving users in testing a series of prototypes

- *Including the organizational context* – orchestrating a design effort in view of simultaneous development initiatives and top management's shifting agenda

C. Møller and S. Chaudhry (Eds.): CONFENIS 2011, LNBIP 105, pp. 1–28, 2012.
© IFIP International Federation for Information Processing 2012

- *Acknowledging that the intentions of an enterprise information system are realized through people* – An enterprise information system only sets the stage for organizational processes.

If adopted in an enterprise, management will be challenged to carry out design activities in a radically different way.

Keywords: Roots and nature of design, New approaches to design of enterprise information systems.

1   Challenges to Design of Enterprise Information Systems

As a scientific and professional discipline, design of enterprise information systems has undergone a remarkable development thanks to the impressive technological achievements and at the same time the acceptance by new users of new types of applications. Today, design of enterprise information systems is well established and widely recognized with a number of approaches and practices. It includes studies of management systems design as well as business processes.

However, significant changes are taking place in society and in companies resulting in new conditions for and requirements to designing new enterprise information systems. To mention some of them:

- Global markets and operations call for design and management of large networks of distribution and sourcing channels as well as of production plants. Companies are challenged to find a balance between branding global products and services and yet offering a local touch.

- Dynamic changes with many unforeseeable events stem from speedy technological development, the emergence of new markets, and political unrest in many parts of the world. This puts pressure on the stable parts of a company such as its organizational structure, management systems and competence profile. The time for reacting to change and for learning new skills has indeed become very short and calls for innovative responses.

- Complexity has increased, partly as a result of the above-mentioned trends. The technological development combined with competition has made it necessary to include knowledge into the design process at a high expertise level putting demands on organizing multi-disciplined teams. Furthermore, global product programs and management systems have become comprehensive with intricate interfaces. Many companies have experienced that it is not sufficient to focus on their own product program, and have engaged in developing complex business models that entail close cooperation with other companies in business networks.

These changes represent significant challenges and will call for radically new approaches to design of enterprise information systems. To be successfully implemented, they will also challenge management's attitude and managerial practice.

Instead of just extending and adjusting current practice, we believe that it is useful to go back to the roots of design in an effort to re-interpret many of the original ideas. This will be the subject of the next section. Furthermore, we shall identify the nature of design in search of new developments and ideas. Before presenting new approaches, we shall discuss common behavioral responses to uncertainty and complexity.

We shall focus on design of enterprise information systems, but shall draw on approaches and practice in other application areas. The notion of design has always been, and still is, related to the solving of complex tasks requiring a consorted effort of several disciplines. The results are not only concepts or drawings, but realized, physical facilities, products or systems. Often design is defined as a transformation from a set of functional properties (requirements) to structural properties [1].

The notion of design has successfully been applied to a wide spectrum of different areas. Several disciplines have made design a central element, such as architecture, engineering, computer science, software engineering, media, art design and information systems. As a consequence, it has become difficult to define a specific set of methods and approaches to constitute design as a scientific discipline. Each application area calls for a specific approach, design process and methods, as reflected in a large number of recent comprehensive textbooks, e.g. [2], [3], [4], [5], and [6].

To illustrate such differences:

- In design of engineered facilities, usually a contract is the starting point for a design effort, and it also serves as a reference through the design process. On the other hand, design of information systems most often is characterized by a rather vague idea of the final result among both end-users and designers.

- Many engineering design efforts are carried out by a rather small group of individuals, whereas the anchoring of a new information system in the organization is a key issue, for which reason user involvement from the very start of the design effort represents an important challenge.

- Visualization of the expected results of a design process may often be rather easy, because the physical artifact lends itself to an intuitive explanation of its proper use. In contrast, design of business processes aims at developing a new way in which people interact in realization of a business model. A prototype or the final design of such business processes can only be visualized by enacting them.

2   Roots of Design Theories

Design may be considered as a scientific and professional discipline in its own right, e.g. supported by [7]. Over the years, several names have been associated with design activities, such as engineering design, design science and design thinking. In the German speaking countries, "Konstruktion" has been widely used for engineering design. The notion of design also includes the more artistic shaping of forms in architecture and industrial design. The various names represent different facets and approaches to design, and we shall try to include them in our discussion. However, for practical purposes, in this paper we shall use the term design as an all-embracing name, justified or not, and maintain a broad view of different application areas. Nevertheless we shall primarily focus on design of enterprise information systems.

It is necessary to view design as a scientific discipline in a different way than traditional disciplines, because of its unique nature of integration. As we shall discuss in the next section, design is essentially concerned with integrating a number of different disciplines and perspectives in such a way that it leads to a useful product or system.

Over the years, design has embedded thinking, approaches, principles, and methods from a number of disciplines. In the following, we shall discuss some of the most significant disciplines.

Problem Solving and Decision-Making

Operations Research and Management Science have made a significant contribution to normative theories of decision-making. Not only were mathematical methods developed and applied, e.g. linear programming and queuing theory, but scholars such as Ackoff [8] and Churchman [9] proposed ways of using scientific thinking to address and solve complex problems. Whereas many OR-researchers increasingly focused on developing techniques and methods for solving well-defined problems, especially Ackoff was concerned with adopting a broad systems approach to defining and scoping a problem. Looking back on his career, he asserts that "it is much better to do the right thing wrong than the wrong thing right, because when errors are corrected it makes doing the wrong thing wronger, but the right thing righter" [10].

Herbert A. Simon [11] and others studied how a rational problem solving process could be modeled. This served in many ways as a foundation for computer programs that would solve complex problems, e.g. playing chess, and thus for the growing field of artificial intelligent systems. But Simon was also very much concerned with adopting a broad multi-disciplinary approach to solving complex problems, which he called designing.

A behavioral approach to decision-making was adopted by Cyert & March [12], and this led them to propose that individuals and groups in fact are satisficing rather than optimizing when they make decisions. A large number of studies of actual decision-making behavior has provided a useful supplement to the normative decision-making theories and methods, most prominently promoted by March, e.g. [13]. This approach also includes studies of decision-making in a political environment, e.g. [14].

Systems Theory

A system is commonly defined as "a collection of hardware, software, people, facilities, and procedures organized to accomplish some common objectives", cf. [3]. The idea of seeing a part of reality as a system with a clear distinction between what is included in the system and what is outside has had a remarkable influence on design, since it has allowed the breaking down of a complex system into a number of more manageable subsystems. It has also encouraged systems designers to look at the world outside the system, representing the environment in which the system eventually will operate. A key feature of systems theory is the working with two contrasting perspectives, respectively a holistic and an analytic approach [1]. A dialogue between these two perspectives is proposed by Riis [15].

In view of the very general nature of systems theory, the proposed typology of various systems by Bartalanffy [16] helped apply systems theory to a large number of different situations. The mutual interaction of parts of a system was studied by Forrester [17] and he developed a simulation program, Systems Dynamics, capable of identifying self-exciting processes and counter-intuitive behavior of systems when studied over time. Later on, this idea was used by Peter Senge to develop a significant contribution to organizational learning [18].

Cybernetics may be considered as a special part of systems theory concerned with steering (control) of systems [19]. With the technological development of computer capability, the underlying pursuit of automated decision-making has led to a renaissance of cybernetic thinking and the emergence of artificial intelligent systems and robots. However, attempts to also automate human thinking and behavior to its fullest extent have often neglected the fundamental difference between goal-seeking systems and purposeful systems (with human beings), as pointed out by Ackoff & Emery [20].

A significant contribution has been made in the area of developing principles and methods for modeling systems, e.g. automation systems as well as planning and control systems, for example IDEF, GRAI, and Systems Modeling Language.

Technical Disciplines

Each design effort draws on contributions from a number of different disciplines, for example IT, electronics, mechanics, city planning, materials, and production. Each discipline has its own concepts, theories, methods, as well as standards for good professional practice. To a large extent this determines the phases of a design process.

Not neglecting this technical and professional foundation for design, it is however a challenge to find a way of integrating them into a combined process, which may be considered the core of a design effort, to be discussed in the next section.

Project Management

The field of project management has experienced a development parallel to design. Essentially, project management is concerned with the planning and organization of an effort to solve complex tasks. This also includes design activities.

In the 70s and 80s, project management focused on engineered facilities as well as product and systems design. Due to its success of introducing a new mode of organizing and managing teams cutting across departmental boundaries of the traditional hierarchical organizational structure, project management was also applied to other types of tasks; for example the introduction of new management methods, e.g. Total Quality Management, Total Productive Maintenance, Lean Thinking, many of which stem from Japan.

In recent years, project management has been applied to organizational development in an effort to increase productivity, globalize its operation, and cooperate with other companies on new business models. This has drawn attention to the inclusion of behavioral elements, such as the creation of ownership, visualization of prototypes and dealing with stakeholders, cf. [21].

The parallel development of design and project management holds potential for a coordinated effort to exploit synergies.

Behavioral Science and Organization Theory

As mentioned above, decision-making has also been studied from a behavioral point of view leading to important insight into human behavior. This also includes studies of design processes, e.g. [22].

Scholars of design have also studied user involvement. For example, Binnekamp et al. [23] present a collaborative decision making process for architectural design, and Riis [15] elaborates on his experiences from a participatory approach to design of manufacturing visions.

Simon & March [24] introduced an interesting way of viewing an organization, namely as a coalition of interests among actors. When joining an organization, an actor is committed to make a contribution and, in return, expects to receive a reward. An organization may be formed and survive if a coalition of individuals or groups finds that it is in their common interest to make a number of complementary contributions with the prospect of being awarded. If for some reason or other the balance between contribution and reward is no longer favorable compared to what the individual can obtain elsewhere, he or she may seriously consider leaving the organization.

This view of an organization may also apply to a design effort because of the existence of a large number of stakeholders with legitimate interests in a design, cf. [3], [23], and [15]. We shall discuss this approach in further detail in the next section.

A recent development, Managing as Designing, views management as a design discipline, [25]. Interestingly, their effort, in effect, also discusses the reverse sentence, that design is about organizing and managing [26].

However, most studies of design appear only to a minor extent to have made use of the potential of creating synergies between a predominantly normative planning approach and a behavioral approach. Two different worlds exist in parallel with their own journals, professional societies and departments at universities, making it daring and risky to survive in the academic world, if one attempts to cross over the ditch and introduce a multi-disciplinary approach. The research teams behind Design Thinking at Stanford and Potsdam address this issue with significant results [22], and in the foreword of [7] optimism is expressed with respect to linking design science and behavioral science stronger in the years ahead.

Business Aspects

When a contract forms the basis of a design effort, it is supposed to include relevant aspects of how the final design will create business value. However, in many design efforts uncertainties require that the business value be defined gradually during the design process. In this way, business aspects become an integral part of designing, and not something that is given at the outset.

The literature on business strategy represents an extensive set of principles, models and methods. An excellent overview of different schools of thought is offered by Mintzberg et al. [27].

In recent years, the notion of business models has emerged, cf. [28]. Although in its infancy, it signifies an acknowledgement that business value no longer may be created only by launching a new product. Rather, after-sales service, logistics, distribution channels (e.g. via internet) offer new ways of successfully doing business. Dell is a prominent example of being innovative in its sales channels. We have also seen that new businesses have been established resting on a close cooperation between companies with different specialties, in this way forming a business network, e.g. [29].

In conclusion, design appears as an amalgamation of a number of scientific contributions. Several thinkers of the root of design offer inspiration for modern systems design, for example to seek to the basics of a problem in order to formulate the "right" problem, to be aware of counter-intuitive effects of complex systems, to adopt a broad view of systems design, and to take note of organizational and managerial issues.

3   The Nature of Design

With the different ways of applying design with approaches and methods suited to the designers' specific situation, it is difficult to point to a generally accepted set of methods. However, it is useful, and necessary, if one wants to maintain design as a scientific and professional discipline, to seek a common understanding of the nature of design. The following is an attempt to do so, with the hope that it may be considered as a contribution to a constructive discussion that eventually my lead to a better understanding of the nature of design.

3.1   Purposeful

Although often tacitly assumed, a design effort signifies a concerted effort to improve current and future conditions. It is not sufficient to discuss issues, understand and explain phenomena, and to make decisions. The effort should lead to actions. This approach is supported by Ackoff & Emery [20] who state that individuals perceive themselves as purposeful entities, acting in such a way that they intend to pursue a set of goals. This leads to a normative approach that is guided by an effort to develop a solution to a given task, it be a facility, a product or a system.

A normative approach does not preclude a descriptive approach. The former aims at assisting decision makers in formulating complex problems and in developing appropriate solutions, e.g. [8], [9]. The latter seeks to explain and understand interrelationships of a complex situation in an organization or in the interplay between several companies, e.g. [13] and [14]. As pointed out by Riis [1], Donaldson & Preston [30] and Hevner et al. [31], the two approaches are mutually supportive because the normative approach provides directions for descriptive analyses, and the descriptive approach offers insight and understanding of how appropriate decisions may be reached.

Of the many obstacles to reach a jointly shared decision, the presence of different perceptions and opinions among a number of actors is perhaps the most significant difficulty. A stakeholder model may provide a framework for dealing with this situation.

A Stakeholder Model

As mentioned by Buede [3], stakeholders define the objectives of a systems design. However, they often have conflicting interests and expectations. A stakeholder model considers a good design as one that is approved by a powerful coalition of stakeholders, not necessarily by all stakeholders. The stakeholder approach seeks to go beyond the specified goals of a design effort by asking who are actually interested in seeing the project realized, and who would be against it, and furthermore, what results do they expect in order that they will call the final design a success. As a consequence, the notion of an optimal design, derived by an algorithm, thus makes little sense.

An implication of the stakeholder model is that a design is viewed as a means for a stakeholder to achieve his/her own goals. It is still important to define goals of a design, because they will indicate to stakeholders what the expected outcome of the design process will be, and thus serve as an important way of aligning stakeholders' expectations.

A stakeholder analysis may include identification of important stakeholders, assessment of their desired contribution and perceived reward, and an estimation of their reaction and behavior, cf. [32] and [21].

The stakeholder model addresses the question of where goals of a design come from, and how robust they are with respect to achieving the necessary support. Since expectations of stakeholders may point in different directions, it is important to develop a common platform, against which each stakeholder can mirror his/her own situation. Instead of focusing only on involvement of end-users, the stakeholder model thus suggests that a broader group of stakeholders somehow be involved.

3.2   A Situational Approach – The Current Situation as Point of Departure

A design effort aims to develop a unique solution to a specific design task. As an implication, much attention should be given to capture the nature of the design task, including an analysis of the current and future situation and environment in which the final design should function.

Based on many years of conversation with industrial managers, our impression is that it is far easier to present and discuss a specific solution than to describe a design task. For this reason there is a need to be able to capture the nature of the design task in a more operational way.

Several methods are available for helping understand a design task. At the very general level, we have identified four different characteristics of a design task which identify the difficulty of dealing with a specific task [1]. They are

(i) *uncertainty*, e.g. to identify the nature of uncertainties in the face of commitments

(ii) *complexity*, e.g. to identify the origins of complexity (interaction of parts, complementary perspectives, or the need to combine different disciplines)

(iii) *repetition and learning*, e.g. to analyze if knowledge and experience exist from similar previous situations, and

(iv) *conflicts of interest*, e.g. to identify the nature of differences in perception, held belief and opinions among stakeholders.

The first two characteristics describe features of the task itself, while the third one captures characteristics of relationships between the design task and the individuals who are to be involved in the design effort, namely the extent to which they have prior knowledge and experience. The fourth characteristic describes interrelationships between individuals (actors).

Another way of capturing the design task is to identify the following three elements [33]:

- *External conditions*, originating from other parts of the enterprise and its environment,

- *Internal constraints*, such as current product portfolio, competences in the organization, and IT systems,

- *Specified objectives*, indicating management's decisions as to overall competitiveness.

Having been involved in developing production management systems in industrial companies for several decades, very often we have seen that there exists no deeper understanding of the overall interaction in an organization. Everybody is busy with his or her own task and takes little effort to discuss with colleagues how the overall processes are carried out. A rather simple method has been developed and widely used called a problem matrix, cf. [34] and [35]. At a workshop, each person or group of persons from the various sections and departments is asked to write down on yellow stickers the problems that he/she experiences. The stickers are placed on a wall under each section and grouped according to the type of problem. Usually, a distinction is made between problems imposed by other sections, internal problems, and problems sent on to other sections. By adding arrows connecting corresponding exported and imposed problems, it is possible to obtain a picture of the way in which sections are interacting. Tracing arrows may help identify and extract a handful of problem chains with self-exciting mechanisms. A common reaction from participants is a realization that, contrary to traditional theories of organization, no single person is to be blamed for the overall mal-functioning, but causes should be found in the interaction of persons.

Using Soft Systems Methodology to draw a Rich Picture is another approach to developing a mutual understanding of a complex situation with many actors [36].

There is much tacit knowledge underlying the complicated interaction of individuals, sections and departments when a business process is carried out, such as handling a customer order, developing a new product or system, or assuring quality and traceability of operations. To unveil this kind of knowledge, it is necessary to enact the pertinent business processes. Development of company-specific role-playing games represents a useful method for establishing a common understanding of the interplay around business processes, cf. [15].

Other methods exist for mapping business processes and value streams, cf. [37] and [38].

To conclude, more methods exist, but despite the ample assortment of methods for describing and analyzing the design tasks, there is a need to understand better why the development of a thorough understanding of current interplay in an organization attracts so little attention in theory and in practice.

3.3   Integration of Subsystems, Perspectives and Time Horizons

An engineered facility, product or system represents a whole that can function as a total of their interacting parts in accordance with desired performance. It is a challenging job to define a set of subsystems that will minimize their mutual interaction. This will also define where the most essential need for integrating subsystems is. A useful means of integration of subsystems is to develop and test prototypes even in the early phases of the design process, for example through simulation and enacting. This will enable the designers of each subsystem to study the interaction with other subsystems.

As already mentioned, many disciplines need to make a contribution and to be integrated in order to achieve a desired functionality. Furthermore, to understand the functioning of a design it should be studied from different perspectives.

Several authors have approached the issue of integrating disciplines and perspectives. Burbidge et al. [39] discuss integration inside a manufacturing function and across function boundaries. In particular, they note that consequences of decisions made in one function show up in other functions and thus call for an extra effort to integrate across functions.

Miles & Snow [40] use an adaptive cycle to describe how an industrial enterprise develops its corporate strategy. They define three generic problems: (i) the Entrepreneurial Problem, (ii) the Engineering Problem, and (iii) the Administrative Problem. By addressing each problem in turn, eventually the adaptive process will lead to a well-balanced strategy. Riis et al. [41] have proposed a model for creating a dialogue between professionals and experts as part of developing a manufacturing vision. The key element is a series of Question-and-Answer sessions in which a facilitator or a participant asks a question pertaining to another domain.

Although integration of subsystems, disciplines and perspectives has been acknowledged as an important issue, little attention has been given to the integration of time horizons. In general, with increased time horizon the degrees of freedom will become larger, primarily due to the fact that a design has to accept constraints imposed by existing systems, products and organization. A longer time horizon will allow for more options. It seems fair to claim that a given design is appropriate for a specific time horizon, and that a series of appropriate designs exists for a given set of time horizons.

On the one hand, a design should be able to solve short-term issues, and on the other hand it should not commit the users in such a way that the design will not be useful in the long run. Thus, a design should include future options and at the same time be useful in the shorter run. This represents a dilemma that may be called integration of time horizons.

The issue of integrating time horizons is related to the requirement of any organization to be able to handle both exploitation and exploration, cf. March [42]. As pointed out by Tushman & Reilly [43], this requires an ambidextrous organization that is capable of hosting multiple and internally inconsistent architectures, competencies and cultures. Along the same lines, Boer [44] and Hyland & Boer [45] have been concerned with combining incremental and radical innovation.

Especially because integration is a positive word with many good and beautiful connotations, it may be tempting to suggest that everything should be integrated. However, it is impossible to achieve this in practice. An important challenge, therefore, is to discuss where integration is needed, and where disintegration should be pursued. Lawrence & Lorsch [46] address this discussion and illustrate that integration along one dimension may, as a natural consequence, leads to disintegration elsewhere, for example to choose between an organizational structure based on divisions according to a product/market segmentation or functions. Hence, it is important to discuss the need for integration and to be innovative with respect to identifying where and how integration should and can be realized.

3.4   Design Process: Understand – Improve/Innovate - Apply

It is understandable that there is a keen interest in finding out how the design process should proceed. There seems to be wide-spread agreement on three generic phases: (1) to understand the present situation and future challenges, (2) to develop a solution that may represent an improvement of an existing design or a new design, and (3) to implement the design in order to achieve the desired functionality and business value, e.g. [22].

In the traditional engineering design, the first effort includes an analysis of the current situation and the perceived need or opportunity for designing a new system or product, i.e. the design task is defined by specifying the desirable end result, cf. for example [47], [48], [49] and [50]. This forms the starting point for seeking one or more alternative design proposals to choose from. With complex design tasks usually the design phase is divided into a conceptual design and a detailed design phase. A proposed design is evaluated and eventually selected and implemented.

At the more specific level, currently there seems to be a clash between a traditional model of design phases and new approaches, primarily stemming from a need to address uncertainties and unforeseeable events. In view of the uncertainty and complexity involved when a design effort is initiated, it is difficult at the outset to clearly define desired functional properties. On the other hand, analysis of a specific solution may serve as an inspiration for defining desired functional properties, i.e. using a circular design process as a sequential dialogue between exploring problem spaces (design task) and solution spaces (final design), cf. [1] and [51].

The traditional design process extends the three generic phases into five to eight phases, e.g. the seven stages in [2] and the Vee model described in [3]. The process is often seen as a one-way road where one phase is supposed to be completed before entering the next phase, indicated by the notion of "waterfall model". In a design environment where the design process is highly predictable, because of both a well-known outcome and experienced design teams, this linear design process seems appropriate. One of its advantages is that all decisions pertaining to a phase are taken before entering the next phase.

However, the waterfall model is difficult to apply when many unforeseeable changes occur during the design process, and when it is difficult to specify the desired functionality of the design in the early phases. Several new models have appeared in an attempt to seek new approaches.

A cascade model was used in an industrial company introducing a new manufacturing vision entailing a new plant layout, management system, and a new organization. In the first place, top management agreed on the introduction of production groups and outlined a conceptual solution. Then production planners were asked to develop a new production planning and control system. Through participation in a workshop, the foremen were asked to design a new plant layout for their own production group, and finally, operators were asked to take part in a role-playing game as an introduction to discussing and planning their daily operations. In this way members of the organization were gradually involved in developing (designing) parts of the new production system. This process created a high degree of ownership.

A parallel design process has been proposed by several persons. Hein & Andreasen [52] proposed a model called Integrated Product Development in which attention to sales/marketing, product design, and design of production system was carried out in parallel. The development of conceptual designs allowed for mutual adjustments and coordination between the three streams. Gudnason & Riis [53] proposed a similar parallel stream process for the design of production systems.

In recent years, the notion of agility has been introduced as a response to a wish to maintain maneuverability in the light of an increasingly dynamic and unforeseeable environment. Disenchanted with the current mode of software development, assuming that customers and users know in advance what they want, a group of American software developers met to develop a manifesto on agile software development. In many ways, the manifesto signals a distinctly different approach to software development by preferring individuals and interactions to formal processes, working software is valued more than comprehensive documentation, customer collaboration is preferred to contract negotiation, and responding to change is valued higher than following plans. Some of the fathers of the manifesto have themselves written books on agile software development, e.g. Beck [54] and Highsmith [55]. Hirschfeld et al. [56] extend agile development processes with elements from the Design Thinking approach to make them even stronger and apply them to geographically dispersed software development teams.

3.5   Modeling

Models and modeling play an important role in design. As a simplified picture of the real world intended to capture certain features, a model is an expression of our knowledge within a certain area by way of the relationships between variables and parameters of the model.

In design, models are used to express our understanding of the current and expected future situation, e.g. a mapping of current business processes, the structure and functioning of a proposed design, either in a preliminary prototype version or as the final design, and a picture of the situation after the new designed system has been implemented.

A model will play different roles. For example, an IDEF model may serve as a blue print for software engineers to design an IT system, or a role-playing game may explain in action how a new management system will function and affect their future working life. We cannot expect that a single model may serve both purposes. To the contrary, we need a broad spectrum of models.

As a consequence, in the design of enterprise information systems many different models are used. IDEF models typically represent the backbone of software systems design, e.g. [3], whereas more soft models are used in discussions with stakeholders, including end-users. For example, Edelman et al. [57] and Luebbe et al. [58] report on the development of TBPM (Tangible Business Process Models) that includes the use of LEGO bricks, yellow stickers and role-playing activities in a series of iterations (prototypes).

Also at the conceptual level we have used models, called production management concepts and manufacturing visions, to express how in principle manufacturing may take place in the future [59]. As part of a participatory approach such models have primarily been used to provide a commonly shared picture of a future daily life, as a basis for discussion and redesign. Emphasis is on telling a story.

4   Common Responses to Uncertainty and Complexity

Over the years, we have observed how companies have responded to uncertainty, unforeseeable events and complexity. Although not based on a specific statistical survey, we shall claim that the following characteristics represent typical reactions that are also reflected in several studies of organizational behavior.

Preoccupation with Daily Operations

In recent decades, Danish companies have demonstrated significant improvements in their operations in terms of better quality, shorter and more precise delivery times, and increased productivity. However, competing companies have managed to do the same.

On the other hand, very little focus has been placed on their capability to learn from daily operations, e.g. to extract patterns from the large amount of operational data that is available, and to systematize knowledge sharing. Furthermore, few companies are aware of increasing their capability of speedy and effective organizational changes. Most companies plunge into initiating major changes, as a response to external demand, without taking note of the organization's capability to change.

Different Degrees of Uncertainty Are Dealt with by the Same Organizational Form

In many of the planning situations involved in daily operations and in many design activities there is little room for including probability statements. Colleagues and external partners expect precise answers to delivery dates, to the manpower needed, to expected future sales of a new product, or to the scope of a new management system, etc. Even if the associated probability can be calculated or estimated, there are some fundamentally difficult issues related to making a decision under conditions of uncertainty. The organizational hierarchical structure, often with detailed performance indicators for each unit, does not encourage the inclusion of probability statements.

In addition, traditional organizational forms do not permit dealing with incidents that are not even perceived. Many organizational procedures and management systems are geared to provide only one response to coping with a broad spectrum of different situations.

Complexity Syndrome

We have often observed that managers and employees are not aware of the intricate interplay taking place in an organization whether it concerns daily operations or product development activities. Traditionally, a manager is supposed to display decisiveness and to be resolute. According to this role model of managers, action is preferred to contemplation. If lack of understanding of the complexity of a system is combined with the expected behavior of a manager, things may become critical. This combination may lead to what we call Complexity Syndrome, not understanding what is actually happening or the underlying behavioral mechanisms, and yet being obliged to make decisions pretending to have a comprehensive systems understanding. The results are a profusion of decisions demonstrating decisiveness, aimed at curing symptoms and not real causes.

Self-excited Complexity

Usually, complexity is considered a consequence of exogenously imposed factors, such as the call for a deeper knowledge of specialists, a multitude of markets with individual requests, and increased outsourcing of activities to international vendors. There are good reasons to take note of these factors. Sometimes, however, complexity is self-inflicted by the behavior of individuals, groups or the whole organization.

Consider a few examples:

- Engineers in new product development usually take professional pride in introducing the latest technology in their line of specialization. This often leads to advanced and complex solutions not necessarily in tune with the requirements of customers.

- Business processes are often adjusted to handle new situations, or improvements are implemented by adding new features. Over the years they may be dominated by a large number of exceptions and add-ons with few traces of the original business processes. Thus, the supporting systems and business processes themselves have become extra complex.

The examples show that complexity may increase inadvertently because of actions by individuals and groups.

Self-sustaining Learning Processes

An observation often made in a company is the existence of self-sustained learning processes that members of the organization are not aware of. One person responds to the activities of another person who in turn reacts to the first person's behavior. Due to informal and not intended feedback loops, such processes may, if not interrupted, lead to either a continuous deterioration or improvement of performance.

Consider two case examples:

- In an industrial company the production manager tried to cope with external changes by issuing many change orders, most often by shooting from the hip. It seemed that all externally imposed changes were sent directly on to production units without any filtering. The foremen were asked to make detailed planning in view of the workload and available capacity. In this way the production manager would be provided with valuable information about the actual and future work load and capacity which in turn would have made his own decisions more consistent. However, in the face of the many changes, the foremen eventually gave up trying to do thorough, detailed planning and resorted to ad-hoc planning decisions. Everybody was working hard and felt a constant pressure to deliver and to act. Sometimes a foreman would ask an operator to tear down the setting for one production order in the middle of its completion in order to do another production job. As a consequence, production performed poorly, and many frustrations indicated that the organization was working under great pressure.

- In an industrial company producing large equipment, the following result of mutual adjustments (organizational learning) could be observed. Sales often experienced that negotiations with customers would take longer time than first anticipated. Nevertheless, the delivery date for the equipment was kept. Engineering started their work when the contract was signed and wanted to do a good job. A master plan was prepared for the customer order, but this was not taken very seriously by engineering. Most often they delivered their detailed specifications late to purchasing and production. With the fixed delivery date, this led production to outsource part of the production processes and to move some of the assembly from being carried out in-house to on-site. As a result, extra costs were incurred, and both production and purchasing were working under great pressure. This was unfortunately not communicated to engineering. When asked about their opinion of the situation, they explained that their planning was guided by notice from production. "When they press us for the third time, we do our best to finish our job. And apparently they are very competent in production, because they always manage to deliver on time." So, engineering had learned that everything was working fine.

In some companies, such not intended inter-personal learning processes represent tacit knowledge and may constitute an essential part of the organization's core competence. On the other hand, they may also lead to overall poor performance and frustrations among organizational members, because they work hard but with unsatisfied results.

Similar learning processes have been presented sometimes under the label vicious and virtuous circles, e.g. [24], [1], [60], and [61].

5   New Approaches and Methods – Seven Propositions

Recent developments, e.g. in design science, design thinking, managing as designing, participatory design, and agile project management, have provided a number of new approaches that in many ways represent answers to the challenges of increased uncertainty and complexity, including the behavioral responses discussed in the previous section. This has given rise to developing seven propositions for systems design in such environments drawing on the recent developments, as well as the root and nature of design. For each proposition we shall give one or two illustrative case examples of how industrial enterprises have applied new approaches and methods.

Understanding Mutual Interplay of Actors – Unveiling Self-sustaining Informal Learning Processes

As discussed earlier, a key feature of design is the situational approach with emphasis on understanding the current situation. Several methods were mentioned, for example the problem matrix, soft systems methodology, and value stream mapping. Also prominent researchers representing the roots of design have pointed to the need to understand the often hidden dynamics of the present interplay in an enterprise, e.g. Forrester's disclosure of counter-intuitive effects of dynamic systems [17], and the need to ask unprejudiced questions in an effort to find the root of the problem, e.g. demonstrated by Ackoff [10].

- Case example: The manager of a small production firm once took time off from his busy daily schedule and filled-in elements of a problem matrix. This enabled him to identify a handful of problem chains with self-exciting elements. He could suddenly see that part of the complexity of managing the firm originated from his own reaction, and he was able to understand the behavior of his foremen.

- Case example: Prior to be engaged in a major turn-around in a midsize enterprise, a seminar was held with managers and employees from all sections. They were asked individually and in groups to identify what caused the greatest problems in their daily working life.

  Contrary to traditional organization theory according to which it is possible to find one individual who is responsible for a problem, the conclusion reached at the seminar was that the main cause of the problems was the mutual interplay between individuals and sections. It had created much complexity and prevented anybody to understand how the organization as a whole reacted, partly because of a number of self-sustaining vicious circles. This revelation created a strong support for and engagement in the subsequent organizational development initiative.

Involving Stakeholders – Clarifying Who Wants to See the Design Succeed

As mentioned earlier, stakeholders define the objectives of a systems design [3]. However, stakeholders often hold conflicting views and expectations. Therefore, the formulated objectives of a systems design may be viewed as an alignment of the wishes of a coalition of stakeholders. In view of the dynamics of systems design with internal and external changes, it is useful once in a while during the systems design project to ask who really wants to see the design project to be a success.

- Case example: In an enterprise information systems design project, the project manager spent much time in the beginning to involve stakeholders and to listen to their views and expectations. A set of objectives was formulated and gained general support. However when testing the conceptual design, the project manager realized that the formulated objectives could not be fully met. Through informal channels, stakeholders learned about the new situation and reacted negatively. The project manager felt very much alone with the project and decided to call stakeholders to a meeting to re-start the systems design project and ask them who actually wanted to stay on to see the project completed and under the new circumstances to discuss how this would be possible. In hindsight he would have wished that he had informed the stakeholders continuously to align their expectations to the real situation.

Accepting Diversity – Working with Several Perspectives in Parallel

Despite the fact that our environment increasingly becomes complex and difficult to comprehend, there is a tendency to ask for quick and simple answers. We are of the opinion that individuals and groups, in fact, are capable of dealing with complex and uncertain issues by drawing on their professional insight, intuition and common sense. But the organization in which they work rarely encourages this.

We shall propose a four-perspective model that encourages designers to adopt a multi-faceted view and thereby better be able to cope with complexity [62]. This is supported by Reimann & Schilke [63] who state that "design thinking can be thought of as a methodology for innovation that systematically integrates human, business, and technical factors in problem-forming, problem-solving, and design."

Each perspective represents a specific angle or point of view and depicts essential features of an enterprise information system.

1. The entrepreneurial perspective. This perspective looks at the utility of the design, its benefits and costs. Attention is focused on clarifying and visualizing the benefit of the effort, and on justifying the cost incurred.

2. The technical perspective. This perspective is concerned with satisfying the technical constraints and requirements necessary for completion of the design effort and attainment of its objectives. Attention is focused on the technical specification, work breakdown structure of technical activities, and interfaces with surrounding systems and installations.

3. The organizational perspective. This perspective focuses on the formal and informal working modes employed, and on the development of motivation and know-how among the persons to become involved in the planning and execution of the design effort.

4. The political perspective. This perspective looks at the stakeholders around the design effort and the potential and real conflicts of interests. Attention is focused on identifying relevant stakeholders and estimating their interests, their potential contribution to the project and their reward, as well as their attitudes, power and expected level of activities. The perspective is concerned with the question: Who wants to see the design completed and with which objectives?

Each perspective is based on a specific set of assumptions and focuses on a specific set of issues and phenomena. Theories and models explain interrelationships and indicate appropriate methods and procedures. Thus, each aspect enables us to draw a picture of the enterprise information system. In one sense it is limited by the angles used for viewing the initiative; in another sense the picture depicts the whole initiative. In the literature, a perspective often represents a certain school of thought; e.g. the entrepreneurial aspect reflects the business case and its strategic positioning and may draw on entrepreneurial strategic management schools providing methods for evaluating the market value of an initiative, cf. [27]. The organizational perspective offers conceptual ideas and theories for understanding the interaction between people involved in the initiative, and the political perspective provides a different kind of rationale based on power and influence.

The four perspectives will lead to four significantly different and complementary pictures. Instead of arguing which of the four perspectives gives the best and most correct picture of the enterprise information system and its situation, we shall maintain that we need all four perspectives to capture the essential features of a change task. However, their weight and importance may vary from one initiative to the other.

As pointed out by Lindberg et al. [51], design of IT systems tends to take place in an engineering expert world. The four-perspective model may be seen as an attempt to encourage the adoption of a broader view. In fact, the four-perspective model has been used in the initial stages of design processes to anticipate where most of the time and energy will be spent. To the surprise of many, the organizational and political perspective called for much attention. Also, in determining the rhythm of the design process, the four-perspective model has led to increased focus on creating ownership in the organization in which the new management system will be implemented, instead of letting technical issues be the primary determinant of the design process.

Dealing with one perspective may support the activities of another perspective. For example, a clear business case may encourage stakeholders to become more engaged and may set a scope and direction for technical issues. Also, involvement of members of the organization may stimulate development of innovative solutions.

- Case example: A group of specialists was engaged in developing a global logistic management and information system. They were very excited about their integrated model and were convinced that everybody would readily accept it. However, the group had not adopted an organizational perspective, because their model did not provide any answer to competences required and incentives. Nor did the group try to address issues like "what is in it for me?" Fortunately, the HR manager succeeded in changing the agenda to include the organizational perspective before the systems design was launched.

- Case example: An international company in the consumer goods industry once introduced the vision of "Direct Ordering" as a new way of fulfilling customers' orders. When a customer at a retailer shop had decided which product and which version to buy, the sales person would make an online request to the logistics department. A promised delivery date would be provided instantaneously, hopefully acceptable to the customer. A great effort in assembly and purchasing to reduce the through-put time had made it possible to guarantee a delivery time in Europe of less than five working days.

  However, the Direct Ordering project dragged on and lasted for almost a year longer than first anticipated. When inquiring about the reason, in hindsight the logistics manager explained that the project had been assigned to the IT department, not realizing that the project would also touch on political and organizational issues. The project would short-cut the communication and have a heavy impact on the jobs of national dealers, district warehouses and the central warehouse. The logistics manager conceded that the project would have been handled differently had it not been perceived purely as an IT project.

Experimenting with New Ideas - Establishing a Playful and Creative Mood among Participants

Based on our experience with developing and running company-specific games and with creative workshops in which elements of a manufacturing vision have been developed, we have seen how organizational members (shop stewards, operators, middle managers, engineering staff, etc.), under proper guidance, are willing to engage in exploring and playing with new ideas. If many persons from the organization are involved, a common understanding is developed of possible directions for the company, including the need for new business processes.

No commitments are necessarily made at this stage. However, if later on an opportunity occurs to move in a specific strategic direction, a broad awareness already exists of potentials and areas in need of attention.

We denote this playing with new ideas for probing into the future, adopted from Brown & Eisenhardt [64]. They talk of exploring unknowable environment located on the edge of chaos at the same time as managing stable operations. To realize this, a spectrum of different working modes is necessary calling for different competencies and managerial mindset. However, practice shows that many companies are reluctant to allow for a more differentiated view of its business processes, guidelines and control mechanisms. Based on student projects, Skogstad & Leifer [65] found that engineering designers gain important insight by experimentation, but managers and organizational procedures discourage them from a more playful exploration of innovative ideas.

We believe that a new managerial mindset and design practice is warranted to probe into the future by a participatory exploration of new business processes.

- Case example: During the process of developing a vision for a production unit that was responsible for making components important for the perception of uniqueness and quality of the products of an industrial enterprise, the relationship with suppliers was a key issue. Two different directions of a vision solution were defined

  o The enterprise employees to be stationed at suppliers to ensure quality
  o Suppliers' employees to be stationed with adequate machining tools at the enterprise to draw on their expertise.

Two groups explored how each of these ideas could be realized and were also asked to identify critical issues. Although the directions were different, it turned out that there were many overlaps in the solution elements and critical issues. This provided a sense of robustness and opened up for a more relaxed approach to the subsequent effort to define elements of the emerging manufacturing vision for the production unit. Thus, as the case example illustrates, it often spurs creativity to simultaneously explore two distinctly different directions.

Enacting Key Features of New Systems Design – Involving Users in Testing a Series of Prototypes

As already discussed, enterprise information systems support management and business processes that cut across organizational boundaries. Thereby it stimulates the mutual interplay between individuals, sections and departments. The planning process and information flow of the systems design may be tested by logical procedures and simulation, for example to study the robustness of a planning system. However, because the enterprise information system eventually will be used by individuals and groups through complex mutual interactions, a real test should involve an enactment of the proposed system among the future users. Following one of the principles of agile project management, a series of prototypes should be developed and tested by involving users.

- Case example: A young, small enterprise experienced a rather chaotic planning situation. An analysis showed that the production manager and planner themselves contributed to the stressful situation. A manufacturing vision was developed and visualized by making an analogy to the rules for traffic circles. In Denmark until the late 1980s traffic should give way to traffic coming from the right. As a result, with heavy traffic a circle would quickly be filled up. New rules for traffic circles were passed according to which the yielding rules were reversed giving way to traffic already in the circle. This meant that cars in traffic circle could easily drive through the traffic circle. Realizing that the company actually had followed the old traffic rules, the new manufacturing vision would follow the new rules cutting in-process inventory and through-put times.

  To test the proposed manufacturing vision, a simple company-specific game was developed with products and processes taken from the real company. It should last at most three hours, and all 45 employees should have an opportunity to play the game. One game run could accommodate 15 players. Methods for estimating the required capacity were introduced, and planning principles were tested. Not only did the participants engage themselves in trying out new ways of planning and executing production, but they were also taking active part in designing elements of the planning and information system.

Including the Organizational Context – Orchestrating a Design Effort in View of Simultaneous Development Initiatives and Top Management's Shifting Agenda

It may be tempting to focus on a single design effort, and much of the design literature does so. However, a survey of internal development initiatives suggested that organizational changes should also be looked at from a corporate point of view [66]. The study supported the observation that at any point in time a company has a wide spectrum of development initiatives in progress, including various design efforts, most of which are competing for the same resources and management attention. This suggests that a broader company-based view be adopted, and we have introduced the notion of orchestration. This indicates that management of internal development initiatives, similar to conducting an orchestra, is about harmonizing the activities of many interested parties into a concerted effort able to continuously shift the balance between actors and focal areas.

As an implication for design efforts, this suggests listening in on which development initiatives are in progress and considering if some of them may support the design effort and be joined into a coordinated development effort. Also, an opposite conclusion may have to be reached, that another initiative is in direct competition with the design project in question and ought to be discontinued.

- Case example: A production manager wanted to initiate a drastic shift in the assembly of his company producing complicated equipment for the graphic industry offered in many variations. Instead of parallel assembly lines producing batches of given products, in the new assembly system the final assembly should be carried out by single operators working in parallel under the motto "One operator should produce one finished product per day". With new short-term inventory located next to the assembly cells, a drastic reduction of through-put time was estimated providing the flexibility that sales had wanted for years.

  Well aware of the required change in mindset, the production manager decided to tie the introduction of the new assembly system to the introduction of a new, advanced product. Everybody knew that the new product was rather complicated and called for special attention. Therefore, it was easy to obtain support for the idea that the new product also deserved a new assembly system.

  The project manager in charge of the new assembly system decided to build a prototype of a production cell next to the existing assembly lines. In this way, operators had an opportunity to ask about the new mode of assembly as the cell was built and tested. This also gave rise to many discussions and proposals.

Acknowledging That the Intentions of an Enterprise Information System Are Realized through People – An Enterprise Information System Only Sets the Stage for Organizational Processes

If a traditional, linear design process is followed, management, the design group, stakeholders and users are asked to make decisions on a weak knowledge basis. It is difficult early in the design process to imagine how the information system will function and affect each stakeholder.

So, even if a participatory approach is adopted with involvement of stakeholders and users, it is necessary to pay attention to visualizing the need to change, the basic idea of a new systems design, and the way in which the new system will function.

In addition, an organizational learning approach will often provide a better background for deciding the scope and objectives of a systems design as well as solution elements. It may be tempting when designing a new enterprise information system to focus attention primarily on the systemic aspects of business processes and to neglect how the people who eventually will use the system will react. This suggests that systems design be viewed as a learning process with several versions, instead of a once-for-all design based on limited knowledge.

- Case example: Supported by external consultants, the production manager of an industrial company wanted to change the plant from a traditional plant lay-out with sections for each type of production process to a manufacturing flow plant. During workshops it became clear that some of the foremen actually had proposed similar ideas years ago, but without gaining any interest from management at that time. Further analysis indicated that, in fact, it was possible to form two flow lines with existing machining tools. Many questions were asked indicating some uncertainty with respect to the effect on the daily working life of foremen and operators. Therefore, instead of asking production engineers to spend a couple of years designing "optimal" flow lines, it was proposed quickly to form one of the two lines of the existing machines and allow for an experimental period in which everybody would be involved in design of the actual processes, procedures and working modes.

- Case example: Two decades ago, management in a large industrial company had been convinced that time was ripe for introducing a new CAD system. Much effort was spent on studying the various commercial systems available on the market, including a comparison of their features. Finally, a system was selected and the implementation process started. After one year, the engineer in charge of this process was asked what he would have done differently if he was given the opportunity to make the decision again. His reply was that a more experimental approach would have been better, giving some groups of employees a 3-D system, another group a 2½-D system, and a third group a 2-D system. This would have offered an opportunity for groups with different requirements to gain hands-on experience and an understanding of its potential, thus providing a broad and solid basis for planning the application of CAD in the near future. He admitted that very few in the organization at the time of the original decision had a good understanding of their needs and the capability of evaluating the various systems features.

The seven propositions do support one another and suggest a broader, multi-perspective approach to design, an effort to understand the current interplay of individuals, sections and departments in business processes, a participatory approach based on stakeholder analysis and user involvement, and an experimental approach to play with new ideas and directions.

6   Conclusion and Implications

In this paper we have focused on how to design enterprise information systems under condition of uncertainty, dynamics and complexity. It was argued that new approaches and methods were necessary. Instead of just extending current practice, we went back to the roots of design to look for inspiration. This led to a review of major contributions to decision-making, systems theory, project management, behavioral science and organization theory, as well as business aspects. Several thinkers of the root of design offer inspiration for modern systems design, for example to seek to the basics of a problem in order to formulate the "right" problem, to be aware of counter-intuitive effects of complex systems, to adopt a broad view of systems design, and to take note of organizational and managerial issues.

To further understand the nature of design, we discussed key features of design, such as purposeful intent based on a stakeholder approach, situational approach, integration of subsystems, perspectives and time horizons, the design process, and modeling.

Recent developments, e.g. in design science, design thinking, managing as designing, participatory design, and agile project management, have provided a number of new approaches that in many ways represent answers to the challenges of increased uncertainty and complexity. The paper concluded by presenting a number of propositions for systems design in such environments, drawing on recent developments, as well as the root and nature of design.

The propositions do support one another and suggest a broader, multi-perspective approach to design, an effort to understand the current interplay of individuals, sections and departments in business processes, a participatory approach based on stakeholder analysis and user involvement, and an experimental approach to play with new ideas and directions.

In its focus on challenges to cope with increased uncertainty and complexity, this paper has argued that new approaches and concepts need to be developed and adopted, in fact a re-conceptualization of enterprise information systems design. This has both theoretical and practical implications. The propositions point to new focal areas for research; for example increased research in the study of

- *Integration of subsystems, perspectives and time horizons.* As the technological development has led to an extensive specialization in all fields of society, a parallel development of means for integrating these areas of specialization has been widely neglected. This is, however, the essence of design, and research on integration needs to be strengthened, in tune with the origins of the design concept. As pointed out, research on integration should be seen as enacting an organizational process, including involvement of key stakeholders. This will require a new approach to design research. A better understanding and means of integration will have a significant impact on many areas of society far beyond design of enterprise information systems, due to the need for systemic and holistic thinking in view of the far-reaching specialization.
- *Coping with uncertainty.* We need more research on how to design enterprise information systems on the edge of chaos aimed at seeking a balance between exploiting existing means and approaches and exploring innovative solutions. This will require a multi-disciplinary effort to organize such a process at the same time as invariant patterns and elements are identified. It should also include the idea of postponing specific commitments to design solutions, yet securing a progressive design process.

Practical implications for design of enterprise information systems include increased focus on describing and understanding the corporate and organizational context in which the system will be developed and implemented, and on organizing the design process. It may be useful to join forces with the area of project management.

Practical implications do not only pertain to designers but also to managers. The new approaches will challenge management to carry out design activities in a radically different way. For example, the design team should be given more leverage to experiment with new ideas, and organizational learning should be allowed to take place before committing decisions are made, for example by developing a systems vision that would allow postponement of key decisions until participants have obtained a clearer picture and understanding of the main idea of the new systems design. Managers would also need to develop organizational forms that can stimulate a systemic and holistic approach in view of traditional organizational forces to specialize in separate organizational units. The case examples have illustrated that it is, in fact, possible to work with new approaches and methods.

References

1. Riis, J.O.: Design of Management Systems – An analytical approach. Akademisk Forlag, Copenhagen (1978)
2. Ambrose, G., Harris, P.: Design Thinking. AVA Publishing, Lausanne (2010)
3. Buede, D.M.: The Engineering Design of Systems: Models and Methods, 2nd edn. Wiley & Sons, New Jersey (2009)
4. Pahl, G., Beitz, W., Feldhusen, J., Grote, K.H.: Engineering Design – A Systematic Approach, 3rd edn. Springer, London (2007)
5. Keinonen, T., Takala, R.: Product Concept Design – A Review of the Conceptual Design of Products in Industry. Springer, Germany (2006)
6. Vaishnavi, V., Kuechler Jr., W.: Design Science Research Methods and Patterns – Innovating Information and Communication Technology. Auerbach Publications, Taylor & Francis Group (2008)
7. Hevner, A., Chatterjee, S.: Design Research in Information Systems – Theory and Practice. Springer, Heidelberg (2010)
8. Ackoff, R.A.: Scientific Method, optimizing applied research decisions. Wiley & Sons (1962)
9. Churchman, C.W.: Prediction and optimal decision. Prentice-Hall (1961)
10. Ackoff, R.L.: On passing through 80. Systemic Practice and Action Research 12(4), 425–430 (1999)
11. Simon, H.A.: The Sciences of the Artificial, 3rd edn. The MIT Press, Cambridge (1996)
12. Cyert, R.M., March, J.G.: A Behavioral Theory of the Firm. Blackwell, Oxford (1964)
13. March, J.G.: A Primer on Decision Making, How Decisions Happen. The Free Press (1994)
14. Lindblom, C.E.: The science of 'muddling through'. Public Administrative Review, 79–88 (1959)
15. Riis, J.O.: Models for Company Development – A participatory approach taking manufacturing as point of departure. Center for Industrial Production, Aalborg University (2009)
16. von Bertalanffy: General Systems Theory: Foundations, development, applications. Penguin, London (1973) (original American publication 1968)
17. Forrester, J.: Industrial dynamics. MIT Press, Cambridge (1961)
18. Senge, P.: The Fifth Discipline. Century Business (1993)

19. Wiener, N.: The Human use of Human Beings: Cybernetics and Society, revised edition. Houghton Mifflin, Boston (1954)
20. Ackoff, R.L., Emery, F.E.: On Purposeful Systems. Aldine-Atherton, Inc., Chicago (1972)
21. Mikkelsen, H., Riis, J.O.: Fundamentals of Project Management (in Danish: Grundbog i Projektledelse). Prodevo, 10th edn. An English summary (2010), http://www.prodevo.dk
22. Plattner, H., Meinel, C., Leifer, L. (eds.): Design Thinking: Understand – Improve – Apply. Springer, Heidelberg (2011)
23. Binnekamp, R., van Gunsteren, L.A., van Loon, P.-P.: Open Design, a Stakeholder-oriented Approach in Architecture, Urban Planning, and Project Management. IOS Press, Amsterdam (2006)
24. Simon, H.A., March, J.G.: Organizations. Wiley & Sons, New York (1958)
25. Richard Jr., J.B., Collopy, F. (eds.): Managing as Designing. Stanford University Press, Ca (2004)
26. Weick, K.: Rethinking Organizational Design. In: Richard Jr., J.B., Collopy, F. (eds.) Managing as Designing, pp. 36–53. Stanford University Press, Ca (2004)
27. Mintzberg, H., Ahlstrand, B., Lampel, J.: Strategy Safari, A Guided Tour Through the Wilds of Strategic Management. Prentice Hall Europe (1998)
28. Osterwalder, A., Pigneur, Y., Tucci, L.C.: Clarifyng business models: Origins, present, and future of the concept. Communications of AIS (16), 1–25 (2004)
29. Lindgren, P., Taran, Y., Boer, H.: From single firm to network based business model innovation. International Journal of Entrepreneurship and Innovation Management 12(2), 122–137 (2010)
30. Donaldson, T., Preston, L.E.: The stakeholder theory of the corporation: Concepts, evidence, and implications. Academy of Management Review 20(1), 65–91 (1995)
31. Hevner, A., March, S., Park, J., Ram, S.: Design science in information systems research. MIS Quarterly 28(1), 75–105 (2004)
32. D'Herbemont, O., César, B.: Managing Sensitive Project. MacMillan Press (1998)
33. Riis, J.O.: The use of production management concepts in the design of production management systems. International Journal of Production Planning & Control 1(1), 45–52 (1990)
34. Johansen, J., Mitens, L.: Methods for Analysis and Diagnosis of Production Management (in Danish). Aalborg University & Technical University of Denmark (1986)
35. Riis, J.O.: Situational production management: a practical theory for the development and application of production management. International Journal of Production Planning & Control 5(3), 240–252 (1994)
36. Checkland, P., Scholes, J.: Soft Systems Methodology in Action. John Wiley & Sons (1999)
37. Rentzhog, O.: Process orientation – A foundation for modern management (in Danish) Studentlitteratur (2000)
38. Bicheno, J.: The Lean Toolbox. Piscie Books, Buckingham (2000)
39. Burbidge, J.L., Falster, P., Riis, J.O., Svendsen, O.: Integration in Manufacturing. Computers in Industry 9, 297–305 (1987)
40. Miles, R.E., Snow, C.C.: Organizational Strategy, Structure and Process. McGraw-Hill, New York (1978)
41. Riis, J.O., Dukovska-Popovska, I., Johansen, J.: Participation and dialogue in strategic manufacturing development. Production Planning and Control 17(2), 176–188 (2006)
42. March, J.G.: Exploration and Exploitation in Organizational Learning. Organization Science 2, 71–87 (1991)

43. Tushman, M.L., O'Reilly III, C.A.: Ambidextrous organizations: managing evolutionary and revolutionary change. California Management Review 38(4) (1996)
44. Boer, H.: And [Jethro] said.. Learning: the link between strategy, innovation and production, Inaugural lecture. Center for Industrial Production, Aalborg University (2001)
45. Hyland, P., Boer, H.: A continuous innovation framework: Some thoughts for consideration. In: Proceedings of the 7th International CINet Conference 2006: CI and Sustainability - Designing the Road Ahead, pp. 389–400. University of Brighton, CENTRIM (2006)
46. Lawrence, P., Lorch, J.: Organization and Environment. Division of Research, Graduate School of Business Administration. Harvard University (1967)
47. Asimow, M.: Introduction to Design. Prentice Hall (1962)
48. Krick, E.: An Introduction to Engineering and Engineering Design, 2nd edn. J. Wiley (1969)
49. Pressman, R.S.: Software Engineering - A Practitioner's Approach, 5th edn. McGraw-Hill, London (2000)
50. Sydenham, P.: Systems Approach to Engineering Design. Artech House, Inc., Norwood (2003)
51. Lindberg, T., Meinel, C., Wagner, R.: Design Thinking: A Fruitful Concept for IT Development? In: Plattner, H., Meinel, C., Leifer, L. (eds.) Design Thinking: Understand – Improve – Apply, pp. 3–20. Springer, Heidelberg (2011)
52. Hein, L., Andreasen, M.M.: Integrated Product Development (in Danish). The Confederation of Danish Industries (1985)
53. Gudnason, C.H., Riis, J.O.: Manufacturing Strategy. OMEGA 12(6), 547–555 (1984)
54. Beck, K.: Extreme Programming Explained. Addison-Wesley (2000)
55. Highsmith, J.: Agile Project Management – Creating Innovative Products. Pearson Education (2004)
56. Hirschfeld, R., Steinert, B., Lincke, J.: Agile Software Development in Virtual Collaboration Environments. In: Plattner, H., Meinel, C., Leifer, L. (eds.) Design Thinking: Understand – Improve – Apply, pp. 197–218. Springer, Heidelberg (2011)
57. Edelmann, J., Currano, R.: Re-representation: Affordances of Shared Models in Team-Based Design. In: Plattner, H., Meinel, C., Leifer, L. (eds.) Design Thinking: Understand – Improve – Apply, pp. 61–79. Springer, Heidelberg (2011)
58. Luebbe, A., Weske, M.: Bringing Design Thinking to Business Process Modeling. In: Plattner, H., Meinel, C., Leifer, L. (eds.) Design Thinking: Understand – Improve – Apply, pp. 181–195. Springer, Heidelberg (2011)
59. Riis, J.O., Johansen, J.: Developing a manufacturing vision. Production Planning and Control 14(4), 327–337 (2003)
60. Argyris, C.: On Organizational Learning. Blackwell, Oxford (1992)
61. March, J.G., Levitt, B.: Organizational Learning. Annual Review of Sociology 14, 319–340 (1988)
62. Riis, J.O., Mikkelsen, H.: Capturing the nature of a project in the initial phase - Early identification of focal areas. International Journal of Project Management 3(1), 18–22 (1997)
63. Reimann, M., Schilke, O.: Product Differentiation by Aesthetic and Creative Design: A Psychological and Neural Framework of Design Thinking. In: Plattner, H., Meinel, C., Leifer, L. (eds.) Design Thinking: Understand – Improve – Apply, pp. 45–60. Springer, Heidelberg (2011)

64. Brown, S.L., Eisenhardt, K.M.: The Art of Continuous Change: Linking Complexity Theory and Time-paced Evolution in Relentlessly Shifting Organizations. Administrative Science Quarterly 42, 1–34 (1997)
65. Skogstad, P., Leifer, L.: A Unified Innovation Process Model for Engineering Designers and Managers. In: Plattner, H., Meinel, C., Leifer, L. (eds.) Design Thinking: Understand – Improve – Apply, pp. 19–44. Springer, Heidelberg (2011)
66. Mikkelsen, H.: Managing the Myriad of Projects (in Danish: Ledelse af Projektmylderet). Børsens Forlag, Copenhagen (2005)

Using Empirical Foundations for Designing EIS Solutions

Robert Winter

Institute of Information Management, University of St. Gallen, Mueller-Friedberg-Str. 8,
9000 St. Gallen, Switzerland
Robert.Winter@unisg.ch

Abstract. From a design science research perspective, enterprise information systems (EIS) are understood as artifacts intended to support organizations in achieving certain goals. Proper EIS design needs not only to be based on solid general foundations ('kernel theories') and valid construction processes, but also should incorporate domain related experience and expertise. One important aspect is to understand which design goals and context factors have lead to which variations in existing solutions in the real world. Another aspect is to understand which design variations can be empirically related to which design goals, and to derive respective design actions. Using examples from enterprise architecture management and process performance management for illustration purposes, we show that existing variations of EIS solutions can be transparently explained and that innovative EIS solutions can be systematically constructed.

1   Introduction

According to Hevner et al. [1] two scientific approaches characterize much of the research in the information systems discipline, namely *behavioral science* and *design science*. Behavioral science addresses research through the *development* and *justification* of theories that explain or predict existing phenomena in a domain. Design science addresses research through the *building* and *evaluation* of innovative artifacts that are intended to solve important, relevant design problems in the domain. Both types of research reflect the respective foundations and methodologies in order to provide guidance for researchers. The knowledge base, as defined in the information systems research framework of Hevner [2] interfaces these approaches. It is composed of foundations and methodologies.

In the wide field of information systems, being concerned with people, task and technology [cf. e.g. 3, 4], different design science research approaches have been proposed over the years. Such approaches aim at constructing and testing various kinds of designed artifacts as solutions to certain classes of design problems in organizations. Since design proposals are often widely varying with regard to foundations, goals, and processes, Hevner [2] introduced a general framework comprising three cycles – relevance, design and rigor cycles –, which should be present and clearly identifiable in every piece of design science research (see Fig. 1).

In the *relevance cycle* the requirements of the problem domain are defined and introduced into the design process. Additionally, the proposed artifacts are established

C. Møller and S. Chaudhry (Eds.): CONFENIS 2011, LNBIP 105, pp. 29–44, 2012.
© IFIP International Federation for Information Processing 2012

in the environment (e.g. by field-testing) in order to demonstrate their problem solving utility. In the *rigor cycle* not only scientific theories and methods as well as existing design products and processes, but also domain experience and expertise are introduced into the design process. Additionally, new generalizable knowledge derived from the design process is added to the knowledge base for reuse. The *design cycle*, which is essentially a solution search procedure, iterates between the core activities of constructing and evaluating design artifacts.

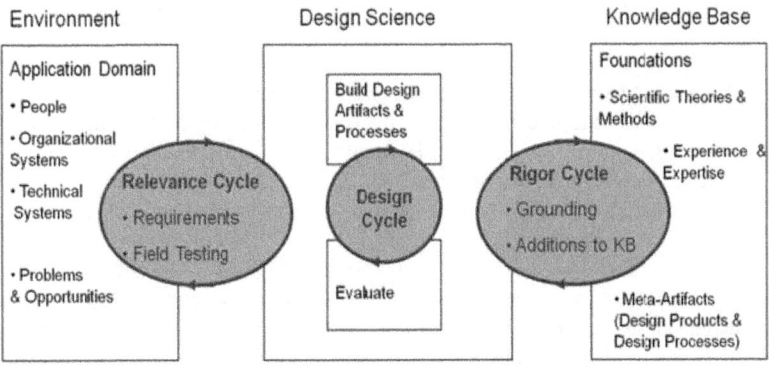

Fig. 1. Design Science Research Cycles [2]

The design and relevance cycles have been subject to many studies and discussions from the early years of design science research on. With more attention being directed to the rigor cycle recently, in particular the role of various types of theories has been investigated [e.g. 5, 6, 7, 8]. Domain related experience and expertise are however often overlooked in the methodological reflection of design science research. The reason might be that, in contrast to theories, methods/processes and other meta-artifacts, domain related knowledge is diverse and not only hard to generalize, but also difficult to obtain and make reusable.

This paper therefore focuses on the role of domain related experience and expertise for design science research in general and for the design of enterprise information systems (EIS) in particular. The goal is to investigate the role and generalizability of domain knowledge for the assessment of existing solutions, the construction of to-be solutions and the transformation process. The relevant foundational concepts are introduced in section 2. For the assessment phase, we present an approach that analyzes existing real-world solutions in a domain to identify possible design goals and relevant context factors for that domain (section 3). For the construction phase, we present an approach that relates design goals in a domain to variations of the respective to-be artifacts and that derives respective design actions (section 4). Examples from enterprise architecture management and process performance management are used in sections 3 and 4 to illustrate that existing variations of EIS solutions can be transparently explained and that innovative EIS solutions can be systematically constructed. The paper is concluded by a discussion and an outlook on further research in this field.

2   Foundational Concepts

Common design artifacts produced by design science researchers in the information systems field are *constructs, models, methods* and *instantiations* [9]. Hevner et al. describe these artifacts as follow: "*Constructs* provide the language in which problems and solutions are defined and communicated [...]. *Models* use constructs to represent a real world situation – the design problem and its solution space [...]. *Methods* define processes. They provide guidance on how to solve problems, that is, how to search the solution space. [...] *Instantiations* show that constructs, models, or methods can be implemented in a working system." [1].

It is important to understand the artifact types of design science research in the information system field not as separate concepts, but as an interdependent system. Winter [10] refers to Chmielewicz's [11] conceptualization of research in social sciences, which may serve as a foundation to explain such dependencies. Chmielewicz differentiates between *ontological facts, theoretical statements, technological statements,* and *normative statements.* These concepts are represented by the artifact types foundational concepts, cause-effect relations, means-ends relations and justifications (for choosing certain goals or preferring certain means to pursue a goal). Chmielewicz's concept system can therefore be easily matched to design science research artifacts.

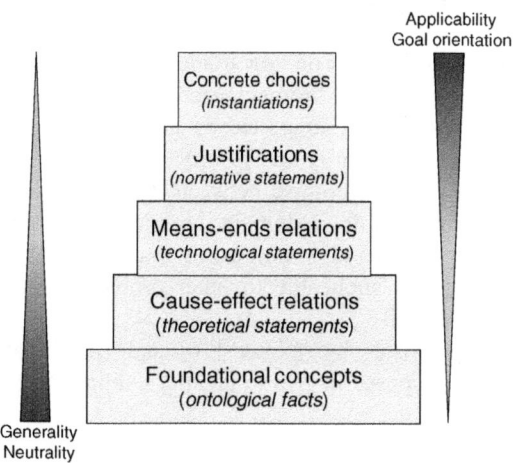

Fig. 2. The interdependent system of concepts for design research

To illustrate the relationships between the concepts and artifacts, the pyramid metaphor can be used: Applicable ontology and meta models define constructs and constitute the foundation for formulating theories for analysis, explanation and/or prediction. Together with domain experience and expertise, valid explanatory and/or predictive theories then constitute the foundation for constructing effective technologies (e.g. reference models or methods). Since alternative means might be effective for the same ends, normative statements are needed to justify which goals to choose and which technologies to apply - Chmielewicz designates this layer "philosophy". At the top of the concept pyramid, concrete goal and technology choices lead to actual design instantiations. Fig. 2 illustrates the concept pyramid.

It is obvious that the presented concepts are fundamentally different regarding the extent they embody certain design goals and regarding their problem-solving power for specific design problems. Goal orientation (vs. neutrality) is strongly related to applicability (vs. generality): Although design artifacts of every type (except instantiations) can be defined on different levels of generality, the typical generality decreases when moving up in the concept hierarchy. In addition to utility, generality is an important quality of design science research artifacts [1]. Baskerville et al. [12] demand a design science research artifact to "represent [.] a general solution to a class of problems."

In addition to applicability / goal orientation vs. generality / neutrality, design artifacts can be classified regarding the problem solution phase they support: While the same system of foundational concepts should be used both in the assessment and construction phases of a problem solution to ensure consistency, instantiations always relates to a specific phase. Certain theories might be used to explain assessment as well as justify design, while others are specific to one of these phases. Since the goals of assessment and construction are different, different technologies will be relevant, and different (yet coherent) justifications will be needed.

3   Assessment: Identifying Contingencies of Existing Solutions

There is some, but not much, work on how to identify contingencies in design science research. For method engineering, "project size", "number of stakeholder groups" or "applied technology" have been suggested as general contingencies [e.g. 13, 14]. Other authors recommend to identify and specify situations individually on a case-by-case basis [e.g. 15]. As a compromise between these positions, we recommend to identify specific contingencies for a domain, i.e. a class of similar design problems, by analyzing existing real-world solutions in that domain. This analysis is not restricted to methods; It is applicable to other problem solutions like (reference) models and constructs as well.

Based on earlier proposals by Winter [16] and Bucher and Klesse [17], the following procedure is proposed in [18] to identify contingencies of existing problem solutions:

Step 1: Preliminary Specification of the Design Problem Class

A rough idea about the delineation of the design problem class is developed. Results of this step are definitions, a description of the system under analysis and ideas about design goals for the respective class of design problems.

After a while, EIS management practice develops a common understanding about the scope of relevant artifacts and about useful design goals for such problem classes. In the remainder of this section, enterprise architecture management (EAM) is used as an exemplary design problem class. In EAM, a considerable amount of consensus exists regarding which artifacts and relationships should be addressed by that approach. Furthermore, design goals like transparency, consistency, simplification or flexibility are established.

Step 2: Identification of Contingency Factor Candidates

A literature analysis is conducted in order to identify contingency factor candidates for the respective class of design problems, i.e. factors which might have influence on how such design problems are solved in practice.

For EAM, such an analysis yields factors like 'EAM's main sponsor is IT or business', 'EAM's main deliverable is maps, analyses or project support', 'EAM's main goal is transparency, consistency, simplification, or flexibility', or 'EAM's role is active or passive'.

Step 3: Field Study

A field study is conducted in order to analyze how design solutions for this class of design problems in practice are actually related to which contingencies. Using principal component analysis on the field study data, the list of potential contingency factor candidates from step 2 is reduced and aggregated into a smaller set of relevant "design factors". Design factors are usually aggregates of several relevant contingency factors and therefore need to be semantically interpreted.

For EAM, principle component analysis on EAM practice solutions yielded eight design factors (like IT operations support, integrative role, business strategy support, or design impact) which aggregate 54 statistically relevant contingencies. E.g., the design factor 'integrative role of EAM' aggregates the contingencies 'EAM takes place in an interdisciplinary team', 'EAM team and business departments continuously exchange information (e.g. in architecture boards)' and 'EAM team and IT departments continuously exchange information (e.g. in architecture boards)'.

Step 4: Redefinition of the Design Problem Class

Every surveyed real-world solution in the domain can be understood as a point in a multi-dimensional coordinate system where every dimension corresponds to a design factor. The design problem class now should be redefined by specifying value ranges for the design factors identified in step 3. This means that "outlier" solutions are excluded from further analysis in order to ensure a useful degree of solution homogeneity.

Step 5: Solution Similarity Analysis

Now ultrametric distances can be computed that represent the similarity (or dissimilarity) of the relevant solutions. Metrics are usually based on Euclidian distance. The observations and their distances can be visualized by a dendrogram-like tree graph. The (dis)similarity of two design solutions corresponds to the generality level of their linkage. If two design solutions are very similar, their linkage is represented on a low level of generality. If two design solutions are very different, their linkage is represented on a very high level of generality.

Figure 3 exhibits a tree graph of 119 observed EAM 'cases' (vertical axis) in 94 different companies. Their ultrametric distances are represented on the horizontal axis. Case 72 and case 73 are very similar, but differ significantly from cases 6, 12 and 104. The generalization of these five cases (B) is still quite homogeneous compared to the overall, "one size fits all" EAM generalization (A).

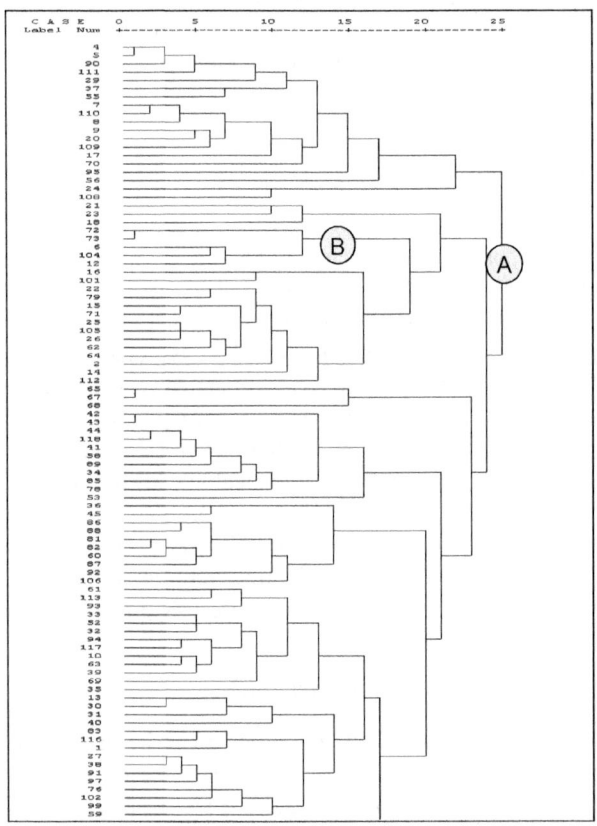

Fig. 3. Visualization of similarities of observed EAM solutions in companies

Step 6: Identification of Representative Design Solutions

In order to not only visualize, but characterize generic design solutions in a domain, a clustering algorithm can be applied to the observation data. By agglomerative clustering, solutions can be specified at any generality level between "full detail" (i.e. one cluster per original observation) and "one size fits all" (i.e. one generic solution description for the entire design problem class). By analyzing the clustering error in relation to the number of clusters, an optimal level of generality (i.e. an optimal number of clusters) can be determined.

For the EAM approaches in 94 companies, the optimal number of clusters is three [19]. This means that, for this observation, three different EAM 'approaches' with specific characteristics should be differentiated (see Fig. 4). With more and broader surveys, this kind of findings might be generalized to the respective design problem domain in general.

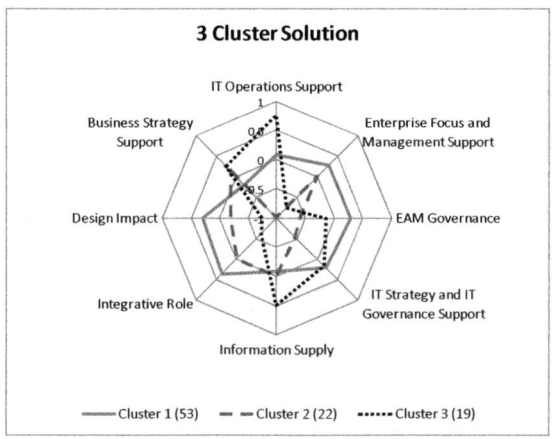

Fig. 4. Problem class decomposition into design situations [19]

Step 7: Specification of Design Situations

For the level of solution description generality chosen in step 6, each cluster represents one design situation. The situations should not only be defined formally (i.e. by specifying value ranges of the respective design factors), but also should be interpreted semantically ("design problem types").

The three EAM clusters differ in particular with regard to their values for the design factors 'IT operations support', 'integrative role', 'design impact', 'enterprise-wide focus' and 'IT strategy support'. These differences are used to characterize one cluster as 'balanced, active EAM', one as 'business analysis' and one as 'IT focused, passive EAM' [19]. In order to interpret the design situations, the cluster centroids have to be analyzed. These can be identified by the mean factor values within each cluster. The mean factor values for each cluster are depicted by the net diagram in fig. 4. The clusters can then be described as follows: [19]

Design situation 1: Balanced, Active EAM
Cluster 1 (solid line in fig. 4) presents a rather balanced approach to EAM. For most factors this cluster shows the highest or at least average values. Especially the similar values for the factors 'IT operations support' and 'enterprise-wide focus' allow the conclusion that organizations within this cluster focus neither on IT support nor on management support. In contrast to the other clusters, the high support of 'IT

operations management', 'IT strategy' as well as the focus on 'design impact', 'integrative role' and 'EAM governance' argue for a high degree of integration within the organization. In particular the values for 'design impact', 'integrative role' and 'EAM governance' are by far the highest between all three clusters. It can therefore be presumed that these organizations have a rather high level of maturity in their EAM approach. It should be noted that this cluster includes 53 out of 94 organizations, which lead to the supposition that this cluster represents a 'mainstream' approach.

Design Situation 2: Business Analysis
The second cluster (dashed line in fig. 4) groups 22 organizations that have an apparent focus on business support in their EAM approach. The factors 'IT operations support' as well as 'IT strategy and IT governance support' are clearly assigned with comparatively low values. Comparing the mean factor values to those of cluster 1, the overall low values imply that the organizations in this cluster do not show a high degree of EAM implementation in any dimension. Two conclusions can be derived from this fact: First, the organizations could have decided to apply a minimalist EAM approach, focusing on management support without putting resources in EAM governance or an active role of EAM. Second, the introduction of EAM could only recently be initiated by management and is not very mature yet. For both cases, literature suggests that a sustainable EAM approach can only be established by realizing an effective EAM governance [20, 21].

Design Situation 3: IT Focused, Passive Approach
Organizations assigned to this cluster (dotted line in fig. 4) clearly emphasize the use of EAM for IT operations as well as the information supply by EAM. In contrast, values for 'management support' are by far the lowest compared to the other clusters. As the factors 'design impact' as well as 'integrative role' are not focused by this approach, it can be described as a passive approach that is most probably realized very locally within the organization. Obviously, this small cluster which includes only 19 of the 94 organizations represents a specialized, IT-centered EAM approach that primarily takes a documentation role. It can be presumed that the EAM approach was initiated by IT departments and has not been disseminated throughout the organization yet.

Examples like [22, 23, 24, 25, 26] show that, for typical design problem classes, between four and eight design factors can be identified which explain the variance of the observed design solutions sufficiently. These design factors span up a solution room where between three and six design situations can be differentiated.

4   Design: Relating Design Goals to Solution Variations

While identifying design situations is of utmost importance to understand the design problem class, the construction of innovative, useful solutions as the core phase of design science research has not been covered yet.

In contrast to as-is solutions that exist in the real world and can be analyzed using field studies or other methods in a descriptive way, to-be solutions need to be constructed and have a prescriptive character. It is therefore necessary to base the construction on (1) valid theories, (2) proven design products and processes, or on (3) domain experience and expertise.

- First, explanatory and/or predictive theories can provide important input for solution construction. E.g., indicators from valid success factor models of the domain at hand provide guidance which properties to-be solutions need to have. Such indicators can often be related to specific design activities.
- Second, existing solutions in the domain can be evaluated, and high-performance existing solutions can be chosen as to-be (reference) solutions. This approach however requires that the design problem domain is already quite mature and high-performance solutions exist. When comparing low-performance as-is solutions with high-performance to-be solutions regarding their design factor values, 'elementary movements' can be determined. These 'movements' represent elementary design steps that need to be composed to construct a better solution – or to be more precise: to change existing design solutions in a way that promises to develop properties of a solution that has better performance.
- If high-performance solutions do not exist or cannot be identified, a third way to determine to-be solutions is to use a field study to define desired solution characteristics. If an as-is solution characterization and a to-be characterization are available for all cases in the field study, solution 'paths' can be identified. These paths constitute the project types for situational artifact construction.

Empirical domain knowledge is essential regardless which approach is taken. Since "one size fits all" solutions cannot be expected to perform in all situations, theory application as well as as-is solution ranking and to-be solution surveys need to relate to the identified relevant contingencies, i.e. to be adapted to design situations. For each design situation, there is a different set of design activities (approach 1) or 'elementary movements' (approach 2) or a situation-specific to-be solution (approach 3). In the following, we illustrate approach 2 using the EAM example and approach 3 using an example from Process Performance Management (PPM).

4.1   Solution Composition from Elementary Design Actions (Approach 2)

First, characterizing design factors have to be identified for every design situation. In the EAM example, only situation 'IT focused, passive EAM' is characterized by high values of the design factor 'IT operations support' and low values of the design factors 'enterprise-wide focus', 'integrative role' and 'design impact'. The situation 'balanced, active EAM', in contrast, exhibits much smaller values for 'IT operations support', but much higher values for 'enterprise-wide focus', 'integrative role' and 'design impact'. With regard to 'information supply', 'business support' and 'IT strategy and IT governance support', these two design situations are not much different, so that these factors are not useful to characterize them.

In a second step, characterizing design factors are linked to design problems. For the EAM example, the description of the clusters implies a characterization of the respective design problems:

- In situation 2 (Business analysis), EAM implementation and impact need to be addressed. Business is the main stakeholder and executor and implementation considerations are widely neglected.
- In situation 3 (IT focused, passive approach), EAM is too IT centric and has not disseminated through the entire organization yet. The characterizing design factors 'integrative role', 'enterprise-wide focus' and 'design impact' can be associated with an EAM setup where the main EAM sponsor is the CIO, the main EAM customer is the IT function, EAM is primarily performed within the IT function, and EAM is widely ignored by business units.
- If EAM is not systematically addressed in the organization at all, either a balanced approach (very challenging) or an IT focused EAM or a business analysis approach can be followed.

Most EAM setups can be easily linked to major EAM challenges as often described in the literature. E.g., missing business involvement and missing business value creation of EAM correspond to the first EAM setup, while missing 'grounding'/'execution' and too much 'locality' of EAM correspond to the latter EAM setup.

In a third step, elementary design actions are derived by comparing design solutions with design problems. Based on the design situation characteristics of the EAM example illustrated by Fig. 4, the following design actions can be derived:

- In situation 2 (Business analysis), 'IT operations support', 'IT strategy and IT governance support' as well as 'EAM governance' need to be strengthened. Since IT topics and EAM governance constitute widely different measures, two different design actions (designated as A and B) should be differentiated.
- In situation 3 (IT focused, passive approach), 'design impact', 'integrative role' and 'enterprise-wide focus' need to be strengthened. Since design impact and IT/business alignment issues constitute widely different measures, design actions C and D should be differentiated.
- If EAM is not systematically addressed yet and an IT focused approach is favoured, 'IT operations support', 'IT strategy and IT governance support', 'information supply' and 'business strategy support' need to be developed foremost. In addition to design action A, a design action E should be defined to address business strategy support and a design action F to address information supply.
- If EAM is not systematically addressed yet and a business analysis approach is favoured, 'enterprise-wide focus' as well as 'information supply' and 'business strategy support' need to be developed foremost. As a consequence, the already defined design actions D, E and F are most relevant.

The final step is to define rules for combining the specified elementary design actions. The fewer characterizing design factors and the fewer design problems have been identified, the simpler the design action configuration will be – and vice versa. For the EAM example, four situated design solutions are configured from, depending on the design situation, up to four design actions out of a total number of six reusable design actions A...F:

- Situated solution I "from business analysis to balanced, active EAM" is comprised of design actions A and B
- Situated solution II "from IT focused, passive to balanced, active EAM" is comprised of design actions C and D
- Situated solution III "initial development of IT focused, passive EAM" is comprised of design actions A, E and F
- Situated solution IV "initial development of business analysis" is comprised of design actions D, E and F

Although not advised because a big maturity leap is necessary, it is possible to combine EAM design methods III and IV to a fifth situated method "direct move to balanced, active EAM" that is composed of design actions A, D, E and F.

4.2   Survey-Based Solution Path Derivation (Approach 3)

Although the above presented approach allows to systematically construct 'better' problem solutions, it (a) requires that such approaches can already be observed and (b) creates no useful solution in cases that already come close to the 'best' solution cluster.

As an alternative, to-be solutions (in the sense of information systems with certain desired properties) could be elicited by means of field studies, i.e. in the same way that is used to identify design situations. In addition to as-is properties of existing solutions, to-be properties of desired solutions are collected and undergo identical analyses.

Using PPM as an example, Fig. 5 illustrates that as-is situations differ significantly from to-be situations. One explanation could be that desired solution properties are

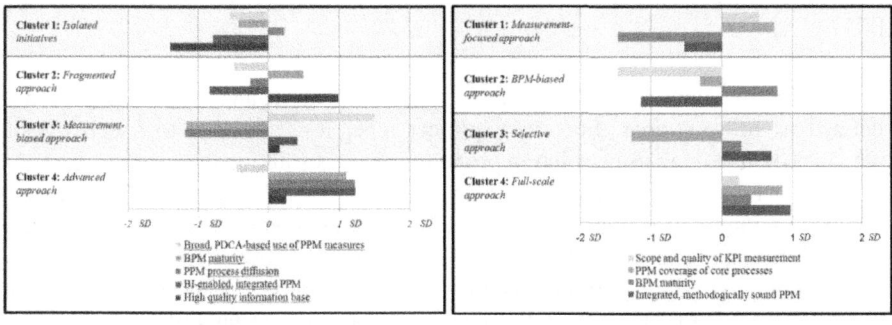

Fig. 5. As-is situations (left) vs. to-be situations (right) for process performance management [27]

more homogeneous than the existing variety of approaches so that cluster analysis generates situations that are less different. This would however require that companies' visions for 'ideal' solutions are very similar which is only true in very mature problem domains. In the majority of domains (including PPM) it can be expected that, if many contingencies exist, companies' PPM visions are quite different so that the variations of to-be solutions is not smaller than the variation of as-is solutions.

From the analysis of as-is and to-be situations, it is not immediately clear which project types result that need to be supported by suitable artifacts. If as-is and to-be data were obtained by the same survey, 'movements' can be analyzed because every case can be assigned to a specific as-is cluster as well as to a specific to-be cluster. Fig. 6 illustrates the aggregated 'movements' for the PPM survey. The number in the lower right corner of each of the boxes indicates the population of each cluster. The thickness of the lines is proportionate to the number of 'movements'. It becomes evident that, although there is a favorite to-be cluster ('full-scale PPM', 23 out of 42 companies), some companies also aim at alternative to-be solutions.

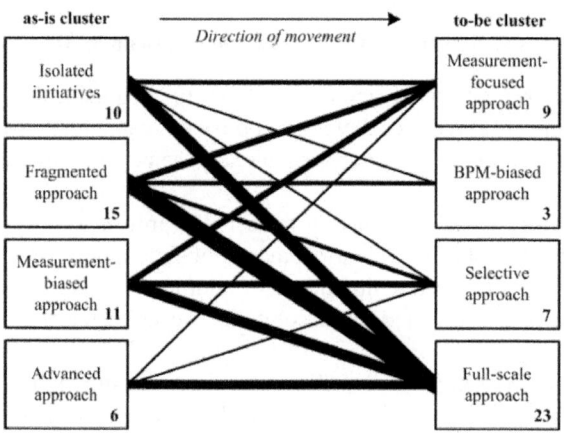

Fig. 6. Project types derived from process performance management design situation analysis [27]

For solution construction, the most significant aggregate 'movements' can be defined as project types. For every project type, it is possible to specify design activities by matching to-be solution properties to as-is solution properties.

To this end a weighted adjacency matrix is used that is based on the items that are grouped by the to-be factors (cf. Table 1). The values represent the arithmetic means of the differences between the to-be and as-is item values across all movers per project type. This allows to identify the areas that require the most change when a company intends to reach a certain to-be PPM approach. Details of this analysis are documented in [27].

Table 1. Adjacency matrix for process performance management [27]

as-is cluster / to-be factors / Items	to-be cluster	Isolated Initiatives		Fragmented (delta)			Measurement-biased (delta)				Advanced (delta)	
		as-is cluster means	Full-Scale	as-is cluster means	Measurement-focused	Full-Scale	as-is cluster means	Measurement-focused	Selective	Full-Scale	as-is cluster means	Full-Scale
Scope and quality of KPI measurement												
Adherence to schedules is measured for processes.		2.2	1.7	2.6	1.7	1.3	3.5	1.0	1.0	0.8	3.0	1.3
Quality is measured for processes.		1.6		2.2		1.4	3.0	0.7		1.4	2.7	
Process cycle times are measured.		1.8	1.7	2.4	2.0	1.5	2.8		1.3	1.2	3.4	0.9
Process costs are measured.		2.1	1.8	2.3	2.0	1.3	2.8	0.7	1.3	1.8	2.9	1.9
Capacity utilization is measured for processes.		2.2	1.3	2.8	2.0	1.1	2.8	1.3	1.3	1.2	3.5	1.0
Process resource utilization is measured.		2.2	1.7	2.5	2.0		3.0	0.7	1.0	1.4	3.1	
Data quality is consistently high.		1.7	2.5	3.4	0.7	1.1	3.1		1.0	1.4	2.7	
A central integrated data base is in place (e.g., an Enterprise DWH).		1.6	2.3	3.6	1.0	1.0	3.1	1.3	1.3	0.8	3.7	0.6
Processes have defined process officers.		2.9	1.2	3.4	1.0	1.0	3.6	1.3	1.3	1.4	4.0	0.7
Defined BI governance responsibilities and processes are in place.		1.6	2.0	2.3	2.0	1.8	2.8	1.0	1.3	1.4	3.9	0.5
PPM coverage of core processes												
PPM is deployed for production processes.		2.1	1.0	2.2	1.7	1.6	2.5	0.3	0.0	1.0	4.0	0.8
PPM is deployed for sales processes.		2.4	1.0	2.8	1.0	1.1	2.0	0.7	0.0	1.4	3.4	1.3
PPM is deployed for purchasing processes.		2.0	1.2	1.9	1.7	1.3	1.6	0.7	6.0	1.8	2.9	
PPM also covers non-financial measures.		2.4	1.0	1.8	1.7	0.9	2.1	0.3	0.6	0.6	3.1	<0.3
BPM maturity												
Process orientation is a central paradigm.		2.9	1.5	3.1	1.0	1.5	3.1	1.0	0.7	1.8	3.6	0.8
Process flows are consistent and transparent beyond functional borders.		2.4	1.3	2.9	0.7	1.8	2.3		2.0	2.4	3.4	1.0
Processes are consistently documented and/or modelled.		2.2	2.2	2.9	1.3	1.5	2.6		2.0	2.4	3.6	1.0
Process flows are consistent and transparent beyond system borders.		2.3	1.5	2.8	1.0	1.6	2.1	1.3	1.3	1.8	3.1	1.3
Integrated, methodologically sound PPM												
PPM is part of the enterprise-wide Balanced Score Card (BSC).		1.7	2.0	1.4	0.3	1.5	2.5	0.0	0.3	1.0	3.3	1.3
PPM is part of the Corporate Performance Management (CPM).		1.7	2.0	1.8	0.0	2.0	2.4	0.0	0.3	1.0	3.4	1.0
The plan-do-check-act (PDCA) cycle is applied for PPM.		1.4	1.7	2.0	0.8		2.7	0.0	0.3	0.8	3.3	

In the PPM example, the most important project type (and the first movement described in the adjacency matrix) is the shift from the "isolated initiatives" approach towards a "full-scale PPM" implementation. Organizations running isolated PPM initiatives are especially characterized by the lack of a high quality information base. Moreover, neither from a business intelligence nor from a business process management perspective have these companies established concepts in place. A more detailed analysis reveals that, in order to realize an effectual PPM concept, these companies explicitly focus (a) on providing an adequate IT infrastructure and (b) on gaining a deeper knowledge about their work by consistently documenting their processes. Besides, in order to bundle thus far isolated initiatives, organizations consider integrating their PPM ambitions with an enterprise balanced scorecard and/or their enterprise performance management program. Organizations starting off from the "fragmented approach" strive for either the "measurement-focused" or the "full-scale" approach. As described above the "measurement-focused" approach emphasizes the use of a broad set of key performance indicators (KPIs) for high quality decision making regarding the improvement of core processes—assumedly often in an on-demand setting based on real-time data. While organizations using the "fragmented approach" show a profound process orientation and possess a high quality information base, the transition to the "measurement-focused approach" requires the development of a set of crucial process performance metrics like process quality, cycle times as well as resource and capacity utilization. Moreover, the change demands a stronger concentration on the measurement of core processes in particular on the basis of non-financial metrics. A shift from the "fragmented" to the "full-scale approach" on the contrary, first and foremost necessitates a more organized and well-planned method. In order to overcome the parallelism of a strong process orientation and an underutilized IT infrastructure, organizations rigorously implement the plan-do-check-act cycle and align their process performance initiatives with enterprise performance management. Bridging the business-IT-divide is further enhanced by making process flows transparent across functional borders for the whole workforce. The "measurement-biased approach"—as the name betrays—is characterized by a strong overestimation of KPI use and measurement. Consequently, each convergence towards another approach—be it "measurement-focused", "selective", or "full-scale" —requires establishing a more sophisticated process orientation. In any case the measurement-biased organization must consistently design and model its processes and make them transparent beyond both functional and system borders so as to enable a comprehensive and successful PPM implementation. The last movement Cleven et al. [27] analyzed in more detail leads from the "advanced" to the "full-scale approach". Due to the fact that the advanced approach already shows a comparatively high maturity, only minor adoptions are required. The analysis reveals that an improvement of the overall data quality becomes necessary. As the measurement level of production processes is already very high, the focus will be shifted to sales and purchasing processes. An increased use of the balanced scorecard and the plan-do-check-act cycle further fosters the holism of the approach.

5   Discussion and Future Research

We presented a generally applicable approach to systematically analyze the mutability of information system solutions and differentiate design situations for a domain. For relating design goals to solution variations, we presented two alternative approaches. While the first approach requires an evaluation of the as-is clusters and then helps to transform inferior solutions into superior ones by specifying respective design actions, the second approach is based on a separate set of as-is and to-be situation specifications which provide the foundation to define project types and then derive appropriate design activities. While the latter alternative provides a sufficient variation of to-be solutions for every domain, it requires surveyed organizations to specify their respective solution vision in great detail – which is not always possible in particular when a domain is immature.

While many solution engineering approaches claim to incorporate situational factors, they do nearly never detail what these situational factors exactly are and how they can be incorporated into solution design and solution component configuration rules. This is the contribution of the empirical approach we presented here. It must however be conceded that every empirical foundation of solution design is only as general as the empirical base supports. Within a specific domain like EAM or PPM, we can reliably specify design factors, design situations, design actions and solution procedures. The less specific the domain is, the less useful the results, and the less effective their application will be. Several broad categories of research opportunities exist:

- First, the proposal needs to be further validated. Although a number of research projects have applied the proposed procedures and many case studies provide evidence that as-is situations, to-be situations, project types and respective design actions are meaningful and realistic in the respective domain, these claims might be invalidated by future studies.
- Both the EAM example and the PPM example comprised several simplifications like the elimination of tradeoffs between design goals and design activities. E.g., the derivation of design actions was straightforward for EAM if implementation

impact and business involvement can be achieved equally. If however tradeoffs have to be observed, solution design becomes much more complex.

- An interesting feature of many design solution analyses that yield a larger number of design factors is that the first factor is often representing many and quite diverse problem aspects that are sometimes not easy to interpret qualitatively. With regard to design solution analysis and solution construction, we interpret this "technically" overloaded design factor as a problem independent aggregation of "generalized" properties and the respective solution component as a basic set of domain-independent problem solution activities like e.g. general project/transformation management. This aspect of our approach does certainly need additional research attention.

- In addition, our approach does not explicitly cover yet the adaptation of situated solutions to specific design problems in an organisation. On the one hand, we consider this extension not too problematic because there is a plethora of adaptation knowledge on reference models which promises to be transferrable to this approach. On the other hand, adaptation efforts might depend on problem properties and influence the 'optimal' level of solution generality that up to now is determined using 'technical' homogeneity/heterogeneity metrics in cluster analysis only.

- Another and probably the most important extension would be to include not only adaptation effort, but also other 'economic' properties like the number of problem instantiations of a type or the attractiveness of design problems in terms of economic gains into the identification procedure of design factors and in particular design situations. This is probably the most interesting – and challenging – avenue for further research.

References

1. Hevner, A.R., March, S.T., Park, J., Ram, S.: Design Science in Information Systems Research. MIS Quarterly 28(1), 75–105 (2004)
2. Hevner, A.R.: A Three Cycle View of Design Science Research. Scandinavian Journal of Information Systems 19(2), 87–92 (2007)
3. Mason, R.O., Mitroff, I.I.: A Program for Research on Management Information Systems. Management Science 19(5), 475–487 (1973)
4. Keen, P.G.W.: Information systems and organizational change. Communications of the ACM 24(1), 24–33 (1981)
5. Gregor, S.: The Nature of Theory in Information Systems. MIS Quarterly 30(3), 611–642 (2006)
6. Gregor, S., Jones, D.: The Anatomy of a Design Theory. Journal of The Association For Information Systems 8(5), 312–335 (2007)
7. Fischer, C., Winter, R., Wortmann, F.: Design Theory. Business and Information Systems Engineering 52(6), 383–386 (2010)
8. Venable, J.: The Role of Theory and Theorising in Design Science Research. In: Proceedings of the 1st International Conference on Design Science in Information Systems and Technology (DESRIST 2006). Claremont Graduate University, Claremont (2006)
9. March, S.T., Smith, G.F.: Design and Natural Science Research on Information Technology. Decision Support Systems 15(4), 251–266 (1995)

10. Winter, R.: Design Science Research in Europe. European Journal of Information Systems 17(5), 470–475 (2008)

11. Chmielewicz, K.: Forschungskonzeptionen der Wirtschaftswissenschaften. Poeschel, Stuttgart (1994)

12. Baskerville, R.L., Pries-Heje, J., Venable, J.: Soft design science methodology. In: Proceedings of the 4th International Conference on Design Science Research in Information Systems and Technology (DESRIST 2009), Philadelphia (2009)

13. Kornyshova, E., Deneckère, R., Salinesi, C.: Method Chunks Selection by Multicriteria Techniques: an Extension of the Assembly-based Approach. In: Situatinal Method Engineering Fundamentals and Experiences, pp. 64–78. Springer, Geneva (2007)

14. van Slooten, K., Hodes, B.: Characterizing IS Development Projects. In: Method Engineering - Principles of Method Construction and Tool Support, pp. 29–44. Chapman & Hall, Atlanta (1996)

15. Mirbel, I., Ralyté, J.: Situational method engineering: combining assembly-based and roadmap-driven approaches. Requirements Engineering 11(1), 58–78 (2006)

16. Winter, R.: Problem Analysis for Situational Artefact Construction in Information Systems. In: Carugati, A., Rossignoli, C. (eds.) Emerging Themes in Information Systems and Organization Studies, pp. 97–113. Physica, Heidelberg (2011)

17. Bucher, T., Klesse, M.: Contextual Method Engineering. Working Paper, Institute of Information Management, University of St. Gallen (2006)

18. Winter, R.: Design Solution Analysis for the Construction of Situational Design Methods. In: Ralyté, J., Mirbel, I., Deneckère, R. (eds.) ME 2011. IFIP AICT, vol. 351, pp. 19–33. Springer, Heidelberg (2011)

19. Aier, S., Gleichauf, B., Winter, R.: Understanding Enterprise Architecture Management Design – An Empirical Analysis. In: Proceedings of the 10th International Conference on Wirtschaftsinformatik WI 2011, Zurich, pp. 645–654 (2011)

20. Aziz, S., Obitz, T., Modi, R., Sarkar, S.: Enterprise Architecture: A Governance Framework - Part I: Embedding Architecture into the Organization (2005)

21. Aziz, S., Obitz, T., Modi, R., Sarkar, S.: Enterprise Architecture: A Governance Framework - Part II: Making Enterprise Architecture Work within the Organization (2006)

22. Baumöl, U.: Strategic Agility through Situational Method Construction. In: Proceedings of the European Academy of Management Annual Conference 2005, München (2005)

23. Bucher, T., Winter, R.: Taxonomy of Business Process Management Approaches: An Empirical Foundation for the Engineering of Situational Methods to Support BPM. In: vom Brocke, J., Rosemann, M. (eds.) Handbook on Business Process Management, vol. 2, pp. 93–114. Springer, Heidelberg (2010)

24. Klesse, M., Winter, R.: Organizational Forms of Data Warehousing: An Explorative Analysis. In: Proceedings of the 40th Hawaii International Conference on System Sciences (HICSS-40). IEEE Computer Society (2007)

25. Lahrmann, G., Stroh, F.: Towards a Classification of Information Logistics Scenarios – An Exploratory Analysis. In: Proceedings of the 42nd Hawaii International Conference on System Sciences (HICSS-42). IEEE Computer Society (2009)

26. Leist, S.: Methoden zur Unternehmensmodellierung - Vergleich, Anwendungen und Diskussionen der Integrationspotenziale. Habilitation, Institut für Wirtschaftsinformatik, Universität St. Gallen (2004)

27. Cleven, A., Winter, R., Wortmann, F.: Process Performance Management – Illuminating Design Issues through a Systematic Problem Analysis. In: The 26th Annual ACM Symposium on Applied Computing, pp. 280–286. Association for Computing Machinery (ACM), Taichung (2011)

A Workshop about the Future
of Enterprise Information Systems

Per Svejvig[1] and Charles Møller[2]

[1] Aarhus University, Business and Social Sciences, Department of Business Administration,
Haslegaardsvej 10, 8210 Aarhus V, Denmark
psve@asb.dk
[2] Aalborg University, Department of Business and Management,
Center for Industrial Production, Fibigerstræde 10, 9220 Aalborg Ø, Denmark
charles@production.aau.dk

Abstract. Enterprise Information Systems (EIS) can be classified into three generations, starting with the application-centric, moving on to the data-centric and then to contemporary thinking, which can be described as process-centric. The overall theme of CONFENIS 2011 was to re-conceptualize EIS. One way of re-conceptualizing is to start with a blank sheet and "think out of the box". This topic was addressed in a workshop at CONFENIS 2011 which focused on the future of EIS. The workshop consisted of a large number of experts from across the world, divided into seven groups, who discussed the topic using LEGO SERIOUS PLAY to facilitate and stimulate the discussions. The group of seven came up with seven challenges for the future of EIS and we propose that the next generation of EIS should be conceptualized as human-centric.

Keywords: Future Workshop, Enterprise Information Systems, LEGO SERIOUS PLAY.

1 Introduction

The Fifth International Conference on Research and Practical Issues in Enterprise Information Systems (CONFENIS 2011) was held in October 2011 in Aalborg, Denmark. CONFENIS is now an established conference with representation from all over the globe. More than 80 experts from around the world were gathered together in Aalborg and to exchange knowledge and discuss EIS. This year's overall theme was Re-conceptualizing Enterprise Information Systems (EIS).

One way to re-conceptualize is to start with a blank sheet and "think out of the box", that is, to try to think differently or from a new perspective. The organizing committee for CONFENIS 2011 decided to hold a workshop about "the Future of EIS" to contribute to the overall theme of re-conceptualizing EIS. This workshop explored the combined knowledge of the participants about the challenges and potential features of future EIS, using the LEGO SERIOUS PLAY method [1].

The purpose of this chapter is to present the process and the results from the workshop.

C. Møller and S. Chaudhry (Eds.): CONFENIS 2011, LNBIP 105, pp. 45–57, 2012.

The LEGO SERIOUS PLAY method was used to facilitate and stimulate the discussions at the workshop [2]. The participants were divided into seven groups and each group was challenged to come up with their view on the future of EIS.

The seven groups each identified their number one challenge for the next five years: (1) Security, (2) Transparency of control, (3) User simplicity, (4) Rights management, (5) Standards, (6) IT and business working in a cooperative environment, and (7) Human business systems. The way these challenges were approached will be explained in this chapter with relation to the group work.

The chapter is organized in the following way. The next section presents the methodology, using LEGO SERIOUS PLAY to stimulate and facilitate the discussion. The seven major challenges are then reported on in the following section. This is followed by detailed presentations of five cases representing the results from five out of the seven groups. Finally we present our view of the next generation of EIS and the paper concludes with implications and suggestions for further research.

2   Methodology

2.1   Brief about the Workshop Process

The workshop took about two hours and consisted of several steps managed by a workshop facilitator. The seven groups were formed ad hoc. First, the facilitator introduced the workshop question "How can we conceptualize the Enterprise Information System of the future?" The facilitator explained that this is not an easy question with an easy answer and therefore there could be a lot of different answers based on different viewpoints. The viewpoints can be expressed metaphorically as different slices of a potato symbolizing the EIS, while the potato is a big and fluffy. The slices make up different images based on the workshop participants' theoretical and practical understanding of future EIS. Then he explained about how our hands and fingers can stimulate our cognitive thinking by building models and prototypes. This approach was taken further by playing (not to be confused with gaming) using LEGO SERIOUS PLAY (LSP) to facilitate and stimulate the play [see also 3, 4]. Working with complex problems and concepts in a playful way can produce a high degree of creativity.

Secondly, the facilitator moved the audience through different exercises in order for them to learn the language of LSP by building small LEGO models.

Thirdly, each workshop participant was asked to build the future EIS in 2016 (five years time from now) as an individual exercise. After the building process, each model was presented for the others in the group.

Fourthly, the final step was to build a shared model in the group by using the individual models, although adding parts to the model and removing redundant parts was still allowed. This shared model represented the team's final and conclusive work. At the end of the workshop, this model was formally presented to the other groups and the main future challenge was identified in each group. The groups were required to name unique challenges (There was no overlap between groups).

Fig. 1. LEGO SERIOUS PLAY workshop session

2.2 Data Collection

One of the authors of this paper had the role of carrying out participant observation [5] and of capturing the workshop by video recording [6]. Several student assistants supported the process by taking pictures from the workshop and video recording the final models prepared by the seven groups and providing formal feedback to the audience. This ensured that the activities that were simultaneously being carried out were sufficiently documented.

2.3 Data Analysis

The videos were transcribed and coded in NVivo [7]. The transcription process contained both visual elements (e.g. annotation of pictures) and verbal elements. Some of the videos were very difficult to transcribe, due to the noisy environment and the multifarious English accents. Pictures were selected to represent the shared models. Videos from the two groups were missing, so the detailed presentations of the group work covered five groups. Videos, pictures, transcriptions etc. were used to theorize about the major challenges with future EIS and to come up with proposals for the next generation of EIS.

3   The 7 Major Challenges of Future EIS

The shared conception of the next generation EIS is remarkably uniform. All groups began by assuming that three of the main challenges of EIS today already would have been solved in the future:

Firstly, EIS is considered to be *ubiquitous*. This on the agenda on this year's CONFENIS conference and we can see in people's minds that the idea of the EIS being available everywhere– easily accessible from the grid– is considered to be a certainty. It is interesting that also this is seen as a potential driver for more green and sustainable IT solutions in the future.

Secondly, EIS is considered to be extremely *flexible*. This is despite one of the prominent challenges of the existing EIS being that they are infamous for being inflexible and thus hindering the business innovation of enterprises locked into systems logic. The LEGO brick itself is considered the ultimate model for IT solutions or services, packed into units with well-defined interfaces making the future of EIS potentially extremely versatile.

Thirdly, EIS is considered to be *relevant*. There are many new technologies today and also new approaches that could leave the EIS as outdated legacy systems. Not surprisingly for EIS researchers, the EIS is viewed as being likely to be present in both the back-office and the front office in terms of playing a new role for business organizations.

This is also the starting point for the first challenge of the next generation of EIS, as characterized by seven inter-related challenges.

3.1   IT and Business Working in a Cooperative Environment

Today there is a lot of attention being given to the gap between IT and business organizations. In the future the participants in EIS, IT and business organizations will work together to solve business problem, with EIS as an underlying technology to support intelligent decision making and solutions.

3.2   Human Business Systems

Today we can define EIS as being mainly a technology for supporting management control systems. In the next generation of EIS, we will see much more emphasis on EIS as a foundation for human centered business systems. This implies the existence of access to EIS by means that are independent from time and space.

3.3   User Simplicity

EIS today is characterized by often being difficult to use by the ordinary and occasional business user. In the future EIS will have to simplify their user interfaces and the logic behind their functionality must be simplified where the user is involved. This challenge also includes including mobile access from gadgets such as iPads and other future smart devices.

3.4   Transparency of Control

The most important way that the next generation of EIS can be made simple is to make the controls transparent. Lack of visibility is one of the major drivers of complexity and creating transparency of control is one way of making it apparent to the users what is cause and what is effect in the business.

3.5   Rights Management

In order to support the new networked business architecture, the future EIS must manage rights in a different way. When we are dealing with smart devices we cannot be sure that one person is in front of a computer or a person requiring information could be outside of the organization, e.g. they could be located at a supplier's. This creates a tremendous challenge regarding the management of rights.

3.6   Security

Various security issues that will have to be managed and solved in order to open up enterprise data to be accessed outside an enterprise. Today a new security update can be considered safe until the bad guys crack the code. Then a new security update is needed. This is not good enough in an enterprise setting. So new approaches to security will be required in the future EIS.

3.7   Standards

Finally, in order to advance the maturity of the EIS, overall standards are needed. These are needed, not only to sustain technological standards but also a process standards. These also point towards achieving flexibility and as such are a prerequisite for flexibility and versatility.

   These seven interrelated and to some extent cascading challenges were considered to be the most important challenges by the participants in the workshop. These can be seen as the major findings from this study. Together they span an opportunity for space for future EIS research.

4   Five LEGO Models Representing different Views on the Future of EIS

This section reports on the immediate understanding and interpretation of future EIS in five out of the seven groups.

4.1   Group 1

Fig. 2, as shown below, captures the conceptualization of the future EIS by group 2. The model is annotated with concepts explained by the group.

   Today we completed our future version of an EIS system in five minutes [assembled however from the individually produced future EIS systems in the group]. Now I would like to present the [future EIS] system. The name of the system is Elephant. An elephant is a symbol of luck and longevity, so our system will survive from generation to generation.

There are five major strengths of our system:

1) *Our system is a bug free system. We can see that the bugs (pointing at the LEGO model) are kept out of the system by the fences and the hem. There is another hem if they break into the first fence, but they cannot get into the second one. We have very tight controls.*

2) *The second feature of our system is versatility. This is a very flexible system in a comprehensive / complicated world. There are many different kinds of features (again pointing to elements in the LEGO model) and it is effective to update and change them.*

3) *The third strength is in monitoring threats. We have a monitoring system with which they can watch the outside world and the system will be able to react to threats.*

4) *The fourth feature is that we will "break the old habits". If you think of existing EIS systems, they are like blocks or circles, but we have different shapes, we have blocks, we have circles, we have triangles, we have elephants - so we can break the old habits!*

5) *Finally the last one is maybe the most important. We can integrate a lot of subsystems so that the world can work happily together.*

This is our version of our future EIS system (applause) - Thank you!

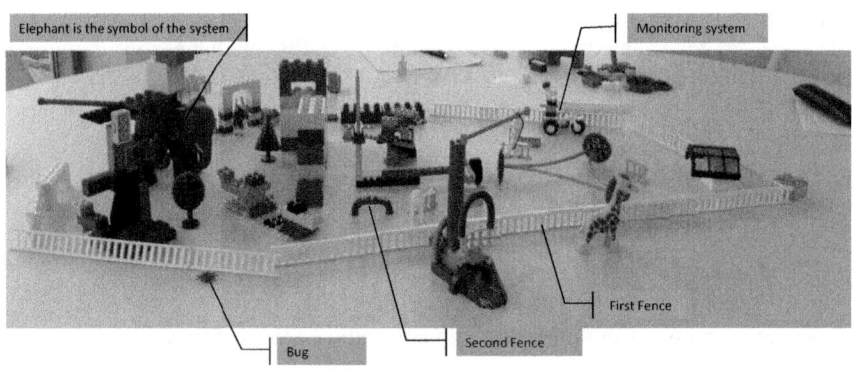

Fig. 2. LEGO Model from group 1

The group decided that *security* is the biggest challenge for future EIS, and this is clearly represented in their LEGO model.

4.2   Group 2

Group 2 came up with the following model in Fig. 3 describing the future EIS. The group describes the model as follows:

What we have here is our conceptualization of the EIS...this is characterized by:

1) *Transparency*
2) *Process factory ability*
3) *Pervasive computing anywhere and any time*
4) *Directions to be able to drive our processes and the processes [delivered by] a process provider. There is a process to drive an organization towards the goal in an efficient way. Adjusting the processes day by day and ensuring that the goals of the organizations can be driven in the right direction*
5) *Flexible sensors to sense what is happening in the outside environment and then to deal with pressure from competitors, the market, and from regulators*
6) *We also have some interaction with mobile devices, so we are very flexible and can see them as a mechanism or as a bridge to an external provider*

We furthermore have controller busses (in the middle of the picture) [to take care of controlling processes]. We have this management information both for the inside and also for the outside, to retain a high degree of transparency. The system also has the horizontal support of processes for manufacturing, sales, finance, and other uses. The system will be very powerful in the future.

Group 2 selects *transparency of control* as the main challenge illustrated by the inside / outside management information system.

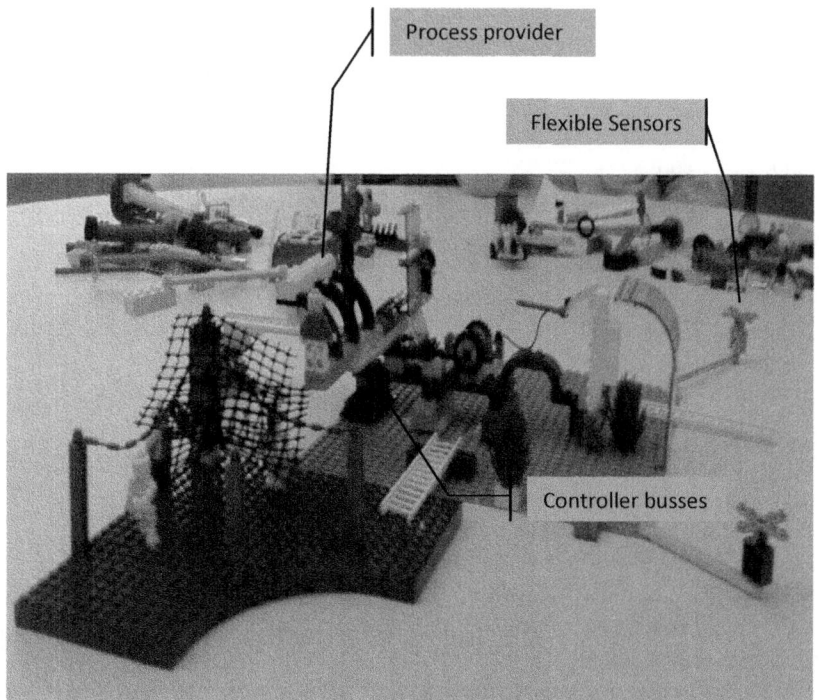

Fig. 3. LEGO model from group 2

4.3   Group 3

Fig. 4 below shows how group 3 conceptualizes the future of EIS:

Fig. 4. LEGO Model from group 3

The group explains the future EIS artifact in this way:

First of all, everything is built around the user: 'humans first' is the motto and it is all placed in a green environment. So we look into the future and in five years' time it is important to consider the green elements within it. Then what we will have is the interconnectivity of the different elements, built on a very simple platform. That green one is the simple platform, but everything is built on stable and flexible pillars using the LEGO building blocks. They are not stuck together in a rigorous or inflexible way, but rather in a flexible way... That is the reason why we say that our artifact is reusable and stable.

The element of the uncertainty [expressed by the lion]... Yes you need to speak about the uncertain. You never know what will happen - security management is also important.

The biggest challenge, according to this group, is *user simplicity*.

4.4   Group 4

The conceptualization from group 4 is shown in Fig. 5:

The group presents their model as follows: *This is a very ecological energy facility where we have all hardware in the computer department and the security and then it is connected to the rest of the world.*

The connection is with the user and the eco system. The ecosystem is the green lawn where users have cover and it is ready to be used as the user wishes.

There are different things (pointing at the model) that can support the user when they connect to something.

And then we have two animals representing all obstacles and new challenges. The elephant is here but it might be attacked by the lion.

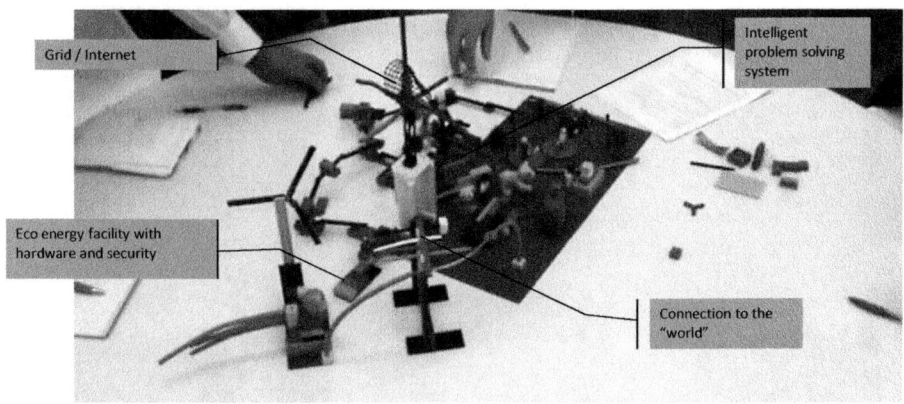

Fig. 5. LEGO Model from group 4

Here is the problem solver with an intelligent problem solving system that is also responsible for solving... new challenges which may arise when using this very flexible model and a sense of the environment, in combining different parts that interconnects together for intelligent problem solving.

Also, in this environment, small pieces of standardized applications can connect to the infrastructure and speak the same language, so as to connect.

All the legacy stuff is hidden in the basement where no one can touch it. Here are two users [Pink platform]. Both are localized and they can work from home. They can recognize their system as being very intuitive, but [they] are also able to travel around the universe using different gadgets to access the data that is hidden somewhere here (pointing...) This is so that security issues can be solved locally and that the users will have access to their data.

And what did I forget? ...Oh yes this is the grid Internet that is actually all over everywhere and this represents the stability that is very standardized, and to which you easily can connect and disconnect.

The biggest challenge for group 4 was *rights management* which is related to security well expressed in the model.

4.5   Group 5

Group 5 conceptualizes the future EIS as shown in Fig. 6:

The group describes their model as follows: *First of all, things must be interconnected. We can make a clear distinction between the two elements [LEGO plates] the system itself with its base [green LEGO plate], the various elements and what the system does [grey LEGO plate] in terms of extending the capability of human beings...alone and in connection with others, so we see the system as being in the sky or the clouds.*

Fig. 6. LEGO model from group 5

We have five challenges:

1. One is people versus technology so we can make it adaptable so that people actually want to use it.
2. Then we have standards, they have flexibility and we can make them applicable to our needs in terms of their use.
3. We have security. It is pretty obvious that vital information should not be revealed (brown knight].
4. A means of safe storing of data ensuring security and privacy, so data is not lost.
5. A mechanism to capture user requirements in a rapid way without it taking five years to develop. That is a real challenge.

Group 5 emphasizes *standards* as their key challenge.

5   Next Generation Enterprise Information System

We have now presented the findings from the CONFENIS workshop on the future of EIS. The workshop methodology has been presented, as have the conceptual models made by the groups. The challenges of future EIS have been presented as an aggregate conceptual model of future EIS. EIS have evolved through different generations and the challenges presented here could point towards the next generation of EIS.

It is possible to classify the three first generations of EIS in this way:

*   First generation EIS can be considered to be application-centric in the sense that the applications contain the data, and the business rules are not necessarily integrated.
*   Second generation EIS can be considered to be data-centric and driven by the integrated databases enabled by the DBMS technology.

- Third generation EIS can be considered to be process-centric and driven by the BPM architecture, supported by the integrated systems.

What characterizes the next generation EIS is of cause yet to be seen, but we can speculate on the challenges based on the three previous generations of EIS.

Table 1. Four generations of EIS

EIS generation	Application-centric	Data-centric	Process-centric	Human-centric
	MRP	ERP	BPM	?
Business Challenge	Efficacy	Efficiency	Effectiveness	Resilience
Organizational challenge	Support of departments	Support of enterprises	Support of supply chains	Support of business networks
Technology Enablers	Databases	DBMS, Client-server architecture	Internet, SOA	Semantic networks, Social Media, Cloud computing
Integrates...	Applications	Data	Processes	Humans
Timeline	Around 80'ies	Around 90'ies	Around 00'ies	Around 10'ies

The evolution of the EIS has been driven by the business challenges and by the resulting organizational challenges. In the discussions in the groups the volatile nature of today's business environment was taken as a premise. Following this premise the organization of enterprises does not follows the hierarchical logic of the past, but is characterized by being network oriented and spanning across organizational boundaries. But mainly the evolution has been driven by the enabling technologies. The role of technology in EIS is an interesting topic to pursue. E.g. this year there was a track at the conference focusing on the impact of cloud computing on EIS. EIS technologies are of cause influenced by the general trends in information technology but in order to become game changers in EIS other factors are required.

Based on the experience of the workshop we can conclude that the next generation EIS will be human-centric. Human-centric EIS are characterized by being: 1) ubiquitous; 2) flexible; and 3) relevant to the business. The seven challenges that were the main findings support the thinking of human-centric and cascading challenges: 1) Standards; 2) Security; 3) Transparency of control; 4) User simplicity; 5) Rights management; 6) IT and business working in a cooperative environment; and 7) Human business systems.

6   Conclusion

This chapter has pursued to illustrate a possible future of EIS. This was addressed in a workshop at CONFENIS 2011 consisting of a large number of experts from across the world, divided into seven groups, who discussed the topic using LEGO SERIOUS PLAY to facilitate and stimulate the discussions. The group of seven came up with seven challenges for the future of EIS, which were overall conceptualized as the human-centric EIS.

There are conceptual and methodological implications from this study. *First*, if we consider other ways of modeling the future through scenario building approaches like the "Shell Energy Scenario 2050" [8] or "Supply Chain 2020" [9], the participants generally share a fairly optimistic view of the future business environment and a positive view of the role of technology in the future. This is perhaps not surprising since most of the researchers are working with various technologies. However this attitude could also have been produced by "group effects" in an atmosphere of enthusiasm for EIS where participants might have a tendency to express accepted views [10]. The workshop should therefore be seen as a creative and thoughtful inspiration for a continued discussion about the future EIS. Further studies involving the EIS community (vendors, consultants, users, researchers etc.) might bring this discussion to a much more refined level.

Second, the research methods used for the workshop are interesting topics itself. The methods combine LEGO SERIOUS PLAY for visualization and cognitive thinking [4] with video documentation [6, 11]. However we encountered several practical and methodological issues (e.g. noisy environment and lack of structured documentation from groups), which has hampered this study. We do nevertheless see the approach as promising for future research and practice as a tool to multimodal imagery which brings together verbal/narrative, visual/imagistic, and kinesthetic/haptic modes [3] documented by video.

Despite the implications and limitations, this study has anyway provided some evidence of trends that may help researchers in selecting topics in the future and for practitioners to make sense of the next generation of EIS.

References

1. Hansen, P., Fradinho, M., Andersen, B., Lefrere, P.: Changing the way we learn: towards agile learning and co-operation (2009)
2. Mabogunje, A., Kyvsgaard Hansen, P., Eris, O., Leifer, L.: Conference SWING-Simulation, Workshops, Interactive eNvironments and Gaming: An Integrated Approach to Improve Learning, Design, and Strategic Decision Making, pp. 277–286 (Year)
3. Bürgi, P., Roos, J.: Images of Strategy. European Management Journal 21, 69–78 (2003)
4. Gauntlett, D., Holzwarth, P.: Creative and visual methods for exploring identities. Visual Studies 21, 82–91 (2006)
5. Myers, M.D.: Qualitative Research in Business & Management. Sage Publications, London (2009)

6. Pink, S.: Doing Visual Ethnography. Images, Media and Representation in Research. Sage Publications, London (2007)
7. Bazeley, P.: Qualitative Data Analysis with NVivo. Sage Publications Ltd., London (2007)
8. Shell International BV: Shell Energy Scenarios to 2050. Shell International BV (2008)
9. CLT Supply Chain 2020: SC2020 Baseline Scenarios. MIT Center For Transportation and Logistics (2009)
10. Bryman, A.: Social Research Methods. Oxford University Press, Oxford (2008)
11. Pink, S.: Walking with video. Visual Studies 22, 240–252 (2007)

Different Instrumental Methods Which Can Be Used in New EIS: Theory and Practical Approach

Roman Veynberg and Victor Romanov

Plekhanov Russian Economic University,
Stremjannyj per., 36, 117997 Moscow, Russian Federation
veynberg@gmail.com

Abstract. In this paper we study Business rules management system (BRMS) approach in Enterprise information systems (EIS) development. The approach is closely connected with Enterprise decision management (EDM) concept and usage of EIS in business and world economy. The paper has survey nature and gives retrospective analysis of today's marketing situation in EIS and BRMS industry. Highlight examples of EIS BRMS modules (ORACLE and SAP), their advantages and goals in the real high-tech industry.

Keywords: enterprise information systems, business rules management systems, enterprise decision management, instrumental methods, Oracle Business Rules, SAP Business Rules.

1   Introduction

Sooner or later top management of any company faced with the problems of systematization of data and process of automation during working with the information. Over time, growth in the volume of data makes within the company problems in creating modern enterprise information systems (EIS), which cover all aspects of the business enterprise. Purchase of EIS is not the final purpose. EIS is only a tool which allows organizations to operate effectively. This applies to work not only ordinary performers, but also top-managers at any company's level [1,2].

Thus, purchase of EIS - is only purchase of a tool to maintain control over the company or to increase the effectiveness of this control. "Automatic Control", unfortunately, does not usually happen. Therefore, if after the implementation of EIS, the process of collecting and processing information is not accelerating and increasing the accuracy and completeness of the data, and management of the organization is not receiving new data, or can not use it properly, then the information remains unclaimed, and it does not lead to more effective solutions. EIS itself does not increase profitability [4]. It can increase efficiency and expedite the processing of data, which can provide information for decision making. Manager can increase profitability from effective solutions based on this information. It is therefore necessary not only to choose and implement EIS, but also learn how to use it with maximum efficiency. Moreover, understanding whether and how the use of EIS should be preceded, more precisely determine the choice of the supplier and the

C. Møller and S. Chaudhry (Eds.): CONFENIS 2011, LNBIP 105, pp. 58–63, 2012.

process of implementing EIS. The main thing that allows manager to make EIS is to unite the activities of the enterprise with its instrumental methods [4]. Author's concept of EIS with instrumental methods is presented in the figure 1. Instrumental methods include: business rules tech., scenario analysis and precedent approach.

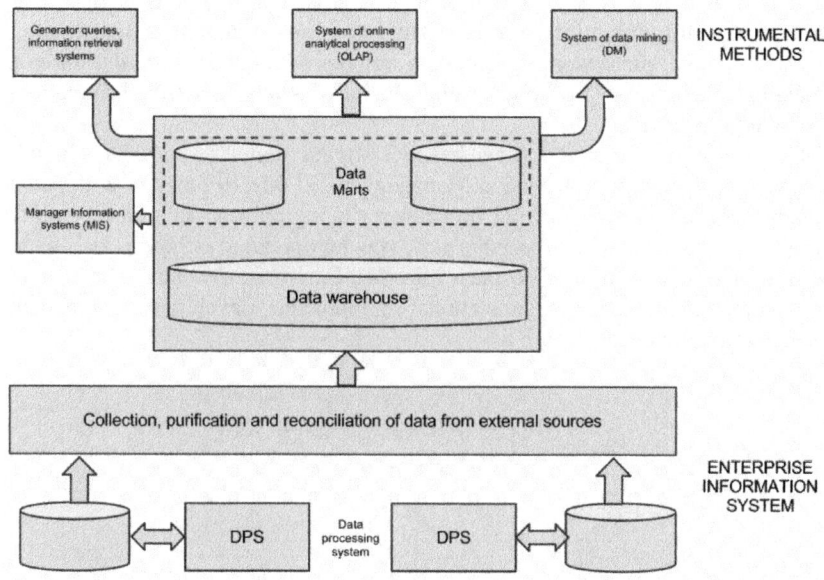

Fig. 1. Enterprise information system with instrumental methods within

For industrial EIS important information is: production data, finance data, procurement, and marketing. Based on the information, manager can quickly adjust and plan the activities of the company. He or she gets a chance to see the whole enterprise and business processes from the inside, to see the basic functioning of the system, where and how he or she can minimize the costs, which prevents from the increasing of the profits. Management team is interested in consolidation of information from the whole branches and central offices of their enterprises, as well as having possibility of monitoring remotely all units.

2   EDM (Enterprise Decision Management) Approach

Since the late 80's companies were focused on improving the efficiency of business processes and building a data structure. In the early nineties has become apparent insufficiency of the approach. Describing the processes and data, the researchers found that there is one other area of expertise, critical for understanding, the nature of any organization - its business rules. Designed to support business structure, control and influence the behavior of businesses, business rules appear as a result of restrictions imposed on business.

This trend popularized by Ron Ross, Barbara von Halle, James Taylor, Tony Morgan and other authors [3,4]. So, it was determined that this approach should include parameters such as terms, facts and circumstances. The concept of business rules are widely used today, there are special groups of organizations, such as, Business Rules Group (BRG), Semantics of Business Vocabulary & Business Rules association (SBVRa) and International Business Rules Forum, which develop different standards for business rules. While no single standard format for business rules was created, there were developed a number of related standards, for example, Semantics of Business Vocabulary and Business Rules (SBVR), Production Rule Representation (PRR).

The integration of business rules and EIS was facilitated to appear in the mid-90's into concept of Enterprise Decision Management (EDM), oriented to a higher degree of automation in decision-making process, replacing an approach based on business process management, when the main task was automatically chosen, and algorithms were presented in the form of business rules [4]. Enterprise Decision Management has three major components: organizational component, developing component and management component (figure 2).

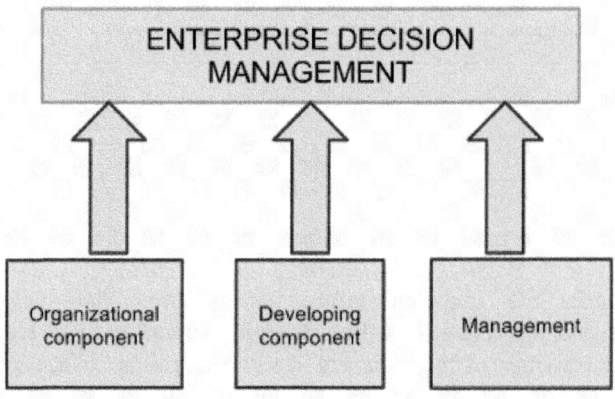

Fig. 2. Enterprise Decision Management approach with its three major components

Due to the complexity of decision-making process within organizations in recent years, EDM has acquired special importance to the business. It must match rapidly changing laws and market situations. To automate the decision-making process, EDM involves pooling of analytical tools, forecasting and automating solutions, business rules, processes and business procedures, electronic control systems and organizational structure. The key points of EDM concept in terms of business rules are:

  1.   business users who have the ability to control key points of solutions in business processes;
  2.   business rules are ideally suited to illustrate the correctness of the decision-making process;
  3.   the possibility of replacing part of the application code for business rules;

4.   visualization of business regulations and their relationships for easy management and the possibility of substitution code.

With the advent of EDM concept, business rules have strong architecture and clear justification from business standpoint, because business flexibility is unstable without right management decisions within the organization. The application of business rules in the way of automating decisions reduces development costs and maintenance; stops the dependence of system's update from IT industry [5].

3   BRMS (Business Rules Management System) Approach together with EIS Leaders

Every company use several hundreds or thousands of specific rules (business rules), such as legislative initiatives, agreements with partners, inside restrictions, certain internal rules of the organization which determine its behavior, business policy and distinguish the enterprise from others. Business rules are indirectly determined by a large number of inconsistent analytical and project documents, and mostly they can be transformed into logic and application programs.

Often they are not available or unconsciousness in general, developers make assumptions about the business rules that may be incorrect and poorly aligned with the objectives of the enterprise, and can not be easily modified and adapted [3]. This fact leads to various inconsistencies and errors and makes it difficult to change business rules, and this is necessary response for change in the external and internal environment.

A leading providers of business rules management systems have been successfully developed their systems in parallel with the suppliers of EIS, and now two markets have become closer [1].

One of the leaders in EIS business is Oracle Corporation, has its own Business Rules module, which consists of three components:

1.   A Rules engine
2.   A Rules SDK for use by applications that modify and/or create Rules.
3.   The Rule Author GUI for Rules creation

Architectural structure of Oracle BRMS is presented in figure 3.

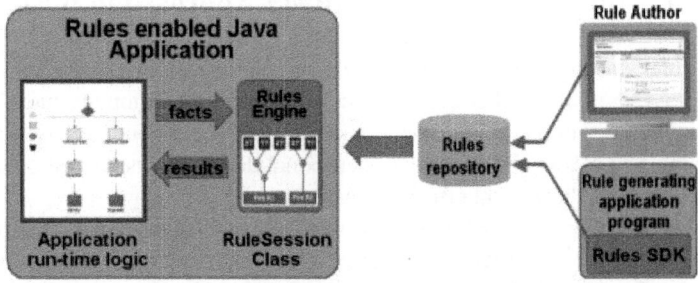

Fig. 3. Oracle Business rules components

Another EIS leader is German company SAP, which provides users with its own BRM system: SAP NetWeaver BRM [2].

SAP NetWeaver BRM helps managers to manage the growing set of business rules in any organizations. Therefore, SAP provides the following tools:

1. **Rules composer** – Enables process architects and IT developers to create and modify business rules via rule representation formats, such as decision tables
2. **Rules analyzer** – Enables business users to test, refine, analyze, and optimize business rules
3. **Rules manager** – Enables business users to edit and manage business rules in a Web-based collaborative environment
4. **Rules repository** – Provides the environment for rules versioning, permissions management, access control, alerts, and additional repository services
5. **Rules engine** – Executes rules, integrated with the run-time technology provided by SAP NetWeaver Composition Environment

Architectural structure of SAP BRMS is presented in figure 4.

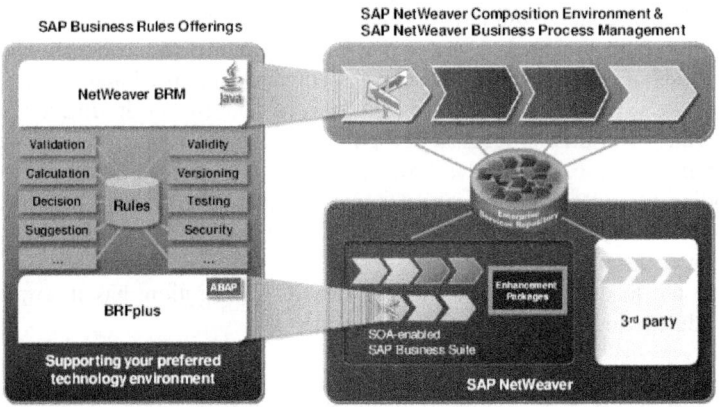

Fig. 4. SAP Business rules components

4   Competitive Preferences of BRMS Approach in Business

Business rules management system speeds up all processes occurring within the enterprise, where it was embedded. As a consequence, the company more favorably responds to changes in the environment or on the global economic crisis. Accelerated decision-making process and automate operational decisions inside and outside of the enterprise which has beneficial effect on business itself [4].

Examples are: the use of BRMS improve business efficiency by 25% in General Electric customer service; 15% of efficiency at the pharmaceutical giant Bayer; Swiss Medical's profit, using BRMS, was increased by 23.5% during the reporting period (second quarter 2010); in Delta Airlines, with the introduction of BRMS, processing speed of customer service was increased by 2.5 times, which resulted in increasing of revenue grows (15.8%). Wodafone, one of the biggest telecommunication companies in the world, implementing BRMS for its order processing system of personalized service packages for customers of different consumer clusters, increased processing speed operational decision-making by 2.5 times, increasing net income by 25 % for the report period (2010, Q2) [3,4].

5   Conclusion

The above description of EIS, its basic definition and practical examples of the following BRMS systems give managers simple possibility to identify problems on time and solve them with immediate actions automatically. Together with BRMS approach Enterprise Information Systems can identify the relationships of objects in the presence of incomplete information, and decrypt the conceptual lattice, obtained by the algorithm which does not require additional knowledge, because of its simplicity.

References

1. http://www.oracle.com/technetwork/middleware/business-rules/overview/index-085313.html
2. http://www.sdn.sap.com/irj/sdn/nw-rules-management/html
3. Harmon, P.: Business Rules //Business Process Trends (2007)
4. Chisholm, M.: How to build a business rules engine. Morgan Kaufmann Publishers (2007)
5. Romanov, V., Veynberg, R., Poluektova, A.: Customer-Telecommunications Company's Relationship Simulation Model (RSM). In: Based on Non-Monotonic Business Rules Approach and Formal Concept Analysis Method//Spring Sim 2011. Program Book (2011)

A Combined Method for Evaluating Criteria When Selecting ERP Systems

David L. Olson[1], Björn Johansson[2], and Rogério Atem de Carvalho[3]

[1] Department of Management, University of Nebraska, Lincoln, NE 68588-0491
Dolson3@unl.edu
[2] Department of Informatics, School of Economics and Management, Lund University,
Ole Römers väg 6, SE-223 63 Lund, Sweden
bjorn.johansson@ics.lu.se
[3] Federal Center for Technological Education of Campos (CEFET Campos),
R. Dr. Siqueira 273, CEP 28030-130, Campos/RJ, Brazil
ratem@cefetcampos.br

Abstract. There are many benefits offered by integrated enterprise computer systems. There are a growing number of options available to obtain such management information system support. A major problem when selecting Enterprise Information Systems, in special ERP systems, is how to deal with the great diversity of options as well as the number of criteria used to evaluate each alternative. There is an implicit tradeoff between cost and system functionality. Total cost of ownership (TCO) is in itself very difficult to calculate accurately, and needs to be considered in light of other criteria. Published criteria for ERP selection decisions in a variety of contexts are reviewed. We also present a method which integrates a multicriteria rating strategy based on the Simple MultiAttribute Rating Theory (SMART) with the meta-method Prepare-Identify-Rate-Compare-Select (PIRCS) framework for driving the selection process. The method is demonstrated with a general ERP selection decision, but is meant as a framework that can be applied with whatever criteria decision makers deem important in the context of their specific decision.

Keywords: ERP selection process, multiple criteria selection, decision criteria.

1 Introduction

Organizations can benefit a great deal from integrated enterprise systems, obtaining increased data accuracy through single-source databases, more efficient operations through business process reengineering, and reduced information technology payroll. The number of options is increasing, beyond top-of-the-line vendor systems such as SAP and Oracle, through more moderately priced vendors such as Microsoft and Lawson [1], to application service providers offering rental of enterprise computing. However, there is risk involved, especially for small businesses [2], [3]. In specific countries, such as China [4], Brazil [5], and elsewhere [6], there are additional local forms of ERP. One option that has become viable in the past decade is the open source alternative providing free software from various business models [7]. There are many enterprise system options available. When selecting an ERP option there is

C. Møller and S. Chaudhry (Eds.): CONFENIS 2011, LNBIP 105, pp. 64–74, 2012.

a general tradeoff between functionality and cost, although total cost of ownership (TCO) is a complex matter that defies accurate calculation [8]. This paper reviews criteria that have been published in the literature with respect to selection of enterprise resource planning (ERP) system. It also demonstrates how the meta-method PIRCS (prepare, identify, rate, compare, and select) [9] can be implemented through the simple multiattribute rating theory (SMART) [10].

2   ERP Selection Criteria

Many papers have dealt with selection among alternative means of obtaining ERP systems. Baki and Çaki [6] reviewed criteria considered by prior studies in manufacturing firms, and conducted a survey of 55 Turkish manufacturing companies concerning the importance of these criteria, adding references, consultancy, implementation time, and software methodology to the criteria used by the prior studies. Baki and Çaki used a 1-5 Likert scale, the mean of which is reported in the last column. A rating of 1 indicated lowest possible importance and a rating of 5 indicated highest possible importance (see Table 1).

Table 1. Comparative Criteria in ERP Selection in Manufacturing Firms

Criteria	[11]	[12]	[13]	[14]	[15]	Mean
Fit with allied organizations					*	4.79
Cross module integration				*	*	4.72
Compatibility with other systems		*				4.28
References						4.24
Vision	*			*		4.22
Functionality	*	*		*	*	4.15
System reliability					*	4.08
Consultancy						4.06
Technical aspects	*	*	*	*		4.01
Implementation time						3.94
Vendor market position				*	*	3.87
Ease of customization		*			*	3.84
Software methodology						3.83
Fit with organization					*	3.83
Service & support	*		*		*	3.77
Cost	*	*	*	*	*	3.65
Vendor domain knowledge			*			3.46

Baki and Çaki analyzed their data for differences between organizations that adopted MRP or MRP-II systems versus those who had not. They found no statistically significant difference between these two groups. Their inference was that prior exposure was not an important factor. The results show that all factors had some positive importance (as 3 would indicate neutrality), but Table 1 indicates that external fit (such as supply chain linkage) and software factors tend to be rated higher than organizational factors such as fit, service and support, and cost.

Open source ERP software is attractive for all small organizations. Three studies were found giving criteria for this domain. Criteria considered varied when selecting open source ERP as can be seen in Table 2.

Table 2. Open Source ERP Software Selection Criteria

Criteria	[16]	[17]	[18]
Technology	Technical requirements	Complexity of technology East of database administration	Database migration
BPR	Business drivers	Ease of business logic implementation	Synchorizing modules to workflow
User interface		Ease of presentation layer implementation	User friendly interfaces
Administration		Ease of administration	Integration with 3rd party software
Cost	Cost drivers		
Others	Flexibility Scalability Business specific	Ease of service exposure Resource utilization	User support

Benroider and Koch [19] sampled 138 small or medium sized organizations in Austria who had selected an ERP system about the criteria they used in their decisions. Small or medium sized was defined on the basis of the number of employees, based upon European Community standards. Large vendors were considered by almost all subjects, but a bit over 47 percent considered smaller ERP vendors. SAP was selected by nearly 70 percent of the samples, and small vendors by a little over 23.3 percent. There was a bias for larger organizations to select SAP. Delphi analysis was used to identify criteria deemed important. Benroider and Koch only reported criteria that had a strong relationship to organization size (focusing on those rated very important to SMEs). SMEs emphasized software adaptability and flexibility and shorter implementation time more than large organizations. Both SMEs and large organizations rated good support and process improvement as very important.

Other studies have looked at specific ERP selection contexts. Table 3 demonstrates further diversity of criteria proposed for consideration in the specific context of outsourcing (or ASP provider selection):

Table 3. ERP Selection Criteria for Outsourcing ERP

Study	Context	Criteria
[20]	Application service providers	Customer service Reliability, availability, scalability Integration Total cost Security Service level
[21]	Outsourcing	Market leadership Functionality Quality Price Implementation speed Link with other systems International orientation

3   Modeling ERP Selection

There are a number of selection models presented in the literature. Conjoint analysis is used in marketing to determine the relative importance of product characteristics to potential clients. Keil et al. [22] conducted conjoint analysis to ERP selection, using software characteristics and implementation attributes. That study received 126 completed responses of 7 software package profiles from MIS managers of large organizations (see Table 4). The study modeled manager likelihood of recommending system acquisition using multiple regression, with a model adjusted R^2 of 0.506.

Table 4. Results of Keil et al.'s Conjoint Analysis

Attribute	Effect	*t*-value	P<0.01	P<0.001
Software Reliability	0.464	20.34	Yes	Yes
Software Functionality	0.457	20.03	Yes	Yes
Software Cost	-0.253	-11.08	Yes	Yes
Implementation Ease of Customization	0.129	5.67	Yes	Yes
Software Ease of Use	0.073	3.19	Yes	No
Implementation Vendor Reputation	0.007	0.29	No	No
Implementation Ease	0.000	0.01	No	No

The results indicate predominance of software factors over implementation factors. Only ease of customization was significant among the implementation factors. In this study, cost was found significant, but not as significant as software reliability and functionality. The subject firms were large. That set of ERP users can be expected to focus on getting the ERP system working. While cost is important, it's unpredictability would naturally be subsidiary to the necessity of obtaining required information system support. Ease of customization was significant, which indicates consideration of long-term life cycle cost. Ease of use was significant at a lower degree, while vendor reputation and ease of implementation were not significant. These last three factors relate to the impact of the system on the organization. MIS managers in the Keil et al. study placed less emphasis on these factors.

A second type of model using criteria is for decision maker selection. Among these models are analytic hierarchy process (AHP) [4], [23] and multiattribute utility theory, to include simple multiattribute rating theory (SMART) [10]. AHP has been the most widely used method in evaluating various aspects of ERP. Ahn and Choi [24] did so in a group context in South Korea, Salmeron and Lopez to evaluate ERP maintenance [25], Kahraman et al. [21] to consider ERP outsourcing, and Onut and Efendigil to ERP selection in Turkey [26]. The related analytic network process [27] was used by Ayağ and Özdemir [28] and Kirytopoulos et al. [29], allowing for feedback relationships.   Olson and Wu [30] applied SMART along with data envelopment analysis to consider information system risk.   One model for ERP selection used the criteria in Table 5 to compare alternative ERP vendors. That study [4] provided a thorough analysis of criteria starting with fundamental objectives for both system software factors and vendor factors, adding evaluation items at a third level, and identifying constraints reflecting means. The methodology was presented in a group decision making context. The hierarchy consisted of: factors, attributes, evaluation items and means.

Table 5. Value Analysis Hierarchy [4]

Factors	Attributes	Evaluation items	Means
System software	Total costs	Price Maintenance Consultant expenses Infrastructure costs	Project budget Annual maintenance budget Infrastructure budget
	Implementation time		Duration Project management
	Functionality	Module completion Function fitness Security	Necessary module availability Currency, language, site issues Permission management Database protection
	User friendliness	Ease of operation Ease of learning	Guidebook Online learning, help
	Flexibility	Upgrade ability Ease of integration Ease of in-house development	Common programming language Platform independence Ease of integration
	Reliability	Stability Recovery ability	Automatic data recovery Automatic data backup
Vendor factors	Reputation	Scale of vendor Financial condition Market share	Financial stability Provision of reference sites
	Technical capability	R&D ability Technical support Implementation	Upgrade service Diverse product line Implementation experience Adequate number of engineers Cooperation with partners Domain knowledge

Another AHP model was applied to selecting an ERP system specific to clothing industry suppliers [31]. Criteria were selected based upon discussion with three such suppliers, as well as literature reviews. Criteria were:

- Cost
- Functionality
- Implementation approach
- Support
- Organizational credibility
- Experience
- Flexibility
- Customer focus
- Future strategy.

Cost benefit analysis was conducted for the first criterion, while AHP was used to generate a synthesis value for the other eight criteria. The ratio of synthesis value to normalized costs was used to rank alternatives.

ANP was applied to benchmarking and selecting ERP systems [32], applying the approach to an actual selection decision (see Table 6).

Table 6. System and Vendor Selection Criteria [32]

System Factors	Vendor Factors
Functionality	Market share
Strategic fitness	Financial capability
Flexibility	Implementation ability
User friendliness	R&D capability
Implementation time	Service support
Total costs	
Reliability	

Kahraman et al. [21] applied fuzzy modeling to a form of AHP for evaluation of selecting an outsourced ERP alternative. Table 7 shows the detailed criteria used by Kahraman et al. through two levels.

Table 7. AHP Hierarchy [21]

Top Level Criteria	Second Level Criteria
Market Leadership	Relevant technology
	Innovative business process
	Competitive position
Functionality	Consumer preference
	Functional capability
	Compatibility with third party
Quality	Reliability
	Security
	Information Quality
	Configuration
Price	Service cost
	Operating cost
	Set-up cost
Implementation speed	Performance
	Usability
	Training
Interface with other systems	Data share
	Compatibility with the system
	Multi-level user
	Flexibility
International orientation	National CRM
	Web applications

4 The PIRCS and SMART Frameworks

PIRCS was proposed for free/open source ERP systems (FOS-ERP) [9]. PIRCS can be understood as a *meta-method*, given that it is composed by a series of procedures that should be adapted for specific purposes, according to the adopter's software evaluation culture and specific needs.

PIRCS is completely compatible with the simple multiattribute rating theory (SMART) model [10]. Olson [33] presented a SMART analysis of an ERP selection decision considering the seven criteria found on Table 3, taken from [20]. It is clear that there are many ways to approach incorporation of multiple criteria in ERP selection models. We have tried to demonstrate the importance of context with respect to the selection of these criteria. In the next section we present a model that aims at demonstrating context such as size of organization as important.

4.1   Demonstration Model for Small Business ERP Selection

It is possible to include many criteria, but it has been argued that a limited number of independent and equally scaled criteria will include the bulk of the relative importance [34].

The PIRCS framework for evaluation of ERP alternatives consists of the following steps:

- **Prepare:** define requirements, establish positioning strategy, identify attributes and constraints on the decision, and measures of attributes to be considered.
- **Identify:** Use searches to identify alternative ERP options and their characteristics.
- **Rate:** Establish the utility (value) of each attribute on each alternative.
- **Compare:** Apply multicriteria methods, such as AHP or SMART.
- **Select:** Consider the comparison analysis from the prior step and make the decision.

The focus of this paper is to demonstrate the use of SMART as a means to implement the Compare step.

We assume the context of a small business considering the criteria and options given in Table 8. The criteria would be identified in the **Prepare** step, and the options in the **Identify** step. The rating entries would be established in the third step, **Rate**. Criteria used here include cost, time, and robustness [9], as well as the most significant criteria identified for SMEs [19]. Ratings are scaled on a 0-1 range, with 0 indicating worst possible performance, and 1 indicating best possible performance. The assignment of these values should be done in the context of the organization, reflecting values of organizational decision makers. Table 8 shows the value matrix from the PIRCS Rate step, which is input to the SMART analysis. The entries in Table 8 are of course demonstrative. Cost values reflect best estimates of total life cycle costs. While OSS without support would be free with respect to software acquisition, there would be costs of implementing as well as training users.

Table 8. Value Matrix

	Cost	Time	Flexibility	Robustness	Support
Large vendor	0.2	0.3	0.1	1.0	1.0
Customize vendor	0.0	0.0	0.8	0.7	0.5
Mid-size vendor	0.4	0.6	0.5	0.5	0.6
OSS with support fees	0.7	0.9	0.6	0.8	0.7
OSS without support	0.6	0.6	0.5	0.4	0.0

The fourth step is to **Compare**. Using the SMART approach, this includes identification of relative weights of importance (scale has been removed by identifying value ratings on 0-1 scales for all attributes). Use of swing weighting would begin by ordering criteria by importance, then assigning the most important criterion a value of 100. The other criteria are assessed in turn on the basis of: if the most important criterion was swung from its worst possible state to its best possible state, how relatively important would the next criterion be worth when swung from its worst possible state to its best possible state. Standardized weights are generated by dividing each assessed relative weighting by the sum of these relative weightings. Our demonstrative developed weights are presented in Table 9:

Table 9. Swing Weighting

Criteria by order	Relative weighting	Standardized weighting (/320)
Time	100	0.312
Robustness	80	0.250
Support	70	0.219
Cost	40	0.125
Flexibility	30	0.094
SUM	**320**	**1.000**

The **Select** step should be done judgmentally, by the organization's decision maker. The SMART analysis should be viewed in terms of decision support (not letting the model make the final decision). However, the PIRCS framework and SMART analysis will provide decision makers with a systematic means to consider important factors and provide greater confidence in the decision. Here the **Select** output would multiply the ratings in Table 8 by the weights in Table 9, yielding the relative scores shown in Table 10.

Table 10. Alternative Relative Scores

Alternative	Score
OSS with support fees	0.778
Large vendor	0.597
Mid-size vendor	0.541
ASP	0.446
OSS without support	0.409
Customize vendor	0.360

The implication is that the relatively moderate ratings over all attributes for the OSS with support fees option led to total value greater than that of the large vendor (which did very well on robustness and support, but very poorly on the other three criteria). The mid-size vendor was moderate on all criteria, but turned out to be dominated by the OSS with support fees option in the assumed context.

5   Conclusions and Future Research

There are many criteria that can be important in the selection of ERP systems. We have tried to show that the context in which such decisions are made is important. While there have been many studies of this matter, there is not universal agreement by any means. Furthermore, each individual organization should be expected to find various criteria critical while other criteria may be more important for other organizations. The ERP environment is also highly dynamic. In the 1990s, ERP was usually only feasible for large organizations. That is changing.

A business case for evaluation of software systems of any type is challenging. Cost estimates involve high levels of uncertainty, and benefits are usually in the realm of pure guesswork. A sound analytic approach is called for, especially given the large price tags usually present in ERP systems. There is a need for a method that can consider expected monetary impact along with other factors, to include risk elements such as project time and system robustness, as well as relatively subjective elements of value such as flexibility and availability of support. The PIRCS process and SMART multiattribute analysis offer a means to systematically evaluate ERP software proposals.

Multiattribute analysis has studied decision making under tradeoffs for a long time. It is quite robust, and can support consideration of a varying number of criteria. It usually is the case that for a specific decision, a relatively small number of criteria matter. If nothing else, the simple fact that if there are seven other criteria more important, the highest relative importance an eighth criterion could have is 0.125, with a high likelihood of a much lower weight [35]. This paper had the purpose of describing how the PIRCS framework could support the critical process of ERP software alternative evaluation, along with multiattribute analysis to consider the inevitable trade-offs that are encountered in such decisions. The demonstration of the combination of the PIRCS framework and the SMART analysis shows that the huge diversity of different options on ERP systems can be managed. The combined framework has a huge potential when it comes to deal with context related factors when making a selection on what option to implement. It also concisely shows tradeoffs among criteria being considered. However, the framework is dependent on that relevant and correct data on every option is possible to have. This is especially true with respect to life-cycle cost, which is very difficult to predict for most organizations, which hopefully do not have to repeat ERP selection decisions very often.

Future research is important in understanding what criteria are important in particular contexts. For instance, free open source ERP systems are emerging, broadening the market for enterprise system support.

References

1. Olson, D.L., Kesharwani, S.: Enterprise Information Systems: Contemporary Trends and Issues. World Scientific, Singapore (2010)
2. Poba-Nzaou, P., Raymond, L., Fabi, B.: Adoption and Risk of ERP Systems in Manufacturing SMEs: A Positivist Case Study. Business Process Management Journal 14(4), 530–550 (2008)

3. Kirytopoulos, K., Voulgaridou, D., Panopoulos, D., Leopoulosm, V.: Project Termination Analysis in SMEs: Making the Right Call. International Journal of Management & Decision Making 10(1/2), 69–90 (2009)
4. Wei, C.-C., Chien, C.-F., Wang, M.-J.: An AHP-Based Approach to ERP System Selection. International Journal of Production Economics 96, 47–62 (2005)
5. De Carvalho, R.A.: Free/Open Source Enterprise Resources Planning. In: Jatinder Gupta, N.D., Rashid, M.A., Sharma, S.K. (eds.) Handbook of Research on Enterprise Systems, pp. 32–44. Information Science Reference, Hershey (2009)
6. Baki, B., Çaki, K.: Determining the ERP Package-Selecting Criteria: The Case of Turkish Manufacturing Companies. Business Process Management Journal 11(1), 75–86 (2005)
7. Johansson, B., de Carvalho, R.A.: Management of Requirements in ERP Development: A Comparison Between Proprietary and Open Source ERP. In: ACM Symposium of Applied Computing, Honolulu, Hawaii, March 8-12, pp. 1605–1609 (2009)
8. Kabassi, K., Virvou, V.: A Knowledge-Based Software Life-Cycle Framework for the Incorporation of Multicriteria Analysis in Intelligent User Interfaces. IEEE Transactions on Knowledge and Data Engineering 18(9), 1265–1277 (2006)
9. De Carvalho, R.A.: Issues on Evaluating Free/Open Source ERP Systems. In: Tjoa, A.M., Xu, L., Chaudhry, S. (eds.) International Federation for Information Processing. Research and Practical Issues of Enterprise Information Systems, vol. 205, pp. 667–675. Springer, Boston (2006)
10. Edwards, W.: Social Utilities. The Engineering Economist 6, 119–129 (1971)
11. Hecht, B.: Choose the Right ERP Software. Datamation 43(3), 56–58 (1997)
12. Brewer, G.: On the Road to Successful ERP. Instrumentation & Control Systems 73(5), 49–58 (2000)
13. Rao, S.S.: Enterprise Resource Planning: Business Needs and Technologies. Industrial Management & Data System 100(2), 81–88 (2000)
14. Verville, J., Hallingten, A.: An Investigation of the Decision Process for Selecting an ERP Software: The Case of ESC. Management Decision 40(3), 206–216 (2002)
15. Kumar, V., Maheshwari, B., Kumar, U.: An Investigation of Critical Management Issues in ERP Implementation: Empirical Evidence from Canadian Organizations. Technovation 23, 793–807 (2003)
16. Reuther, D.: Critical Factors for Enterprise Resources Planning System Selection and Implementation Projects within Small to Medium Enterprises. In: International Engineering Management Conference, pp. 851–855 (2004)
17. Rittammanart, N., Wongyued, W., Dailey, M.N.: ERP Application Development Frameworks: Case Study and Evaluation. In: Proceedings of ECTI-CON, pp. 173–176 (2008)
18. Baharum, Z., Ngadiman, M.S., Haron, H.: Critical Factors to Ensure the Success of OS-ERP Implementation Based on Technical Requirement Point of View. In: Third Asia International Conference on Modelling & Simulation, pp. 419–424 (2009)
19. Benroider, E., Koch, S.: ERP Selection Process in Midsize and Large Organizations. Business Process Management Journal 7(3), 251–257 (2001)
20. Ekanayaka, Y., Currie, W.L., Selsikas, P.: Evaluating Application Service Providers. Benchmarking: An International Journal 10(4), 343–354 (2003)
21. Kahraman, C., Beskese, A., Kaya, I.: Selection Among ERP Outsourcing Alternatives Using a Fuzzy Multi-Criteria Decision Making Methodology. International Journal of Production Research 48(2), 547–566 (2009)
22. Keil, M., Tiwana, A.: Relative Importance of Evaluation Criteria for Enterprise Systems: A Conjoint Study. Information Systems Journal 16, 237–262 (2006)

23. Saaty, T.L.: A Scaling Method for Priorities in Hierarchical Structures. Journal of Mathematical Psychology 15, 234–281 (1977)
24. Ahn, B.S., Choi, S.H.: ERP system selection using a simulation-based AHP approach: A case of Korean homeshopping company. Journal of the Operational Research Society 59(3), 322–330 (2008)
25. Salmeron, J.L., Lopez, C.: A multicriteria approach for risks assessment in ERP maintenance. Journal of Systems & Software 83(10), 1941–1953 (2010)
26. Onut, S., Efendigil, T.: A theoretical model design for ERP software selection process under the constraints of cost and quality: A fuzzy approach. Journal of Intellilgent & Fuzzy Systems 21(6), 365–378 (2010)
27. Saaty, T.L.: The Analytic Network Process: Decision Making with Dependence and Feedback. RWS Publications, Pittsburgh (1996)
28. Ayağ, Z., Özdemir, R.G.: An intelligent approach to ERP software selection through fuzzy ANP. International Journal of Production Research 45(10), 2169–2194 (2007)
29. Kirytopoooulos, K., Voulgaridou, D., Panopoulos, D., Leopoulos, V.: Project termination analysis in SMEs: Making the right call. International Journal of Management & Decision Making 10(1/2), 69–90 (2009)
30. Olson, D.L., Wu, D.D.: Multiple criteria analysis for evaluation of information system risk. Asia-Pacific Journal of Operational Research 28(11), 25–39 (2011)
31. Ünal, C., Güner, M.G.: Selection of ERP Suppliers Using AHP Tools in the Clothing Industry. International Journal of Clothing Science and Technology 21(4), 239–251 (2009)
32. Perçin, S.: Using the ANP Approach in Selecting and Benchmarking ERP Systems. Benchmarking: An International Journal 15(5), 630–649 (2008)
33. Olson, D.L.: Evaluation of ERP outsourcing. Computers & Operations Research 34(12), 3715–3724 (2007)
34. Olson, D.L.: Decision Aids for Selection Problems. Springer, New York (1996)
35. Miller, G.: The Magical Number Seven Plus or Minus Two: Some Limits on Our Capacity for Processing Information. Psychological Review 3(2), 81–97 (1956)

Deployment of Open Source ERPs: What Knowledge Does It Require?

Björn Johansson and Vadim Koroliov

Department of Informatics, School of Economics and Management, Lund University,
Ole Römers väg 6,
SE-223 63 Lund, Sweden
bjorn.johansson@ics.lu.se, v.koroliov@gmail.com

Abstract. Enterprise resource planning (ERP) systems are rapidly becoming a de facto standard in business activity. While large and medium-sized companies have the luxury to afford proprietary ERP solutions, small companies are struggling with resource poverty which maybe makes them consider available open source ERP products which are free from licensing fee. However, there is little knowledge available on open source ERP adoption in small companies. In order to spread some light on the first phase of ERP adoption, an experiment on open source ERP deployment was conducted. The experiment aimed at investigating what knowledge is required to successfully deploy open source ERP systems. The experiment was based on a research framework, the Technology Acceptance Model 2 (TAM2), and considered usability testing and user training and education factors. The factors of Perceived Ease of Use (PEOU) and Perceived Usefulness (PU) were used to determine the ease of deployment process, and the usefulness of the open source ERP deployed in relation to the made effort. The findings suggest that user with advanced computer skills perceive open source ERP deployment process as easy, and the deployed open source ERP was seen as being useful to organizations business activities.

Keywords: Deployment experiment, Enterprise resource planning systems, ERPs. , Open source, Small organizations, SMEs.

1   Introduction

In organizations, there is a growing need for managing information to become competitive and sustain such advantage over a longer period of time. Therefore, many organizations have implemented extensive enterprise information systems, such as enterprise resource planning (ERP) systems, to obtain a better control over information and thereby acquire advantages over its competitors [1] by, for instance, getting better and faster access to information stored. However, deployment can be problematic for organizations since it can take long time and cost a lot of money; and there is also a high risk that it may fail [1-3]. Despite that, there is an increased interest in ERPs among organizations which also has created an interest in developing

C. Møller and S. Chaudhry (Eds.): CONFENIS 2011, LNBIP 105, pp. 75–91, 2012.
© IFIP International Federation for Information Processing 2012

simplified versions of ERPs. These simplified versions are developed both by proprietary ERP vendors, such as Microsoft Dynamics or SAP, as well as by new vendor organizations in the open source (OS) area. The open source ERP projects could be seen as an alternative to traditional ERP proprietary systems available today. In general it can be suggested that OS have grown large and still continues to grow strongly as more and more organizations become interested in how they can benefit from OS in their organization [4]. Therefore, it could be suggested that organizations, in their search for having an ERP system implemented in their organization, could consider an open source ERP system. Consequently, an interesting question follows if this is doable or not. From an earlier investigation done by Johansson and Sudzina [5], we know that there are a lot of open source ERPs available for download from an online service such as SourceForge. On the other side, what we do not know is, if this is done or if it is feasible for an organization to do so? This directs to the question discussed in this paper which is: What knowledge is required to successfully deploy open source ERP systems?

To be able to say something about this, Section 2 defines open source ERP and open source ERP deployment. Section 3 presents the research conducted, which could be briefly described as a controlled experiment of downloading and making a first usage test of an open source ERP system. The experiment aims at describing knowledge needed to successfully deploy open source ERP systems. Section 4 analyzes the results from the experiment and discusses the knowledge required to successfully deploy open source ERP systems. In the final section some conclusions are provided, and some future research questions in the context of open source ERP deployment are suggested.

2   ERPs, Open Source ERPs and Open Source ERP Deployment

Enterprise Resource Planning systems (ERPs) are major investments for organizations, and according to Morabito et al., [6] have high attention among practitioners, academia, and media. They state that ERP research primarily focuses on two aspects: 1) organizational and economic impact of ERP implementation, and 2) how to best manage implementation. There are a number of key characteristics that more or less all ERP system share making them a unique subtype of information systems. Firstly, ERP is defined as a standardized packaged software [7] designed to integrate entire organization [8-10], its business processes and ICT into a synchronized suite of procedures, applications and metrics which transcend organizational boundaries [11] and that can be bought (or rented) from an external provider and adapted to firm's specific requirements.

The fact that ERPs are assumed to integrate the organization (both inter-organizationally as well as intra-organizationally) and its business process into one package, feeds the complexity of ERPs when it comes to development and implementation as well as usage [12]. Millman [13] posits that ERPs are the most expensive but least-value-derived implementation of information and communication technology (ICT) support. The reason for this, according to Millman, is that a lot of ERPs functionality is either not used or is implemented in a wrong way. In addition, wrong implementation results from ERPs being customized to fit the business processes, instead of changing the processes to fit the ERP [13], described by Hammer and Champy [14] as "paving the cow path".

Several studies on inspiring success [15], but also failures [16, 17], associated with implementation and utilization of ERPs [18] exist. Benefits are only related in part to the technology, and most come from organizational changes such as new business processes, organizational structure, work procedures, integration of administrative and operative activities, and global standardization of work practices leading to organizational improvements, supported by the technology [19]. It can definitely be said that implementation of ERP systems is a difficult and costly organizational "experiment" [18], and implementation of ERP systems can be described [20] as "perhaps the world's largest experiment in business change" and for most organizations "the largest change project in cost and time that they have undertaken in their history". The implementation is a necessary but insufficient prerequisite for benefits and value, at least for having competitive parity [21].

According to Wieder et al. [22] there is no significant performance difference between ERP adopters and non-adopters either on process or overall firm levels. In conclusion, it can be claimed that there are different opinions on benefits and advantages of ERP systems adoption.

Nevertheless, the market tendency shows that ERP adoption is growing and will grow among organizations worldwide. Jacobson et al. [23] denote - in their report on ERP market sizing - that ERP investments among large corporations as well as small and medium-sized enterprises (SME) are continuously increasing. The ERP systems became in practice an industry standard [24] and, as argued by Shehab et al., [25] considered to be the price of entry for running a business.

From this it can be said that the ERP products market have grown. Up to recent years, the ERP systems offer has been primarily characterized by proprietary software products. The largest ERP vendors to present are SAP, Oracle, Infor and Microsoft. In the same time, the industry witnessed the proliferation of open source ERP packages as well. The open source ERP packages, and namely community-based versions, provide a free alternative to commercial ERP packages. Some notable examples are OpenBravo, Compiere, TinyERP, OFBiz, Adempiere, xTuple/PostBook and others, and the majority of them target SMEs.

One would wonder why they are free. Usually, the companies who stand behind these products earn money in a different way, other than traditional. Along with the community version, which is completely free, there are commercial versions with better support, updates and upgrades.

In brief, open source ERP vendors bring a couple of reasons of why to choose open source ERP. Firstly, there are no upfront licensing fees. Anyone can download the software from vendor's website and try the product for free. Thus, assess whether it suits or not the company's needs. Secondly, open source offers free control of software customization with the support of contributing communities and organizations. There is also professional-quality support available from companies working with that specific ERP. And one of the last arguments is that open source reduces the specification risk, characteristic to custom built software; and loss of vendor risk (Opentaps.org, 2011). Not less important is the promise of "be up and running with a full system in 10 minutes" (xTuple.com, 2011) – this, in particular, makes it very interesting to challenge.

Fougatsaro [26] presents the following seven reasons of why organizations should choose open source ERP:

- Flexibility – the available source code makes it easier to customize and integrate the open source ERP with existing systems.
- Quality – as a result of commitment of vendors and communities to development efforts.
- Ability to adapt to business environment
- No hidden costs – as opposed to proprietary ERP systems, where changes scalability issues might be imminent.
- Ability of specific developments – freedom of customizing and development
- Free of vendor dependence – the support is provided both by community and commercial vendors.
- Freedom to upgrade or not.

Fougatsaro [26] claims that despite all these benefits, open source software also has disadvantages. The comparison of proprietary and open-source (community/free) ERP advantages and disadvantages, as well as a total cost of ownership analysis have been researched to a limited extent. As stated by Carvalho [27] the full picture of open source ERP's issues and benefits still has to be covered. Therefore, it might be difficult to evaluate which type of ERP brings the most value. However, this of course impacts the decision when adopting or not, but this is outside the scope of this paper that focuses on open source ERP deployment and knowledge required for doing that.

2.1   Open Source ERP Deployment in SMEs

In recent years, ERP systems have become very attractive to SMEs, i.e. the SMEs' interest towards ERP system has increased. And this happened due to a number of reasons. Firstly, ERP vendors have shifted their development efforts focus from mainly large customers - today a saturated market, to small and medium sized companies – a promising market both in cash and in customers. Consequently, the range of ERP packages offer has considerably increased, adjusting to the needs and pockets of various companies [28]. Secondly, it is the highly dynamic business environment which requires ERP adoption in order to gain competitive advantage over rivals [28]. In the same context, Jacobson et al., [23] mention that ERP adoption among SMEs comes as a response to new customer requirements, as well as to the wish to participate in a highly global market. And finally, ERP systems offer unprecedented advantages over any other traditional models of managing businesses [29].

However, before any further statements are made about SMEs and ERPs, it is important to define SMEs. In this context SMEs are defined as: companies from 10 to 49 employees are considered to be small, companies from 50 to 249 employees are considered being midsized, and companies having 250+ employees are considered to be large companies. This definition is consistent with how the European Commission [30] defines SMEs. However, this paper regards organizations with less than 10 employees (micro) as small, the reasons are that constraints and objectives of ERP systems in this group of organizations could be considered the same [31]. However, as Laukannen et al. state, there are significant differences between small and medium-sized companies and therefore they should not be considered as a homogeneous category. The same is claimed by Carvalho and Johansson [32].

In terms of general constraints, small companies, in comparison to medium-sized, have a lower user IT competence and insufficient information, but are less sensitive to changes enforced by ERP implementation. In terms of ERP objectives, medium-sized companies feel eager to develop new strategic ways of doing business, and are more interested in expanding its business activity [31].

It can also be said that small companies, despite having a growing interest for ERP, have a low actual rate of ERP adoption. Laukannen et al. [31] point out that resource poverty is one the main constraints of ERP system adoption, i.e. they cannot afford one. Small companies, in comparison to mid-size and large enterprises, have limited or scarce resources. Then the logical question arises: so why not chose the free ERP?

Somewhat apparent, the financial factor can be crucial and decisive for small companies. However, Johansson and Sudzina [5] mention that cost is not the only factor affecting the selection and adoption processes of an open source ERP. Laukannen et al. [31] suggest that knowledge is another determinant barrier lying in the way of ERP adoption in small companies specifically, whether it is IT competency, enough information for decision-making in ERP selection or system usage.

It is crucial to understand that knowledge requirements change along various stages of ERP life cycle and embrace a large set of skills, experiences, abilities and perspectives [33]. In other words, type of knowledge required in implementation phase, for example, would be different from what knowledge is needed in the system use phase. However, there is no scientific support whatsoever for knowledge requirements for open source ERP deployment.

Given that a small company intends to adopt an open source ERP for free, it would be both interesting and challenging to find out how much knowledge is needed or how easy it is to deploy – choose, implement and use - an open source ERP, and when deployed if it meets the expected outcomes/benefits.

3   The Open Source ERP Deployment Experiment

The objective of the open source ERP deployment experiment was two-folded. On one hand, it was to find out the required knowledge in the open source ERP adoption process in small companies, and namely, the actual prerequisites, needs and issues with an open source ERP in the early stage of adoption, i.e. its deployment. The prerequisites, needs and issues are to cover the time and knowledge aspects. On the other hand, it is also interesting if the open source ERP is found useful in relation to the effort required to deploy it.

The data collected was based on TAM2 model developed by Venkatesh and Davis [34]. In other words, TAM2 model was used as lens for assessing the open source ERP deployment process (Perceived Ease of Use) and its primary impact on business and its users (Perceived Usefulness). The experiment focused on three questions:

- How much effort – time and knowledge - does it take to deploy an open source ERP?
- What is the perceived ease of use in the deployment stage?
- What is the perceived usefulness of open source ERP in the deployment stage?

3.1   The Foundation of the Experiment

In the realities of small companies, where the resources and knowledge are limited, open source ERPs seem to be a viable solution. First of all, the product is free regarding license cost, so initial costs could be said are low. However, the problem of knowledge still remains, because it is still unclear how much knowledge is required to adopt and use an open source ERP. Therefore, it would be interesting to find out how much effort is required to deploy and start using open source ERP systems. In order to address this issue, the Technology Acceptance Model 2 was used.

3.2   Technology Acceptance Model 2 (TAM2)

TAM2 comes as an extension to the initial Technology Acceptance Model (TAM) developed by Davis [35]. Both of the models or both versions address the subject of system usage. The model helps to understand and evaluate the reasons and factors which affect the use and adoption of new systems or existing systems. Also, the TAM model is viewed as a tool to measure users will and intention to adopt a system. In this research papers, TAM2 will also serve as a measuring tool to assess the ease and usefulness of an open source ERP.

The initial model was limited to two factors, which in opinion of its author, affect the intention and use of a system: perceived ease of use (PEOU) and perceived usefulness (PU). Despite its popularity and use, Venkatesh and Davis [34] suggested an extension. The extended features take into consideration the external factors which affect perceived usefulness (see Figure 1). Venkatesh and Davis [34] explain that external factors have social and cognitive character.

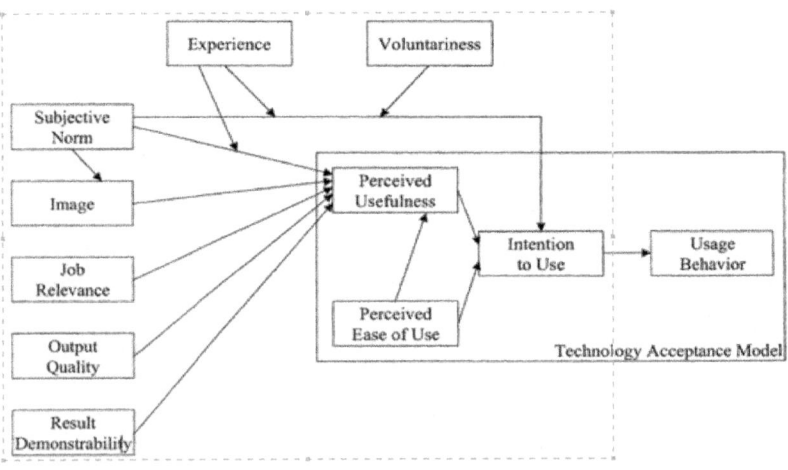

Fig. 1. The TAM2 model and scope of this research [34]

Perceived usefulness is the extent the user thinks the systems helps her or him to perform the tasks, i.e. job activities. *Perceived ease of use* measures the effort required to use a system, i.e. how easy it is to perform the job tasks. PEOU affects the PU and the *Intention to Use*. One user's intention to use affects in turn the actual usage of the systems, i.e. determines the *Usage Behavior*.

The external factors are explained by Venkatesh and Davis [34] as follows: *Subjective norm*, is a "person's perception that most people who are important to him think he should or should not perform the behavior in question". The key idea behind is that persons are susceptible to other people' ideas and views. That is why some persons perform actions motivated by other people.

Voluntariness is "the extent to which potential adopters perceive the adoption decision to be non-mandatory" [34]. In other words, voluntariness determines if system use is perceived as obligatory and unwilling or opposite to these.

Image has a positive effect on perceived usefulness, if the use of the system is to enhance user's social status or image; otherwise it has a negative effect on perceived usefulness. *Experience* might also have a positive or negative effect on PU. It is considered that a system is most like to be perceived useful if the user is experienced.

Job relevance, as defined by Venkatesh and Davis [34], is "an individual's perception regarding the degree to which the target system is applicable to his or her job". In other words, job relevance measures whether a system use is important to daily job tasks.

Output Quality measures the quality level of the tasks performed by the system. In other words, if the task performed by the system is perfect, then the perceived usefulness of the system is appreciated higher.

And ultimately, *Result Demonstrability* measures the tangibility of the results given by a system. Venkatesh and Davison [34] explain that "even effective systems can fail to garner user acceptance if people have difficulty attributing gains in their job performance, specifically to their use of the system". That is why it is important for users to see direct results of their system use, in order for the system to be perceived as useful.

This research paper's scope is limited to the deployment of a system, i.e. the installation and first use of an open source ERP system. That is why the use of the TAM2 model would be partial (the dotted line in Figure 1). And namely, the interest lies on perceived ease of use and perceived usefulness of the open source ERP in its installation and first use.

Consequently, the paper will focus on defining the effort needed for and usefulness of deploying an open source ERP in the realities of a small company, in terms of time and knowledge.

3.3   The Pre-study of Open Source ERP Deployment Experiment

The pre-study started with finding information about available open source ERPs on WWW. Having taken the suggestion of Johansson and Sudzina [5], the first source to look for open source software was www.sourceforge.org, which is the largest project promoting open source software. Using this portal's search function, the keywords "open source ERP" were queried. Over 13,000 hits came up, all of these were obviously not relevant.

According to sourceforge.org, the two most popular and downloaded open source CRM & ERP solutions were OpenBravo and PostBooks. So the next logical step was to check out the website of respective projects, and the information provided.

Both of the websites made a professional impression. OpenBravo impressed by the number of customers, and both of the open source ERPs have a large community of users. With no previous experience related to ERP and its activity, the deciding criteria for choosing one was the technical criteria and requirements. It was relatively easy to find the download page and proceed to downloading. Both software products offered solution for cloud, Linux and Windows platforms, however PostBooks/xTuple offered also for Apple/MAC OS users.

Having consulted the available documentation, first difficulties appeared. OpenBravo promised a very simple, one-click installation for Linux users, but more complicated installation paths for other platforms, i.e. advanced computer skills are needed. xTuple software promised easy installation on all platforms. Having available only Linux and Windows operating systems, it was decided to try out OpenBravo on Linux and xTuple on Windows XP. Indeed, the installation process was very easy for OpenBravo, but with no transparency whatsoever. Only, advanced computer users could be able to follow the installation procedure. After installing, OpenBravo on Linux/Ubuntu the software ran in web browser successfully. Regarding, xTuple the installation procedure was as easy, plus the level of procedure transparency and clearness was quite high. The user is guided by explanatory instructions with options of choosing elements to be installed. By default, all elements are being installed. The software also ran with no errors on Windows XP. The approximate time for both installations was ten to fifteen minutes, with high speed internet available. At this point, it is important to mention that from the technical standpoint, the requirements are not high. The computer properties available were 1GB RAM, 10GB free space on hard drive, and Windows XP. The basic needs for installation are mentioned on the vendors' websites.

It was decided to proceed with xTuple. The argument behind was the availability and spread of Windows operation systems, so that theoretically most small companies would have a computer running Windows. The next step was to get acknowledged with xTuple open source ERP.

The log-in procedure was very easy. However, potential users have to pay attention to details while installing, because important information is given, such as credentials, which would be of use later on.

After log-in, the first thing was to get accustomed with menus available in the software. xTuples offers a very pleasant user interface, with large buttons and well organized modules, such as sales, inventory and other. For screenshots please visit www.xtuple.com.

After getting to know the software, the decision was to consult available documentation and tutorials on how to work with the ERP. There are many videos available; some of the videos are introductory, and some of them give detailed instructions on the internals and functions of the system. From the video tutorials, it was found out that following steps were required in order to get a valid invoice[1]:

---

[1] The following experiment aimed at having students downloading, installing and print an invoice with data from a business case.

1. Register a new user for the company
   a. Create separate account
   b. Enter details such as address, company info, logo etc.
2. Register the new customer with according details
3. Create a new product/item
4. Configure the taxation settings
5. Create a new sales order containing the product created
6. Ship and print out the invoice.

These steps were enough to print an invoice valid for Swedish standards, i.e. having required information. From the knowledge gained so far the actual deployment experiment took place.

3.4   The Study of Open Source ERP Deployment

There were two methods used for data collection, a structured questionnaire; that gathered data on students' general information profile, as well as on computer experience and knowledge. The purposes of questionnaire was to establish whether experiment participants had any previous experience which resembled the experience required in accomplishing the task, i.e. installing and using software.

The other data collection method was semi-structured interviews, giving the freedom to express the issues and thoughts regarding the easiness of deploying an open source ERP. The interviews were audio recorded, and after completion immediately transcribed.

The experiment involved three students, who were asked to download an open source ERP system; and then proceed with installing it. In the next phase, the students were asked to print out an invoice. In order to simulate a real business situation, a business case with enough data to print the first customer invoice was provided to them. And for the case to resemble a real business situation, all data contained were enough to make a valid invoice by means of Swedish regulations, i.e. VAT, Address details, Organizational number etc. During the experiment, the participants were continuously asked to assess the level of knowledge and effort required to complete a certain task. Printing of invoice was not set as the ultimate goal, but rather as a guiding objective which would take an amount of effort and user interaction with the software. Of great interest was the whole process, from its start to its end – printing the invoice. It is important to mention and understand, that this experiment shares features with observational studies and usability tests. Firstly, the intention of the experiment is to answer to the research questions posed by observing its participants in the settings close to reality, i.e. in front of the computer in an office. Lastly, the experiment shares the features of a usability test, where the system is tested for ease of use. However, the focus of this study is not the interface nor the productivity, but rather the whole experience of the participants from the very moment of deciding to look for an open source system to the very last moment of printing the first invoice.

The sampling technique was influenced by the organizational characteristics of small companies. According to Laukannen et al. [31] , size is the most significant factor which shapes the attitude of organizations towards ERPs. The attitude is expressed in terms of constraints and objectives for ERP adoption. In their study, a small enterprise was characterized by an average of 29 employees, with low IT competence, resource poverty, and representing a variety of industries: wholesale, logistics, retail and manufacturing. This tells that there are no strict requirements on choosing participants, as long as types of companies studied are various, and there are no strict requirements for IT skills. However, in order to avoid bias or misinterpretation accurate profiling of participants computer skills have been made.

The questions in the interview were constructed around two important aspects: 1) Perceived Ease of Use and 2) Perceived Usefulness.

The profiling questions, as previously mentioned, had the purpose of establishing the background of participants and their level of computer skills.

The questions related to Perceived Ease of Use had the purpose to assess the level of ease perceived in the open source ERP deployment process. As TAM2 is a quantifiable model, the participants were asked to answer PEOU questions on a scale from 1 to 5, were 1 was ranked as very easy and 5 – very difficult. Also, clarifying questions followed in order to get better explanation of why participants gave specific grades. The questions related to Perceived Usefulness were designed to assess the positive or negative influence of TAM2 external factors on PU.

The TAM2 model has been applied in two ways. The interviewees were first asked to grade the Perceived Ease of Use related to deployment experiment stages on a Likert-scale. This was done in order to assess the effort and knowledge needed to evaluate the process for the amount of effort needed to complete the tasks. After that, the interviewees were asked to elaborate on the effect of external factors on Perceived Usefulness, whether it was negative or positive. That was done in order to determine if the open source ERP delivered the benefits expected.

4   Analysis of the Deployment Experiment

In this section a summary of the empirical results will be presented. The structure follows the theoretical model and research questions, and, thus, the data will be arranged accordingly into the following parts: Profiling, Perceived Ease of Use, Perceived Usefulness. Perceived Ease of Use will cover subtopics: Finding and Choosing an open source ERP, Installing and Configuring an open source ERP, Accomplishing the Business Case tasks.

The interviewees who took part in the deployment experiment are all master students within Information Systems field. The computer experience has been assessed as between intermediate and advanced levels, with computer experience being seven years on average. Having been asked on their use of computers, they commonly replied that internet and studies are the main reasons. Only one of the students used computer for work and multimedia also. All students confirmed that they have successfully installed software on computers. Regarding software usage, all students have been using one or more software products for a long time, five years or more; and all of them have advanced skill level with the product they have been using over that period of time.

All students were given a business case, used as a guide in the deployment experiment. In brief, the experiment participants were asked to choose, install, configure and accomplish the task of printing the first invoice. These stages have been assessed for knowledge and time effort.

4.1   Finding and Choosing an Open Source ERP

Having been asked to find and choose an open source ERP, all students searched for one on Internet. The most common search keywords used were "open source ERP", "open source ERP free" and "open source ERP download". Asked to explain the logic behind the search actions, students clarified that they were willing to evaluate the search results given by Google according to their relevance. In other words, the students chose the first results on the Google's webpage, after having queried for open source ERP. The resulting webpage included for instance OpenBravo, xTuple, Compiere, Opentaps.

To the question on how easy it was to find an open source ERP, they all stated that finding one was very easy.

The students proceeded with looking at the websites available in the search results. Asked how the students evaluated different OS ERP choices, they gave different answers. One student took into consideration the professionalism of the website. In other words, he considered the looks and the design of the website. The rest of participants did not have any explanation for the choice. Ultimately, the users selected to proceed with xTuples/PostBooks open source ERP.

However, it is crucial to mention that none of the students took into consideration the technical parameters and requirements of the open source ERP.

4.2   Installing and Configuring an Open Source ERP

All students showed the same behavior during installation process. None of them gave too much consideration to installation and configuring information. They all proceeded with preconfigured elements.

One of the students explained that this behavior is due to lack of knowledge about certain parts of software, such as databases offered and other elements; adding that "sometimes this is scary just because there are things configured you don't know anything about it". But in order to be on the safe side, the students chose to install all elements suggested. Also, the rush can be explained by the wish to run and try out the software at once, skipping the configuration and installation details.

When asked to share the first impression about the installation and configuration process, they expressed that the process was very easy and took little time and effort.

4.3   Getting the First Invoice

This part of assignment was the most challenging and most complex for the students. Some of the issues happened right in the beginning of the task, when they could not find the credentials needed to login to the enterprise resource system. However, all three found the interface of the software very "handy" and pleasant.

Having familiarized themselves with the interface and menus, they proceeded with the task. During the task, they all stated that the software was intuitive and helped them in achieving their goal. However, it also created partial confusion due to multiple reasons such as lack of knowledge, lack of supporting help, and no process transparency from the software. The last reason specifically is related to the save function of the software which was not notifying about its results, such that creating confusion whether the data was saved or not.

Before accomplishing their task, only one of the participants decided to turn to available help on Internet, video tutorials and ERP documentation on the vendor's website. It is interesting to mention that the same respondent used the same technique, googling, for solving issues whenever a problem appeared. The other two used their intuition and the menus available in the software.

Ultimately, the experiment participants succeeded to print out the first invoice. It is crucial to mention that the resulted invoices lacked all data required in the business case.

4.4   Perceived Ease of Use

Generally speaking, students graded the deployment process as relatively easy. The average grade, on a scale of one (very easy) to five (very difficult), was two. The most difficulties were faced when configuring and working with the ERP in order to type in necessary data and print out the invoice. Finding, downloading and installing the open source ERP was described as a very easy task. However, more transparency in the process was seen as necessary.

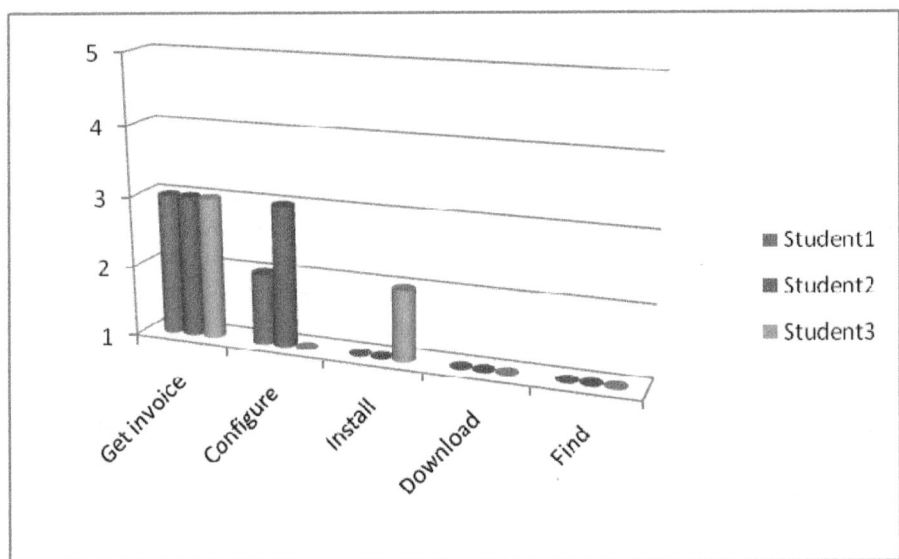

Fig. 2. Perceived ease of use on a likert scale 1-5 (1 very easy) (5 very difficult)

The students mentioned that in order to accomplish the tasks of finding, downloading, installing the open source ERP not much knowledge is needed. Although, they believe that more knowledge is required in learning the system.

Generally, the deployment process of the open source ERP was assessed as easy. It can be claimed that there are multiple reasons for that. First of all, students mentioned that finding an open source ERP was very easy, as they could Google and pick the most relevant results. The key to finding relevant results were queering the right keywords. When it comes to ERP selection, students mentioned that it was very easy as well. However, most of them judged the quality of the software by Google results. None of the participants has thoroughly assessed the advantages and disadvantages of one product comparing to others, nor did they evaluate the product's technical requirements. Such decisions could affect the overall performance of any open source ERP, if the minimum technical requirements are not met.

Students mentioned throughout the experiment that the software had a very "handy" and good user interface, comparing it to regular software products like Microsoft etc. They also mentioned that the installation and configuration procedure was intuitive and guiding. In other words, they could get clear instructions. Generally, these indicate clear signs of good usability practices as suggested by Nielsen [36].

However, the students felt lack of transparence and information during installation. They felt that more knowledge is required to understand all installation and configuration details. Nevertheless, all three participants succeeded with the installation, being able to run the application. That in turn indicates that little knowledge is needed to install and configure the software, and the role of the user becomes as assisting the process or monitoring, rather than obliged to decide.

The first difficulties came when literally working with the ERP user interface. After having familiarized themselves with available menus, two of the students proceeded immediately with the task using the trial-and-error method. Only one of the students tried to get better informed about the available functions and workflows. That is why the former two had consumed more time and committed more errors while executing the task. The latter used information available on Internet, particularly information on the vendor's site.

Consequently, the appropriate use of software documentation and tutorials might have helped students perform their task faster and with higher qualities. That also supports the idea that users with appropriate training find systems easier and relevant to their job performance. However, Nielsen [36] supports the idea that easy to use system should support learnability, i.e. accomplishing task easily at first encounter with the application.

On one hand, the problem might lie not specifically in the interface design, but rather in the complexity of the ERP software systems. The students confessed that for better usage more knowledge and training is required. On the other hand, the poor performance of two students in terms of time and errors might be also explained by the rush of trying out the system.

Nevertheless, all three students have succeeded to place a sales order, ship and print out the invoice. The resulted invoices do miss important parts of data, and that suggests that they partially neglected the assignment. The problems appeared at creating a customized user for the company, i.e. register the company profile, and adding a product to the sales order. In one case, the students blamed the interface of the software, as they could not track the changes to the system.

These problems resulted due to lack of training and proper education of the users. As Bueno and Salmeron [37] mention training and education are necessary before, during and after the system implementation. Consequently, the last task of getting the first invoice was rather hard even for our participants, despite their large experience with other software and high levels of computer skills. Thus, relevant amount of knowledge of the ERP system is a key to perform better job. In terms of time, the deployment assignment was completed in less than one hour.

4.5   Perceived Usefulness

The experiment participants perceived the open source ERP as useful. All of the students believed that the software would enrich and help perform the job tasks, as well as reduce useless paperwork.

However, students believed that in order to get better output quality, one should get to learn the system first. The beliefs about result demonstrability were shared. Some of the students believed that at the moment the results are very limited because of the amount of work done. However, they were satisfied to see tangible results in the form of the invoice.

Regarding the image, one of the students mentioned that adopting an open source ERP is becoming a necessity, as well as affect the status and the image of the company in general.

Generally speaking, the perceived usefulness of the open source ERP has been received as positive. That is why two of the students stated that if they were to choose freely, then they would certainly use such software in their company. The left respondent hesitated to give an answer, explaining that it depends on the company and its activity.

In general, perceived usefulness of the ERP system tested was evaluated as positive. In other words, the open source ERP system has delivered the expected benefits, and all of the students find it advantageous for any small company.

All students found the ERP system as beneficial to their job performance, even though they have encountered it for the first time. One of them mentioned that this particular ERP brings more benefits than just rather using Excel or doing paperwork. Of course, it is hard to assess the benefit of a system in such a short time. Rather usefulness is a variable of time, and needs a longer period of time. The same idea is expressed by many scientists in the domain, who claim that majority of company cannot realize the benefits in the first period of time.

The image, voluntariness, result demonstrability factors have also affected positively the perceived usefulness. This can be explained by the background of the students who are all studying information systems. Thus, their general knowledge about ERP and their benefits might have affected their perceived usefulness of the product. However, the students claimed that in comparison to the effort, they could see clear results in the end.

The resulted invoices are a clear indicator of what can be achieved in shorter than one hour with an open source ERP. Although, the invoices lacked much of the important data, they indicate that with a certain amount of knowledge and training more benefits to the company and overall performance can be gained.

5   Conclusions

The research has shown that in order to deploy an open source ERP a relatively short amount of effort – time and knowledge - is needed. The perceived ease of use of the process has been evaluated as relatively easy, with main difficulties appearing in interacting with ERP workflow due to lack of training and little amount of knowledge. However, if appropriate user training and education is applied, greater job performance and output quality can be achieved.

The study has also shown that the output results of the open source ERP are perceived as beneficial to the company and its activity. The students evaluated the perceived usefulness as mostly positive. The factors of job performance, output quality, result demonstrability, voluntariness and image have positively affected the perceived usefulness of the open source ERP system.

References

1. Verville, J.J., et al.: ERP Acquisition Planning: A Critical Dimension for Making the Right Choice. Long Range Planning 40(1) (2007)
2. Daneva, M.: Understanding Success and Failure Profiles of ERP Requirements Engineering: an Empirical Study. In: 33rd EUROMICRO Conference on Software Engineering and Advanced Applications, EUROMICRO 2007 (2007)
3. The Standish Group, CHAOS Report 1995 (1995)
4. Rapp, J.: Ökat intresse för Open Source. Logica (2009)
5. Johansson, B., Sudzina, F.: ERP systems and open source: an initial review and some implications for SMEs. Journal of Enterprise Information Management 21(6), 649 (2008)
6. Morabito, V., Pace, S., Previtali, P.: ERP Marketing and Italian SMEs. European Management Journal 23(5), 590–598 (2005)
7. Xu, L., Brinkkemper, S.: Concepts of product software. European Journal of Information Systems 16(5), 531–541 (2007)
8. Lengnick-Hall, C.A., Lengnick-Hall, M.L., Abdinnour-Helm, S.: The role of social and intellectual capital in achieving competitive advantage through enterprise resource planning (ERP) systems. Journal of Engineering and Technology Management 21(4), 307–330 (2004)
9. Rolland, C., Prakash, N.: Bridging the Gap Between Organisational Needs and ERP Functionality. Requirements Engineering 5(3), 180–193 (2000)
10. Kumar, K., Van Hillegersberg, J.: ERP experiences and evolution. Communications of the ACM 43(4), 22–26 (2000)
11. Wier, B., Hunton, J., HassabElnaby, H.R.: Enterprise resource planning systems and non-financial performance incentives: The joint impact on corporate performance. International Journal of Accounting Information Systems 8(3), 165–190 (2007)

12. Koch, C.: ERP-systemer: erfaringer, ressourcer, forandringer, p. 224. Ingeniøren-bøger, København (2001)
13. Millman, G.J.: What did you get from ERP, and what can you get? Financial Executives International 5, 15–24 (2004)
14. Hammer, M., Champy, J.: Reengineering the corporation: a manifesto for business revolution, 1st edn., p. 223. Harper Business, New York (1993)
15. Davenport, T.: Mission Critical: Realizing the Promise of Enterprise Systems. Harvard Business School Press, Boston (2000)
16. Larsen, M., Myers, M.D.: When Success Turns into Failure: A Package-Driven Business Process Re-engineering project in the Financial Services Industry. Journal of Strategic Information Systems 8, 395–417 (1998)
17. Scott, J.E., Vessey, I.: Implementing Enterprise Resource Planning Systems: The Role of Learning from Failure. Information Systems Frontiers 2(2), 213 (2000)
18. Robey, D., Ross, J.W., Boudreau, M.-C.: Learning to Implement Enterprise Systems: An Exploratory Study of the Dialectics of Change. Journal of Management Information Systems 19(1), 17–46 (2002)
19. Hedman, J., Borell, A.: ERP systems impact on organizations. In: Grant, G. (ed.) ERP & Data Warehousing in Organizations: Issues and Challenges, pp. 1–21. Idea Group Publishing, Hershey (2003)
20. Davenport, T.: Holistic management of mega-package change: The case of SAP. Center of Business Innovation, Ernest & Young LLP, Boston (1996)
21. Johansson, B., Newman, M.: Competitive advantage in the ERP system's value-chain and its influence on future development. Enterprise Information Systems 4(1), 79–93 (2010)
22. Wieder, B., et al.: The impact of ERP systems on firm and business process performance. Journal of Enterprise Information Management 19(1), 13–29 (2006)
23. Jacobson, S., et al.: The ERP Market Sizing Report, 2006-2011. AMR Research (2007)
24. Parr, A.N.: A Taxonomy of ERP Implementation Approaches (2000)
25. Shehab, E.M., et al.: Enterprise resource planning: An integrative review. Business Process Management Journal 10(4), 359–386 (2004)
26. Fougatsaro, V.G.: A study of open source ERP systems. School of Management. Blekinge Institute of Technology (2009)
27. Carvalho, R.A.: Issues on evaluating Free/open source ERP systems. In: Research and Practical Issues of Enterprise Informations Systems, pp. 667–676. Springer Verlag New York Inc., New York (2007)
28. Bajaj, A.: ERP for SMEs (2008),
    http://knol.google.com/k/erp-for-sme-s#
29. Sammon, D., Adam, F.: Justifying an ERP investment with the promise of realising business benefits. In: 15th European Conference on Information Systems, pp. 1655–1668. University of St. Gallen (2007)
30. European Commission, SME Definition: Recommendation 2003/361/EC Regarding the SME Definition (2003)
31. Laukkanen, S., Sarpola, S., Hallikainen, P.: Enterprise size matters: objectives and constraints of ERP adoption. Journal of Enterprise Information Management 20(3), 319–334 (2007)
32. De Carvalho, R.A., Johansson, B.: ERP Licensing Perspectives on Adoption of ERPs in Small and Medium-sized Enterprises. In: Chaudbry, S. (ed.) The IV IFIP International Conference on Research and Pratical Issues of Enterprise Systems (CONFENIS), Rio Grande do Norte, Barcellos de Andrade, Inez (2010)

33. Suraweera, T., Remus, U., Wakerley, S.: Dynamics of Knowledge Leverage in ERP Implementation. In: ACIS 2007 Proceedings. Paper 58 (2007)
34. Venkatesh, V., Davis, F.D.: A theoretical extension of the technology acceptance model: Four longitudinal Field Studies. Management Science 46(2), 186–204 (2000)
35. Davis, F.D.: Perceived usefulness, perceived ease of use, and user acceptance of information technology. MIS Quarterly 13(3), 319–340 (1989)
36. Nielsen, J.: Usability 101: Introduction to Usability (2011), http://www.useit.com/alertbox/20030825.html (cited May 1, 2011)
37. Bueno, S., Salmeron, J.L.: TAM-based success modeling in ERP. Journal Interacting with Computers 20(6), 515–523 (2008)

Towards the Development of Large-Scale Data Warehouse Application Frameworks

Duong Thi Anh Hoang[1], Hieu Tran[1], Binh Thanh Nguyen[2], and A Min Tjoa[1]

[1] Institute of Software Technology and Interactive Systems, Vienna University of Technology
Favoritenstrasse 9-11/188, Vienna, Austria
{htaduong,tran.hieu,amin}@ifs.tuwien.ac.at
[2] International Institute for Applied Systems Analysis (IIASA)
Schlossplatz 1, A-2361 Laxenburg, Austria
nguyenb@iiasa.ac.at

Abstract. Facing with growing data volumes and deeper analysis requirements, current development of Business Intelligence (BI) and Data warehousing systems (DWHs) is a challenging and complicated task, which largely involves in ad-hoc integration and data re-engineering. This arises an increasing requirement for a scalable application framework which can be used for the implementation and administration of diverse BI applications in a straight forward and cost-efficient way. In this context, this paper presents a large-scale application framework for standardized BI applications, supporting the ability to define and construct data warehouse processes, new data analytics capabilities as well as to support the deployment requirements of multi scalable front-end applications. The core of the framework consists of defined metadata repositories with pre-built and function specific information templates as well as application definition. Moreover, the application framework is also based on workflow mechanisms for developing and running automatic data processing tasks. Hence, the framework is capable of offering an unified reference architecture to end users, which spans various aspects of development lifecycle and can be adapted or extended to better meet application-specific BI engineering process.

Keywords: Business intelligence, Data warehouses, Application framework, Large-scale development.

1   Introduction

Within the application scope of developing DWHs, it is necessary to implement the underlying data basis whereupon this task comprises selection and configuration of relevant software and hardware components for the DHWs architecture [5]. Based on the requirements definitions, the design specification develops suitable database schemas, selects adequate system components, determines partitions of data base tables and specifies ETL processes. The size and complexity of DWH systems are increasingly involved in enabling large data service to scale when needed to ensure

C. Møller and S. Chaudhry (Eds.): CONFENIS 2011, LNBIP 105, pp. 92–104, 2012.

consistent and reliable operations. Therefore, it is difficult to design and maintain large-scale application framework with its own characteristics (dynamicity, scalability, etc) [1] over heterogeneous environments.

The existing systems available in the market already offer pre-built data models, preconfigured applications and prearranged contents for common business domains, e.g. customer analytics, financial analytics, HR analytics and supply chain analytics. Moreover, the systems also enable various kinds of data integration and information delivery. Several BI suites also offer deliver ready-to-use templates and include features to build own ones. However, these approaches still tightly bound to the BI solution products. As the analysis of various multi-dimensional modeling methods shows, libraries comprising reusable elements of DWH reference models are mostly specialized on particular model element types [4].

Although these various emerging services have reduced the cost of data storage and delivery in DWHs, DWH application development still remains a non-automated, risk prone and costly process. Much of the cost and effort for developing a complete enterprise DWH stems from the continuous re-discovery and re-invention of core concepts and components across the BI industry. In this context, there arise the requirements for an generic application framework that can enable an asset base of reusable information models and a structured platform to develop and incorporate DW and BI applications, in a cost effective manner and in the available set of tools and technologies.

Within the scope of this paper, a large-scale DWH application framework lays the groundwork for a new paradigm to specify, design, host and deliver standardized BI applications, with common consistent procedures such as data processing defined as consistently reusable components. The basis of the framework is the metadata-based architecture, including generic data models libraries and pre-built application libraries along with the associated mappings. Integrated with the data modeling components, the application framework enables an integrated set of services that collaborate to provide a reusable architecture for a family of DWH eco-system formed of a large numbers of decentralized data analysis services. On this basis, the application model can then be executed and replicated up to the deployment model in a flexible way, enhancing reusability as well as enabling diverse data model preprocessing and analyzing, thus reduces the implementation time and improves the quality of the BI applications.

The rest of this paper is organized as follows: section 2 introduces some approaches related to our work; in section 3, framework architecture and its core component are presented, along with the its design principles. In section 4, the mechanisms of using the framework in developing DWH applications is analyzed. Section 5 illustrates our experimental design to highlight the feasibility of proposed framework. At last, section 6 gives a summary of what have been achieved and future works.

2 Related Works

The concept of the application framework have been proposed to describe a set of reusable designs and code in the development of software applications [8]. However, currently, there is still a lack of concepts for designing and implementing a possible adaption of large-scale context to the DWH application frameworks. To sketch the background of the presented research, this section discusses approaches proposed in the domain of BI and DWHs, which could help with large-scale development.

The key to a BI application development, in the large-scale context, depends on scalable, configurable and well-maintained application models. In this context, the scalability can range from complete BI applications down to atomic functional blocks, from data models, ETL tools to deployment packages. Research efforts are very much aware of this trend, and there are no fewer than a dozen companies in recent years that build specialized analytical data management software (e.g., Netezza, Vertica, DATAllegro, Greenplum, etc.), along with the known systems available in the market such as Sybase PowerDesigner, Business Objects Foundation, Oracle BI, etc.

However, within the scope of our knowledge, reference application model of Data Warehouse projects mostly refers to an ad-hoc modification of existing information models [6]. A traditional approach proposed either by industry and academia for applying application and data framework is one of manually assembling and configuring a set of compatible elements as a reference application model [4]. Most of these frameworks still demand a vast amount of repetitive and tedious work to implement similar parts of a DWH application; these products are tied to their own extraction and information delivery tools and lack of pre-built data mappings. This is in part because in current reference DWH models, neither the data models nor the application models has any awareness of the other and these layers operate independently. Therefore, it is difficult to design and maintain DWH applications in large-scale context, especially as the data application models change heterogeneously.

Moreover, to solve the data management problems in large-scale development context, technologies have been developed to manage high volumes of data efficiently, e.g. Google Bigtable (http://labs.google.com/), Amazon Dynamo [3], and so on. Recent years have seen an enormous increase in MapReduce adoption, a Google's programming model to solve the problem of massive explosion in data. Due to its convenience and efficiency, MapReduce is used in various applications as a basis for data frameworks. For example, Apache (http://apache.org/) Hadoop framework is commonly used on a scale-our storage cloud to perform the data transformation necessary to create the analytics database. Hive is a data warehouse infrastructure built on top of Hadoop that provides tools to enable easy data summarization, ad-hoc querying of large datasets stored in Hadoop files.

In this context, this paper is aimed to develop a structured application framework that enables a comprehensive, hosted BI solution tailored to scale and reshape to meet the needs of changing business needs and requirements. Integrated with the data modeling components, the DWH application framework can support implementation and deployment of the DWH applications by leveraging pre-built modeling and application framework, providing a high degree of re-usability, and configurability.

3   Large-Scale Data Warehouse Application Framework

The proposed application framework enables users to develop DWHs by enabling framework reuse across application designs and platforms. The design of DWH application, along with the tool suites, simplifies the ability to add and remove analytic features without taking into account the underlying framework logic. This section presents an integrated DWH application framework (DWHAF), providing a flexible, scalable solution to enable the rapid development of differentiated DWHs.

3.1   Component Analysis of DWHAF

A typical method for implementation and maintenance of DWH application comprising the steps of: analyzing the critical subject area, existing data models and data needs; designing in sequence the logical data modeling and physical database; developing back end services and end user applications; deploying database implementation, initial load and validation of the data warehouse. In this context, it needs to be taken into account the fact that developing BI applications requires an efficient application framework of tightly interoperating components along with a scalable data modeling framework.

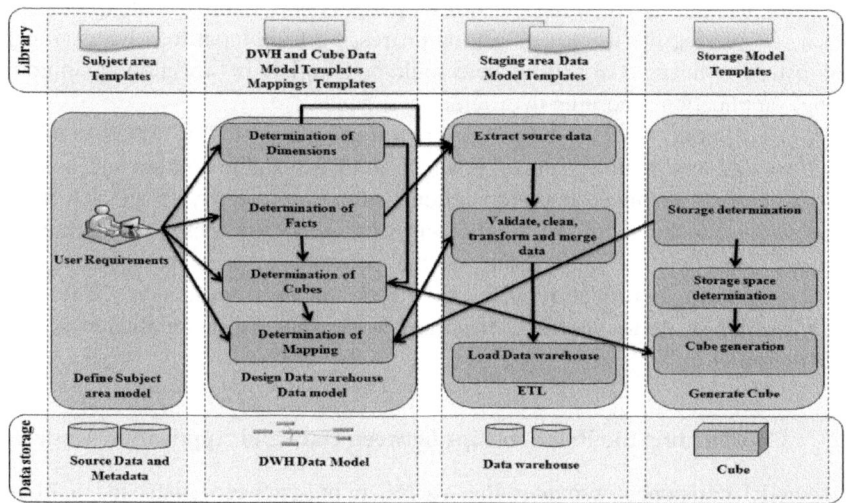

Fig. 1. The required DWH application framework

Figure 1 shows the required application framework with typical development processes resulted from a comprehensive literature review we have conducted. The DWH application framework comprises the phases of Subject area model Definition, DWH Data model Design, ETL and Cube Generation. Phases are subdivided into activities. Within the Subject area model Definition phase, basic questions concerning user requirements and scope of the DWH are answered, in comparison with existing environment templates. To model Data warehouse data model, logical data model and database as well as mappings from source to target are designed. This way an information model of the required DW is created. This information model can be analyzed and the results can be used as a basis for ETL phase. Finally, subject to the development phase is a continuous adaptation and maintenance of the cube models.

The data modeling framework enables end users to define the logical data model using a series of graphical user interfaces (GUI) or application-programming interfaces (API), then dynamically translates the logical data model into a corresponding physical data model. Because the application framework is integrated with the data modeling framework, the application framework features are automatically available to end users, enables them to configure various application features and data management operations also by terms of UI and API. Through the API, BI applications can interact with the application framework, which in turn interacts with the logical data model.

It is clear that the common business domains require common application processing functionality, e.g. data delivery provides users with processing results tailored to their specific needs, for example what data format they accept, what are the relevant parameters they want to retrieve, etc. The required application framework also supports the description and execution of application-specific data processing workflow as well as predefined workflow patterns between distributed components. When considering the whole application processing from input to delivery it appears that instead of a single workflow there could be a variety of workflow definitions for a single application according to different user needs.

In this context, the DWH application framework, including the data modeling functions and application features, is aimed to be a scalable architecture to serve as the warehouse's technical and application foundation, identifying and selecting the middleware components to implement it. New business requirements or changed requirements may result in the addition of new components to the framework and a modification of the existing framework components. Therefore, it takes a series of iterations to get the framework right for the applications that are built on top of it.

3.2   Constructing the Relationships between Data and Application Models

The model component provides the access to pre-packaged data and application models, enabling end users to reconfigure and customize as well as provide aids to dimensional modeling in the DW and BI context. The data models can be distinguished as the model that stores fact and its related dimensions and the model that defines cube structure or relational schema [5].

The data model component of the system offers the means to capture all the possible dimensions and their respective attributes/properties as well as establish mappings between the analytic facts and dimensions. Meanwhile, built-in dimensional models representing the best practices for comprehensive analysis relating to particular business functions. Moreover, data model can be generated based on definitions of dimensions, facts and analytical needs. End users can thus reconfigure these data models via user interfaces.

Meanwhile, metadata associated with a application model used to describe of a template of the interface and functionality of the application. These templates consist of ETL and warehouse design, mappings, data storage, deployment templates or application specifications. An example of application metadata model can include defined options to personalize the DWH applications, which are used in the runtime reconfiguration process when it is instanced in a specific application. This metadata can be executed at run time to provide the design interface for the designer, and to deploy the model into the output data storage structure in DWH applications.

In accordance to the requirements of integrated framework, the variability of the application configuration should be based on the consistent variability of application/business models, i.e. data models, application models or domain models. By merging the application constraints with the data model constraints, we obtain a unified set of constraints that is used by the configuration tool to ensure that the template model generated is consistent and up to the business domain.

The first step towards the construction of a relationship is to capture the variability of a given domain by means of a data modeling service. Similarly, this data model should be represented by configurable data exchange and data store services model, respectively. Application specification should be identified with the variants of the applications and constraints should be defined to ensure the correctness. Once data model, application specification and their constraints have been identified, it is possible to define the mapping by means of the impact analysis:

— from data model to application: given a data model specification, we need to estimate what are the implications to the setting in the application model;
— from application to data model: given a change in application specification, we need to consider which data model are impacted.

A valid mapping is constructed when a valid application specification is defined with respect to the data model. The specification space is obtained by the intersection of the two specification spaces (data and application) via the mapping. By representing the data model variability in a separate model, we can avoid capturing the interdependencies of the data model in the configurable application model, as these interdependencies are propagated to the application model via the valid mapping. Once each customized data model has been configured, a set of service specification, attached to the application specification that captures the selected data model, are performed on the application model to define a configuration.

3.3   Architecture of Proposed DWH Application Framework

The system architecture consists of abstract services that are the core components of DWHAF applications namely Application, Client, DWH and Platform services. Specifically, the framework also contains the main components: the metadata services, the management services and the libraries. The Client layer contains top-level component such as Application interfaces, Service APIs, as well as specific services related to Application service framework.

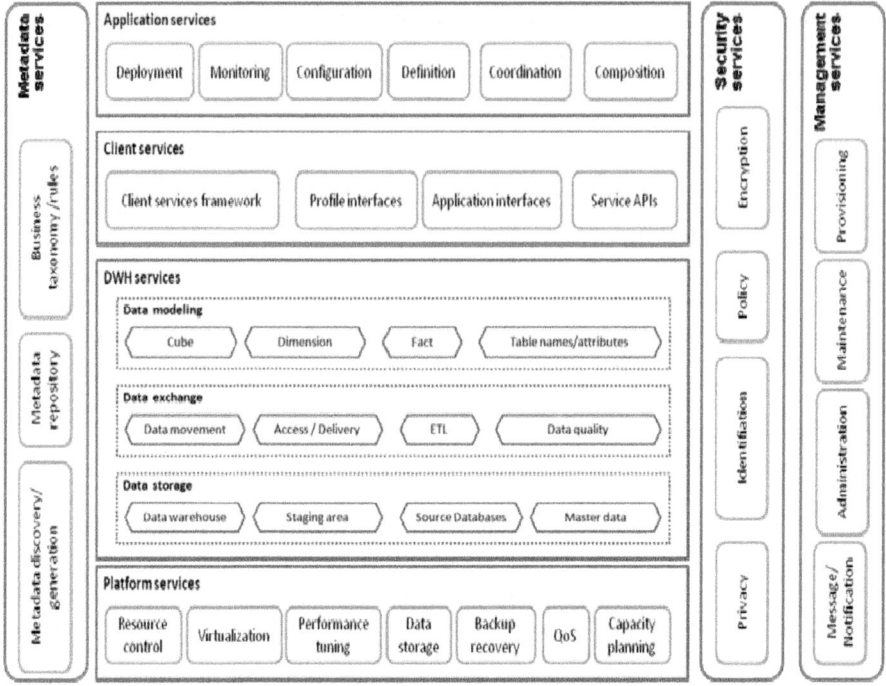

Fig. 2. DWHAF conceptual architecture

3.3.1 Application Services

DWH reference models are the deliverable end result of an application developed in DWHAF. This layer is where context-aware DWH configuration are implemented. The DWH application designer can extend the services by means of the API libraries. All instantiated application models, both native and third party, and other supplementary components, reside in this layer. The application layer runs within the system run time, using the templates and services available from underlying layers.

3.3.2 Client Services

This layer is the place where the context information is processed and modeled. This context information acquired by the components at this layer helps services to respond better to varying user activities and environmental changes. Additionally it serves as an "inference engine" that deduces and generalizes facts during the process of updating context models as a result of information coming from Profile interfaces.

3.3.3 DWH Services

This layer provides the services used to develop DWH applications as well as a generic abstraction for platform access and manages the user interface and application resources. Built around API connectivity, the proposed framework also includes pre-integrated DWH solutions, validated on multiple platforms, cutting down the time cost to launch DWH model. Moreover, customers can plug in components of their choice, with minimal impact on system integrity.

3.3.4 Platform Services

To ensure efficient development, customization and administration of DWH applications, the platform layer offers application delivery. Specifically, DWH development relies on a variety of core services, i.e. security, performance tuning, data storage, visualization packages, data analysis tools, and basic environments. Along with the libraries, this layer forms the deployment basis for the application framework. For example, the Management Services offer application configuration and reporting capabilities; Virtualization delivers abstraction between physical and functional elements in service management.

3.3.5 Metadata Services

As presented in the component analysis process, there's a clear separation of different kinds of metadata, i.e. metadata that describes the data model, the application model, the base functionality of an application, and the customizations. The Metadata repository provides a central, shared source of metadata including pre-built metadata, enabling reduction in implementation and maintenance costs. The metadata repository also serves as a key repository of all mappings between application models and function specific data models housed in the data model component.

Along with the data model component, the system enabling user interfaces to reconfigure the reference models, preventing the risks associated with being locked into a specific configuration. Meanwhile, the library layer contains repositories of pre-built templates for DWH application development. This layer will grow as development of the framework continues and common themes are identified. Specifically, the architecture provides common practice solutions to reduce the effort of data modeling, in which they can be used as a starting point for the construction of application-specific models. Meanwhile, a metadata repository supports application implementation, i.e. definitions of data objects, application components, runtime customizations, etc.

4   Applying DWHAF in Application Development

Built on top of the framework, DWH application service provides the design for specific applications and the query interface required by the DWHs solution. The application service provides both the tools and applications that enable predefined and ad hoc collection, analysis, and presentation of end user's data by means of user interfaces and service API. The result of this design service includes an application prototype, recommended design templates and development tools to support implementation, and deployment plans for the required applications.

Fig. 3 provides an overview of our proposed framework for generating DWH application architecture. DWH designers interact with the service composition environment through a composition user interface, navigating through the generated

DWH reference models, edit the process, and deploy DWH applications. The back-end includes major components that process the contextual information, generate reference processes and analyze historic usage data to recommend DWH templates.

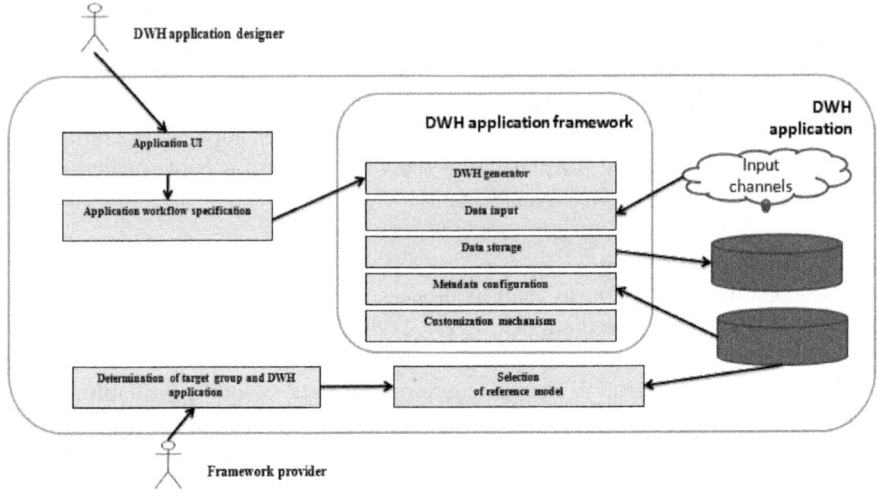

Fig. 3. DWH application framework and application service

From the modeling viewpoint, the ability to use history data is an important feature. An intuitive view to application-specific DWH design would be to satisfy the need for (non-existing) DWH services by bringing together existing ones. We aim to reuse development knowledge and provide a starting template for the users. This knowledge can be based on past successful deployment, and can be seeded by domain-specific knowledge and task-specific knowledge about the core types of information processing activities.

In this context, the presented application framework enables designers to develop DWHs by enabling pre-built service libraries reused across application designs and platforms. The design of DWH applications, along with the tool suites, simplifies the ability to add and remove analytic features without taking into account the underlying framework logic. The result of the architecture design is the Reference Architecture, which is an architectural framework along with a set of middleware elements facilitating the integration of services, and context modeling. An example of adapting the generic component for the implementation of an ETL specific component is presented in Figure 4. The example shows the implementation of the selective data storage service, and the other components can be implemented in a similar manner.

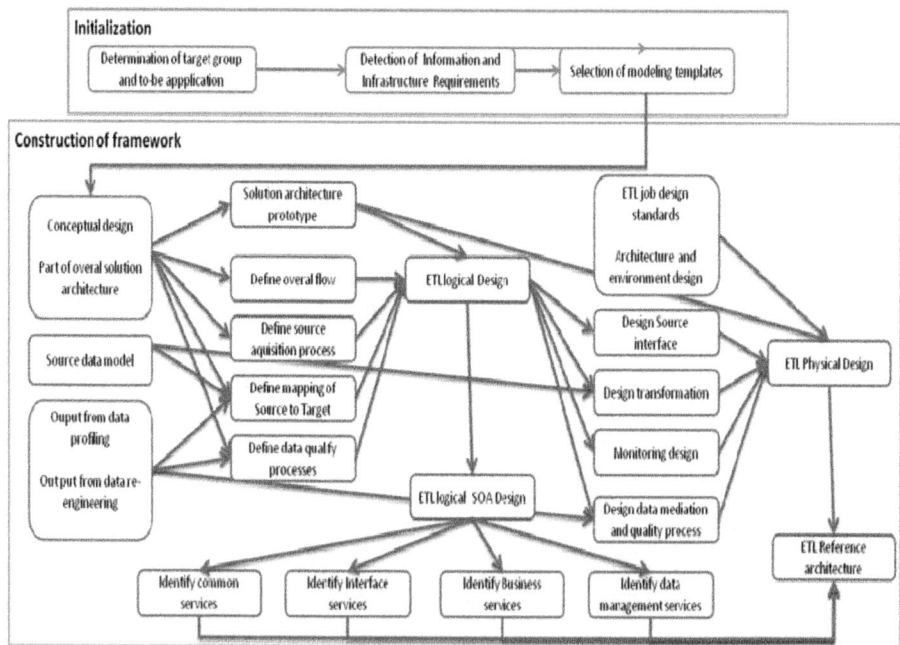

Fig. 4. Example process of defining ETL reference architecture

The application framework aims at providing a reference template configured to enable end users to leverage prebuilt practices and to avoid designing and developing DWH applications from scratch [9]. Moreover, we focus on the stage of dynamic template instantiation, in which we need to identify specific service instantiation for each of the generic service in the template. The focus of supporting end users means that, we aim to automate only the main aspects of the process: selecting suitable services for each task and working out compatibilities between services in terms of data flow, pre- and post-conditions. For example, for querying services, the related pattern can be defined as Warehouse GUI to en-queue queries, check status and retrieve results.

5   Illustrative Example

To establish the practical feasibility of our framework, we have designed a toolset that provides end-to-end support for DWH application model configuration. In this case study, we take advantage of Hadoop environment, which based on MapReduce programming model, in optimizing data warehouse performance. Specifically, experimental ETL application acts as a transformation engine, taking the extracted data from multiple data sources and processing this large-scale data into a common format for integration into the data warehouse. As a proof of concept, a data warehouse of Climate subject area will be deployed, in which we use Pentaho BI suite which extends their ETL (Pentaho Data Integration – PDI) to support processes that exploit Hadoop structures. Figure 5 provides an overview of the toolset's architecture.

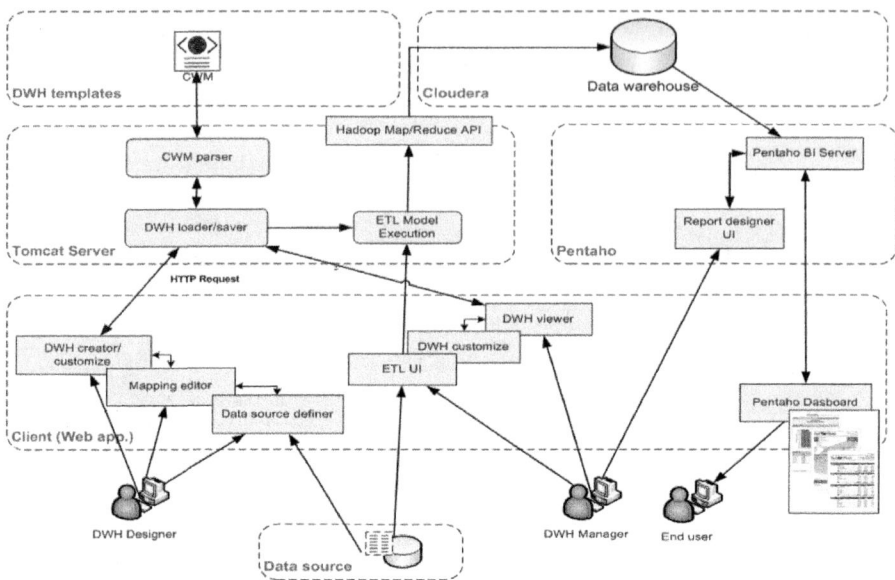

Fig. 5. Prototype implementation architecture

The U.S. National Climatic Data Center (NCDC, http://www.ncdc.noaa.gov/) provides free data on a set of meteorological elements, relating to *Daily Normals of Temperature, Precipitation, and Heating and Cooling Days* for the period 1971-2000 for stations of the U.S. Climate Reference Network (USCRN). These systems were considered as data sources for implementing the core of data warehouse, in which the dimensions can be:

— Time: time key, day number in month, month, season of the year
— Division: division key, region, state
— Weather station: station information (Station Name, State, Division, Call) , location (Latitude, Longitude, Elevation, Elements)
— Climatic variable: variable key, name (Minimum Temperature, Maximum Temperature, Average Temperature, Heating Degree Days, Cooling Degree Days), description, measurement units (deg F, Hundreths of an Inch, none), type (Temperature, Precipitation, Degree Days)

The fact tables can be defined from various subject areas, such as the value of a variable measured at one station an on a date given station key, time key, variable key, and measured value, monthly sum.

There is also a version management used to relate the instances of the model back to the generation of application template. Every time a application is instanced from that template, the instanced application gets a copy of the version attribute that describes which version of the template was used. When a designer customizes an instance of the application, these customizations are stored with the instanced application, they are not propagated back to the template.

6 Conclusions and Future Works

The rising demand for BI and DWH applications is fostering the need to support flexible deployment models for all BI application services. With ever growing data volumes and deeper analysis requirements, it also follows that DWH application framework must be able to scale out to meet operational and technical requirements of hosting and delivering applications. In this paper, a metadata-driven application framework is presented as the core that enable the platform to deliver configurable and scalable DWH applications. The core of this framework is that the application framework is tightly integrated with data modeling components, thus supports an associated and centralized logic to ensure the consistency of the DWH applications.

Focusing on the potentials of semantic technologies [10, 11, 12], we are working on applying sound formal techniques to represent and automate the mapping between domain data model and application model. To establish the practical feasibility of our framework, we have designed a toolset that provides end-to-end support for DWH application model configuration and conducts DWH development experiments with various subject areas to empirically evaluate the applicability and impact of the proposed configuration approach on the deployment process.

Acknowledgments. This work is supported by a Technology Grant for South East Asia of the *Austrian Council for Research and Technology Development* and *ASEA UNINET*.

References

1. Chuck, H., Jeff, W., Karen, C.: Navigating the Next-Generation Application Architecture. IT Professional 11(2), 18–22 (2009)
2. David, P., Awais, R., Alexandru, T., Andreas, S.: An architectural pattern for designing component-based application frameworks. Software: Practice and Experience 36(2), 157–190 (2006)
3. Giuseppe, D., Deniz, H., Madan, J., Gunavardhan, K., Avinash, L., Alex, P., Swaminathan, S., Peter, V., Werner, V.: Dynamo: amazon's highly available key-value store. In: Proceedings of Twenty-First ACM SIGOPS Symposium on Operating Systems Principles, SOSP 2007, pp. 205–220. ACM, New York (2007)
4. Goeken, M., Knackstedt, R.: Multidimensional Reference Models for Data Warehouse Development. In: Proceedings of the International Conference on Enterprise Information Systems, ICEIS, pp. 347–354 (2007)
5. Kimball, R., Ross, M., Thornthwaite, W., Mundy, J., Becker, B.: The Data Warehouse Lifecycle Toolkit. Wiley Publishing (2008)
6. Knackstedt, R., Klose, K.: Configurative reference model-based development of data warehouse systems. In: Khosrow-Pour, M. (ed.) Proceedings of the 16th Information Resources Management Association International Conference, RMA 2005, pp. 32–39 (2005)
7. Luján-Mora, S., Trujillo, J.: Comprehensive Method for Data Warehouse Design. In: Proceedings of the 5th International Workshop on Design and Management of Data Warehouses, DMDW 2003, pp. 1.1–1.14 (2003)

8. Mohamed, F., Douglas, C.S.: Object-oriented application frameworks. Commun. ACM 40(10), 32–38 (1997)
9. Oracle. Enabling Pervasive BI Through a Practical Data Warehouse Reference Architecture (2010)
10. Oscar, R., Alberto, A.: Automating multidimensional design from ontologies. In: Proceedings of the the ACM Tenth International Workshop on Data Warehousing and OLAP, Lisbon, Portugal, pp. 1–8. ACM (2007)
11. Oscar, R., Diego, C., Alberto, A., Mariano, R.M.: Discovering functional dependencies for multidimensional design. In: Proceedings of the The ACM Twelfth International Workshop on Data Warehousing and OLAP, Hong Kong, China, pp. 1–8. ACM (2009)
12. Spahn, M., Kleb, J., Grimm, S., Scheidl, S.: Supporting business intelligence by providing ontology-based end-user information self-service. In: Proceedings of the the First International Workshop on Ontology-Supported Business Intelligence, pp. 1–12. ACM (2008)

Adaptive EIS with Business Rules Discovered by Formal Concept Analysis

Victor Romanov[1], Alina Poluektova[1], and Olga Sergienko[2]

[1] Russian Plekhanov University, Russia, Moscow
{victorromanov1,poluektovaau}@gmail.com
[2] Software Group IBM East Europe/Asia
Russia, Moscow
Sergienko@ru.ibm.com

Abstract. Business rules component became essential part of such software as ORACLE, SAP, IBM and Microsoft and this fact signifies new stage in the Enterprise Information Systems development and applications. The efficiency of application such new tools depends from business rules development technology. The new generation of EIS software requires not only deployment strategy, but also tools for extracting business rules from description of existing practice. Along with manual business rules extraction from mountains of documents there exists the possibility to apply data mining technology based on formal concept analysis. In this paper we are presenting, how supplier and customers data, being accumulated in data base, may be used in CRM system for fitting services and relations to customer and supplier profile.

Keywords: Enterprise Information systems, business rules, formal concept analysis, system adaptation, customer profile.

1   Introduction

The modern enterprises' business processes are very complex, especially for medium and large business. They contain many conditions, restrictions and rules that are implicit and hidden in numerous documents, job manuals, applications codes and experience of employees. Such sparse rules dissemination creates difficulties to company to rebuild the business in time, because of time spending for documents finding, the conditions and rules reveal, rewriting instructions and regulations, and to make changes to the IT components and applications. Great number of business rules and its variability urges the companies to allocate business rules as independent part of the business description [1]. The collecting business rules together as a separate IT components managed by Business Rules Management System increases the response speed to the changing of competitive environment and speed of decision making.

The companies, such as Oracle, SAP, IBM and Microsoft, which are producing software for enterprise information systems during last two years the main effort have been focused at the problems of integrating broad spectrum of the different their

C. Møller and S. Chaudhry (Eds.): CONFENIS 2011, LNBIP 105, pp. 105–117, 2012.

software products, such as Web-applications, SOA, Collaboration suite, Data Warehousing and so on. In the same time such business intelligence tools as Data Mining, Knowledge Discovery, and Business rules were regarded for a long time how not essential part or as special software and even were not included into structure of EIS software.

So there arose a situation, when very complex and expensive software was oriented on the secondary tasks in the business management, that is on the routine tasks of data processing, not on the tasks of top managers for strategic planning. As a result in many cases the efficiency of enterprise information systems implementation being compared with expenses was not sufficient and did not satisfies users.

Meanwhile the concepts of EDM - Enterprise Decision Management [2] and ADS –Automated Decision Support [3] were proposed as an approach for possible automated decision making. Having in mind implementation business rules approach at the some enterprise, we will concentrate our efforts on the problem of including business rule capability on CRM business processes. Only in recent years the companies mentioned have included a component of business rules in their software. It is important to note that rule-component has been integrated into business processes component and Data miming tools are applying for rule discovery. Let's consider some essential features of BRMS components EIS software of these vendors.

2   BRMS Component of the Leading EIS SOFTWARE Companies

2.1   Oracle Business Rules

Oracle Business Rules [4] is a new product that provides all features needed to realize the "agility" and cost reduction benefits of Business Rules. Oracle Data Mining can analyze historical transaction data and suggest business rules. Oracle integrate Business Rules integrates with SOA/BPM facilities.

The Rule Author is a Graphical User Interface tool for creating and updating Rules. The programmers use the Rules Author to create a business rules, extracting it from documents and practice and converting these business terms to Java or XML expressions. Rule Author provides a web-based graphical environment that enables the easy creation of business rules via a web browser.

The Rules engine is implemented as a Java Class, and is deployed as a Java callable library. Java programs directly call the Rules engine. The Rules engine implements the industry standard Rete algorithm making it optimized for efficiently processing large numbers of Rules. There are many types of services including "decision support" services.

2.2   SAP NetWeaver Business Rules Management

The SAP NetWeaver Business Rules Management [5] component complements and accelerates SAP NetWeaver Business Process Management. Together they have become important components of Enterprise SOA.

The Rules Composer is the rule modeling and implementation environment of SAP NetWeaver BRM. Because it is integrated within SAP NetWeaver Developer Studio, the Rules Composer is the most efficient way for developers to build rules-based applications targeted at the SAP NetWeaver platform.

The Rules Engine is the run-time engine of SAP NetWeaver BRM, available as a predeployed stateless session bean in the SAP NetWeaver Application Server (SAP NetWeaver AS) Java of SAP NetWeaver CE. This tool gives IT developers the ability to generate reusable rules services out of the box, which is particularly helpful for integrating rules into composite applications.

The Rules Analyzer, a targeted environment for business analysts, will allow them to model, test, simulate, and analyze business rules without assistance from developers

2.3   MS BizTalk Server

BizTalk Server includes the Business Rules Framework [6] as a stand-alone .NET-compliant class library that includes a number of modules, support components, and tools. The primary modules include the Business Rule Composer for constructing policies, the Rule Engine Deployment Wizard for deploying policies created in the Business Rule Composer, and the Run-Time Business Rule Engine that executes policies on behalf of a host application.

The Business Rule Composer enables you to create rules by adding predicates and facts and defining actions. You can add facts and actions by dragging them to the Business Rule Composer design surface. The actions update the nodes in the specified document. You can also add AND, OR, and NOT operators to conditions to create complex comparisons.

The Business Rule Composer helps you create, test, publish, and deploy multiple versions of business rule policies and vocabularies to make the management of these artifacts easier.

2.4   IBM ILog JRules

Rule Studio JRules and Rules for .NET [7] provide a rule application development environment called Rule Studio. From within Rule Studio, a developer can:

• Create a logical business object model (BOM) for the application, and map it to a customized, domain-specific rule vocabulary.
• Create business rules in a natural language syntax, which can be expressed in one or a more localized versions (for example, English or Spanish).
• Create rules in the form of decision tables and decision trees
• Create technical rules in a platform-specific syntax.
• Separate rules in a rule set into tasks, and specify a rule flow to orchestrate the execution of these tasks.

The rule authoring and management environment for business analysts and policy managers is called IBM WebSphere ILOG Rule Team Server (RTS), a thin-client Web-based environment with a scalable, high-performance enterprise rule repository. The repository provides the BRMS with a central "source of truth", addressing the specific needs of rule-based business policy management.

The WebSphere ILOG BRMS offerings include Rule Execution Server (RES), a managed, monitorable execution environment for rules that can be incorporated into an application by being deployed to a J2EE or .NET application server, or embedded directly in an application.

3   Business Rules Application for CRM

The most promising domain for application of business rules software at   the current time is Customer Relationship Management   (CRM). CRM is a business strategy, directed at the sustainable   business building, the kernel of which is "client-oriented" approach. CRM also includes technology of customer retention   and client-enterprise interaction history database maintenance. This strategy based on collecting information about clients at all stages of service life cycle, extracting   knowledge from it and using this knowledge for business   amelioration.

In this paper we will consider how business rule management conception can be applied to one of the Russian enterprise – Podolsk (town) Electromechanical Plant - PEMP   (http://www.i-mash.ru/predpr/1250),   which   is   producing   hydraulic equipments. This enterprise is specialized in   the supply of hydraulic and pneumatic equipment for energy companies, construction, transportation and industrial complex. The firm is producing various hydraulic equipment (pumps, motors, etc.), designed for application in marine hydraulics, transportation systems, facilities for the repair of wells, as well as railway equipment (locomotives). All the necessary spare parts and rubber products for this equipment are also manufactured .

The problem, nowadays facing the company, consists from reducing the amount of orders for products and customers churn. In modern conditions the market is saturated with offerings, and the struggle for the client retention becomes one of the major problems of each company. Analysis of customers data, selecting different customer categories and corresponding business rules, providing to customers by services, relevant to the customer's consumption profile.   Flexible system of discounts and offers for client will allow the company to increase sales, identify and select the most valuable and reliable customers and, accordingly to their score, focus on them, as result to improve the sales department efficiency and business in general.

Business rules manually could be derived from several sources, and the mainly three sources are described as following policy statements and objectives of organization, business process and external factors (e.g. laws and regulations). The tracing the sources of business rules can help to the personnel to discover the need of changing BR. If the content of the source is changing, the rule relating to this source has to be modified or removed.

Business rules can be described in simple natural language or by mean decision tables or decision trees. If simple natural language would be chosen the rules must be readable and accessible to all interested parties: business owner, business analyst, technical architect, and so on

According to business rules for each category of customers the company is offering different set of products and services according to different customer's profile.

Table 1. PEMP customer relationship business rules

Business rule	Formalized rules	Source Type
If the volume of sales order from 80,000 to 120,000 rubles and the status of the client "risk", then give a discount of 5%	IF 80 000<order_value< 120 000 and status = "bad" THEN set discount 5% IF 80000 <order_value <120 000 and status = "bad" THEN set discount of 5%	Corporate policies, dynamic
If the volume of customer order less than 80 000 rubles, then do not give a discount	IF order_value<80 000 THEN set discount 0% IF order_value <80000 THEN set discount 0%	Corporate policies, dynamic
If the industry of the client equipment, then to appoint a corporate rating of 2	IF otrasl = "1" THEN score:=score+2 IF otrasl = "1" THEN score: = score +2	Corporate policy, static
If the industry of the client shipbuilding, then assign a corporate rating of 8	IF otrasl = "3" THEN score:=score+8 IF otrasl = "3" THEN score: = score +8	Corporate policy, static
If the term of the client in this sector from 11 to 20 years, to appoint a corporate score equal to 14	IF 11<srok<20 THEN score:=score+14 IF 11 <srok <20 THEN score: = score +14	Corporate policy, static
If a corporate customer rating greater than 25, then a status of reliable customer	IF score>25 THEN status:="good" IF score> 25 THEN status: = "good"	Corporate policy, static

We have been elaborated the business rules of this enterprise in the next stages:

- ➢ Defining the main sources of business rule analyses,
- ➢ Rules formalizing and catalog creating,
- ➢ BRMS market analyses and choosing appropriate system,
- ➢ Creating a model in the BRMS environment,
- ➢ Elaborating database and store products and customers data,
- ➢ Testing the model,
- ➢ Integration with EIS.

As a result of this work hundreds of business rules were selected, several examples of which are presented in the Table 1.

We suppose that the business model, based on business rules, makes possible for the plant quickly adjust production and services to changing conditions of market environment by mean procedure of clients clustering according to their significance. The results of such clustering are used for risk rating evaluation and for using flexible discount system, that makes possible to held profitable clients from churn to another companies and eventually for providing to the company additional profit.

In our work for experimental research BRMS Visual rules Modeler was selected and installed. The next structure of the database, containing products and customer data, was developed   (figure 1).

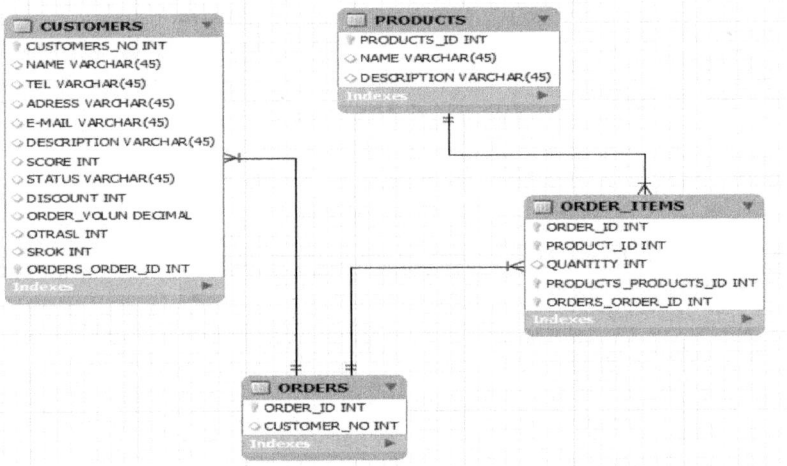

Fig. 1. Database structure

In this data base table «CUSTOMERS» contains the clients legal entities data such as title, description, legal address, phone number, email address, branch of the enterprise, the term of operation of the client on the market, besides the table contains several computed field to store such data as score, the volume of orders and size of the discounts computed as a result of the business rules application. Data about customer's orders are saved in tables «ORDER» and «ORDER_ITEMS». Table «PRODUCTS» contains   the hydraulic products items catalog company.

With application   Visual Rules Modeler was created business rules stream "Discount Assign", depending from order volume and client status. Stream rules "Discount Assign" illustrates the rule set, which is assigning   discounts to customers. Business Rules allow management to create a flexible system of discounts, value which is easy to modify (figure 2).

As can be seen in the data base and views into data fields score, status, and the order volume discounts values have been inserted in accordance with the developed model business rules for certain customer and logic of the discounts assignment decision to the different users. So through the developed business rules model, companies can quickly adapt to changing environmental conditions and dynamic competitive environment.

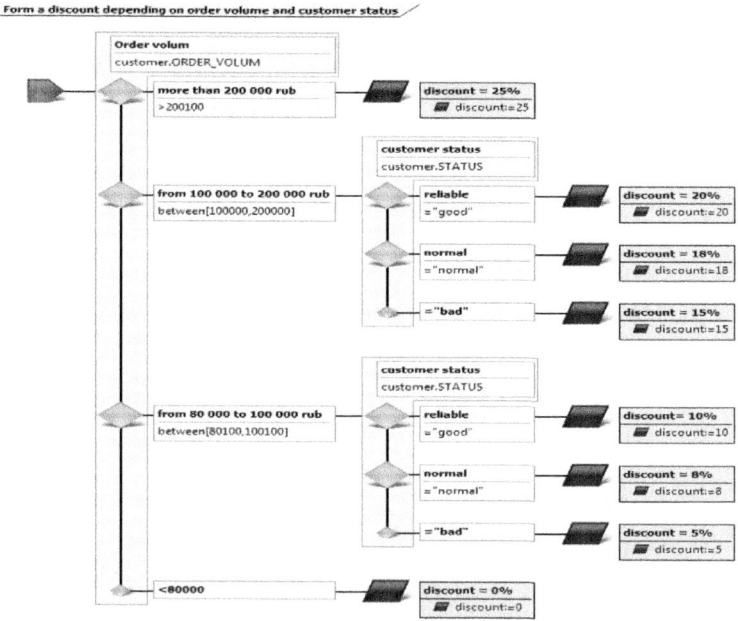

Fig. 2. Business Rules, that assigned the discounts to the clients

The data, prepared for the model testing, which were loaded to the data base and then the discount percents values were computed according business rules to different customers are presented at figure 3.

	NAME	TEL	UAD...	E-MAIL	DESCRIPTI...	SCORE	STATUS	DISCOUNT	ORDER_VOLUM	OTRASL	SROK
1	ООО «Ги...	325...	1155...	Gidros...	выполняет ...	10	bad	15	125600	1	8
2	ООО «Ги...	544...	М.О....	gidro...	бурение ск...	10	bad	5	97000	1	5
3	ООО «Ст...	456...	1256...	stroim...	Алмазное ...	24	normal	0	52000	2	3
4	ООО «Б...	545...	1900...	bibus...	компания ...	24	normal	0	72900	2	25
5	ОАО «Ир...	242...	6640...	iztm@...	работы по ...	24	normal	15	193000	2	40
6	ОАО «Ад...	812...	1901...	admi...	Предприят...	28	good	25	224000	3	32
7	ОАО Суд...	812...	Рос...	sever...	продукции ...	28	good	0	54000	3	26
8	ЗАО "Ас...	851...	РФ, ...	zavod...	При ремон...	28	good	25	320400	3	30
9	ЗАО "Во...	883...	Рос...	office...	Выполняет...	28	good	0	80000	3	31
10	ЗАО «Об...	812...	1960...	kb@o...	особое ме...	24	normal	0	15000	2	25
11	ОАО "Ам...	421...	6800...	office...	нет	22	normal	15	175800	3	12
12	ООО «М...	421...	6800...	mail@...	комплексн...	24	normal	15	108000	2	32
13	ОАО Лен...	411...	6779...	direct...	перевозки ...	28	good	5	88000	3	25
14	АО «Ирт...	381...	6440...	info@i...	Нарядус п...	28	good	5	94500	3	22
15	ЗАО Зап...	838...	6300...	OAOZ...	Основные ...	28	good	25	248500	3	23

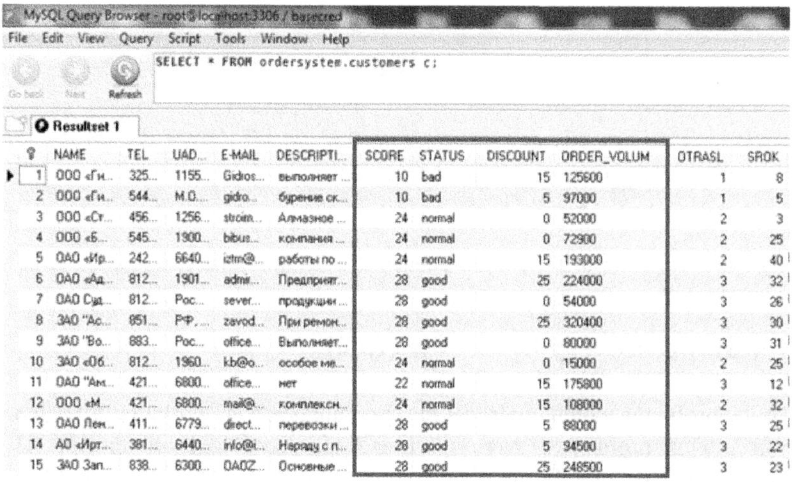

Fig. 3. Clients discount percents data, computed according business rules

Rules stream at figure 4 shows that business rules stream is actually displayed as graphic interface for making the program, containing as business rules for conditions checking as data base SQL commands, performing in the definite order.

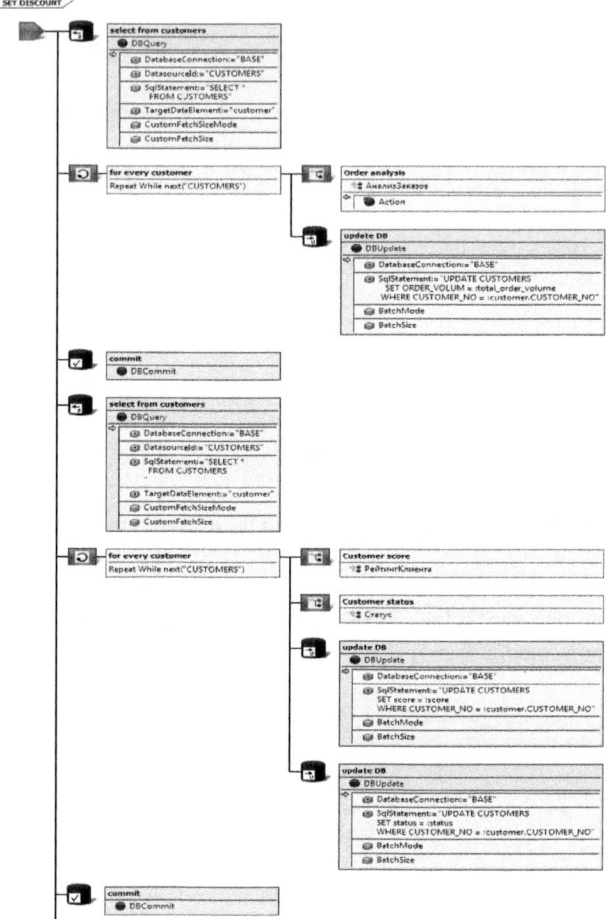

Fig. 4. Rule stream as a program, containing business rules and SQL operators

4   Rules Discovery by FCA Method

One of the problems which confronts business analytics is   problem of business rules discovery. This problem is very hard and has very high dimension. The data mining method that may be used for extracting rules from client and services data (figure 5).

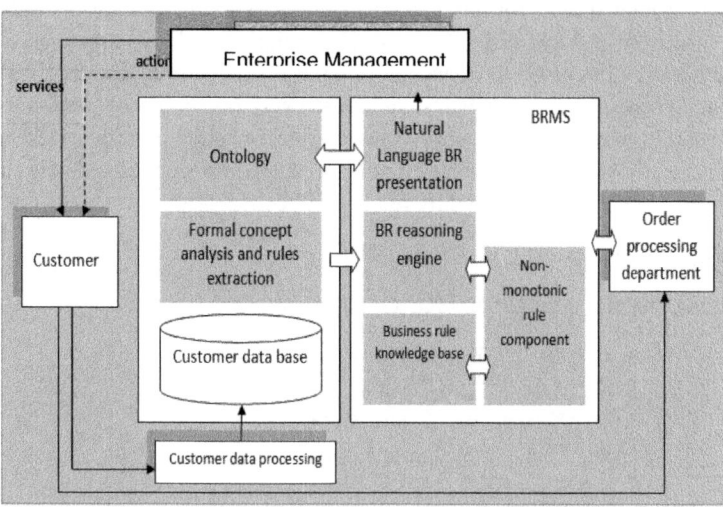

Fig. 5. Adaptive EIS, self-adjusting to the customers' consumption profile and motivation customers to increase volume of consumption

At the figure 5 is presented adaptive EIS, where feedback loop used for adjusting EIS services on the base of analyzing customer's data and applying the results for correcting services and products to customer consumption profile. The formal concept analysis is one of such method.   Formal concept analysis was primary proposed by R. Wille in 1982 year [8] and it finds its application at the different domains for discovering data structure.

Aside from selection clients group and its visualizing this method provide possibility for search attributes dependencies in form of implications. The clients may be regarded as objects and their personal data, kinds of services, intensity services consumption and performed with them marketing actions as a attributes, which customers have. Upon this data, the set of objects with common attributes values may be discovered.

The data are presented as formal context that is as a table, the rows of which correspond to object and the columns – to attributes. If some object has definite attribute value then at the intersection is placed one (or cross). The essence of this method consists in the next [9]. Formal *context K:=(G,M,I)* consists from sets *G,M* and a binary relation $I \subseteq G \times M$, where *M* –attribute set, *G* –objects sets,   expression *(g,m)* $\in I$ - signifies that object g has attribute *m*.

Formal context may be presented as binary matrix, rows of which correspond to object and column – to attributes values. Let us define the mappings for $A \subseteq G$, $B \subseteq M$:

$\varphi: 2^M \rightarrow 2^G$ *u* $\psi:$ $2^G \rightarrow 2^M$.

$\varphi(A)=def\ \{m \in M \mid gIm\ \forall g \in A\}$, $\psi(B)= def\{g \in G \mid gIm\ \forall m \in B\}$, $A \subseteq G$, $B \subseteq M$.

   If $A \subseteq G$, $B \subseteq M$, *then*

pair(A,B)- is named as a formal concept of context K, if $(A) = B$, $\psi(B) = A$ (or another notation: $A' = B$, and $B' = A$). The object set A is named as extent and attribute set B – intent of the concept. Therefore, the formal concept it is a set of objects and corresponding attributes, such that every object has all attributes from the attribute set. In case, when extent of concept C_2 is included into the extent of concept C_1, that is $Ext(C_2) \subseteq Ext(C_1)$, we say that C_1 is a superconcept and C_2 – is subconcept. The concepts hierarchy is defined by relation subconcept-superconcept:

$$(A_1,B_1) \leq (A_2,B_2) \Leftrightarrow A_1 \subseteq A_2 \, (\Leftrightarrow B_1 \supseteq B_2).$$

For formal context (G,M,I) and $X \subseteq G$, $S \subseteq M$,

$$1.\ X_1 \subseteq X_2 \ \Rightarrow X_1' \supseteq X_2' \text{ для } X_1, X_2 \subseteq G,$$
$$2.\ S_1 \subseteq S_2 \Rightarrow S_1' \supseteq S_2' \text{ для } S_1, S_2 \subseteq M,$$
$$3.\ X \subseteq X'' \text{ и } X'=X''' \ \text{ для } X \subseteq G,$$
$$4.\ S \subseteq S'' \text{ и } S'=S''' \ \text{ для } S \subseteq M.$$
$$5.\ X \subseteq S' \Leftrightarrow S \subseteq X'.$$

The ordered set of all formal concepts of (G,M,I) is denoted by $L(G,M,I)$ and is called the concept lattice of (G,M,I). Infimum and supremum of the $L(G,M,I)$ are given by:

$$\bigwedge_{j \in J} (X_j, S_j) = (\bigcap_{j \in J} X_j, (\bigcup_{j \in J} S_j) \,''),$$

$$\bigvee_{j \in J} (X_j, S_j) = ((\bigcup_{j \in J} X_j) \,'', \bigcap_{j \in J} S_j).$$

The most important problem is: how to build the concept lattice for the context (G, M, I). We obtain the most simple answer, creating (X'', X') for all $X \subseteq G$ or (S', S'') for all $S \subseteq M$.

In practice, in this paper we use the program Concept Explorer (http://sourceforge.net/projects/conexp/). The context for our PEMP example is depicted at

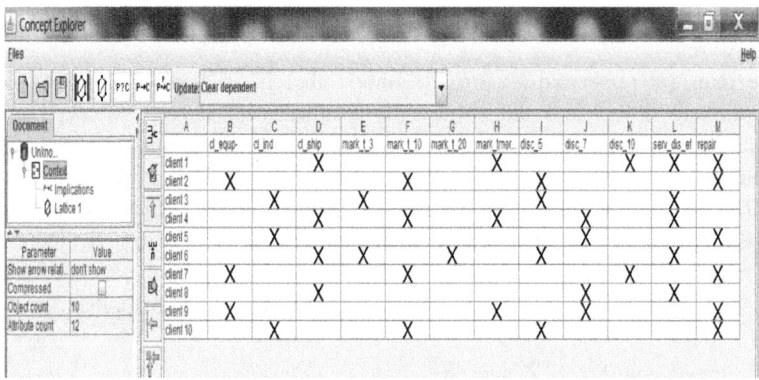

Fig. 6. The context, describing customers of the PEMP

figure 6, where data about customers, their consumption profile, values of score for clients, the efficiency data of preferences and discounts are contained.

The concept lattice for our case is presented at figure 7. This lattice provides us an opportunity to explore and interpret the relationship between concepts.

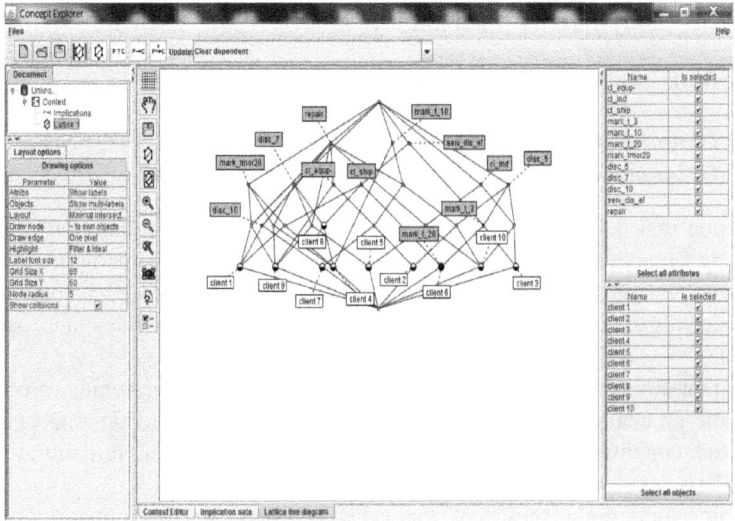

Fig. 7. The concept lattice

The dependency notion between attributes is based on the next idea: if for all objects in the context, for which some property P is true, some another property C is also true, then implication $P \rightarrow C$ is valid. More precisely, the implication $P \rightarrow C$ is valid in a context $K = (G, M, I)$, where $P \subseteq M$ and $C \subseteq M$ iff $C \subseteq P''$.

5   Rules Quality Criteria

The implication means that all objects of context which contain attributes P also contain attribute C. That is in the situation P manager must make decision C. Let us define the next measures of rules quality:

- *Support: $supp(P) = Card(\psi(P)/Card(G)$* – the rate of objects, containing nonempty values of attributes P, comparing to all number of objects.
- *Confidence: $conf(P \Rightarrow C) = supp(P \cup C)/supp(P)$,*
- *Lift: $lift(P \Rightarrow C) = supp(P \cup C)/supp(P) \times supp(C)$,*
- *Conviction : $conv(P \Rightarrow C) = 1 - supp(C)/1 - conf(P \Rightarrow C)$.*

The implication set, discovered by Concept explorer, are business rules, some example of which are presented below. Business rules with confidence 100%:

- *IF branch of the client = equipment THEN repair_discount_5%;*
- *IF time on a market > 10 THEN repair_discount_5%;*
- *IF time on a market > 20 THEN repair_discount_10% and service_discount and consulting_free;*
- *IF branch of client = shipment AND   time on market> 20 THEN serv_discount AND sale_discount = 10% AND repair_discount.*

The rules with confidence less than 100%:

- *IF branch of client = shipment THEN serv_discount;* (confidence 80%)
- *IF branch of client = industry THEN consulting_free;* (confidence 60%)

We assume that data may be incomplete or contradictory and therefore implication derived by Conexp software should be considered within the frame of non-monotonic logic, and realized as defeasible theory rules. Defeasible logic is practical non-monotonic logic, containing facts, strict rules, defeasible rules and supporting relations.

Non-monotonic reasoning is an approach that allows reasoning process with incomplete or changing information. More specifically, it provides mechanisms for taking back conclusions that, in the presence of new information, turn out to be wrong and for deriving new, alternative conclusions instead.

The non-monotonic subset of the rules is obtained by computing the lattice corresponding to the subcontext consisting of the original context without those attributes which do not apply to the set of all objects. FCA computes the minimal base of implications corresponding to the actual context and asks the user if each single implication is valid in the universe of objects or if a counterexample is known. The counterexamples are than added to the context and the implications are newly computed until all implications are accepted.

6   Conclusions

In this paper we have considered the conception of adaptive EIS, which has possibility of tuning its business rules set by mean customer's data mining with applying formal concept method. This approach is especially important when number of business rules, which are changed with time, counts by thousands.

We have shown that on the way of including into the structure of modern EIS means for automated decision making, the essential role may play Formal Concept Analysis method, which can help to find out specific dependencies between observed customers' data and services, provided by business, usability data.

The next step may be research the adaptive   EIS with varying structure, including data base structure, procedures and semantic concepts of language, describing the domain of application.

References

1. Romanov, V., Veynberg, R., Polujectova, A.: Customer-Telecommunications Company's Relationship Simulation Model (RSM), Based on Non-Monotonic Business Rules Approach and Formal Concept Analysis Method. In: SpringSim 2011, p. 54. Program Book, Boston (2011)
2. What IS Enterprise Decision Management or EDM? FICO Decision Management Blog, http://dmblog.fico.com/2006/06/what_is_enterpr_1.html
3. Will Automated Decision Support Tools Replace the Business Analytics? http://thinkup.waldenu.edu/finance-and-accounting/financial-business-systems/item/11860-will-automated-decision-support-tools-replace-business-analytics
4. Oracle Business Rules Overview, http://www.oracle.com/technetwork/.../business-rules/.../index-085313.html
5. SAP Netweaver Business Rules overview #sapteched09 — JT on EDM, http://jtonedm.com/2009/10/13/sap-netweaver-business-rules-overview-sapteched09/
6. Microsoft BizTalk Server Business Rule Framework, http://www.microsoft.com/biztalk/.../business-rule-framework.aspx
7. IBM ILOG JRules | ILOG JRules Tutorial | ILOG JRules Interview ..., http://www.javagenious.com/.../ILOG-JRULES-TUTORIALS
8. Wille, R.: Restructuring lattice theory: an approach based on hierarchies of concepts. In: Rival, I. (ed.) Ordered Sets, pp. 445–470. Reidel, Dordrecht (1982)
9. Ganter, B., Stumme, G., Wille, R. (eds.): Formal Concept Analysis Foundation and Applications, p. 349. Springer, Heidelberg (2005)

Enterprise Information Systems Security: A Conceptual Framework

Peggy E. Chaudhry[1], Sohail S. Chaudhry[1], Ronald Reese[2], and Darryl S. Jones[2]

[1] Department of Management and Operations/International Business,
Villanova School of Business, Villanova University, Villanova, PA 19085 USA
{peggy.chaudhry,sohail.chaudhry}@villanova.edu
[2] Graduate Program, MBA, Villanova School of Business, Villanova University,
Villanova, PA 19085 USA
{ronald.reese,djones21}@villanova.edu

Abstract. Over the past half a century, organizations have implemented information systems for managing their business processes. These information systems have now evolved into what are more commonly known as enterprise information systems. An important facet of implementing an enterprise information system in an organization is the development of security related issues within the information system for the business processes. In this paper, we review the relevant literature related to the security policies that are associated with the use of enterprise information systems within organizations. Based on this literature review, we identify four major issues which are security policy documentation, employee awareness, top management support, and access control. A conceptual framework based on these four issues is then presented within the context of corporate governance for the security of the enterprise information systems. We conclude our work with the future direction for this research.

Keywords: Enterprise information systems, security, conceptual model.

1   Introduction

Enterprise Information Systems (EIS) are companywide Information Technology (IT) systems that companies use to combine multiple business functions information into one data warehouse. They "enable a company to integrate the data used throughout its entire organization [1]" Enterprise information systems can include data from the various functions of an organization such as Finance (Accounts Receivable and Payable, General Ledger, Profitability Analysis, and the like.); Human Resources (Payroll, Personnel Planning, Travel Expenses, etc.); Operations and Logistics (Inventory, Purchasing, Shipping, etc.); and Sales and Marketing (Order Management, Pricing, Sales Management, etc.) [1]. The plethora of information technologies developed and improved over the last few decades has made business decisions easier for managers who now have all of the relevant information available from one access point without the fear of missing or overlapping information.

C. Møller and S. Chaudhry (Eds.): CONFENIS 2011, LNBIP 105, pp. 118–128, 2012.

A problem that results from this convenience is that all company information is now available in one location. This centrality makes a company's intellectual property, one of its core competitive advantages, more vulnerable. Security breaches (malicious or unintentional) can result in continuity disruption, poor reliability of information, lowered effectiveness and efficiency of processes, and can even have legal implications. The current events of *external* information security problems related to information access, such as the hacker who obtained the personal information of 77 million consumers at Sony's PlayStation Network is testimony to the problems that companies will continue to face with security breaches [2]. Likewise, the malware files attached to the NASDAQ's Directors Desk is clearly another recent example of outside hackers creating security violations [3]. However, in this paper, we are not addressing so-called "Hack attacks" but will be evaluating the risk of *internal* information security dilemmas, such as employees of the firm either intentionally or unintentionally compromising the data stored.

Overall, firms must safeguard their employee access to the "keys to the kingdom" (e.g., accounts and passwords) that protect an array of information ranging from credit card data, human resource personnel data, internal financial reports and research and development plans [4]. For example, in 2010, an employee of the General Services Administration of the U.S. government unintentionally compromised the social security numbers of its 12,000 staff members to a private email address that made the government agency provide identify theft coverage and credit monitoring to its employees [5].

More research on this topic is important because of the paradigm shift that we are currently facing. Until recently, most of the concern regarding security in enterprise information systems was more of a technical nature (e.g., viruses, worms, Trojans, etc.), however, more research is finding that human interaction with the systems is the real cause of most breaches [6], [7], and [8]. In fact, Sachlar Paulus, Senior Vice-President of Product and Security Governance of SAP (a global EIS provider) has stated that "The weakest link is still people ... the biggest problems occur wherever technology comes into contact with people who need to administer, manage, or even use IT security functionality [9]."

The purpose of this paper is three-fold. First, we will briefly review the past work that has been done regarding security in Enterprise Information Systems and provide a succinct literature review. Next, we present a new conceptual framework that businesses can use to properly secure their data through Enterprise Information Systems. Finally, the paper concludes with a brief synopsis of plans for future research.

2   Literature Review

Up until the last few years, most of the research done on corporate dealings with security in EIS focused mainly on the technical aspect of IT such as firewalls and anti-virus software which rely more on technology than the employees using the systems [10]. In fact, as recent as 2005, Siponen [10] believed "the importance of the socio-organizational nature of (E)IS is not recognized seriously enough by traditional Information Systems Security methods." Researchers are now starting to realize that the human interaction with the EIS of the firm is just as important, if not more, than the technical -and that information security cannot be achieved solely through these technological tools [11].

The threat of external hackers and malicious attackers of information systems are still a major issue for information security and widely reported in the current events and highlighted in practicing managers' publications, for example, see [12]. However, many researchers now believe the biggest threat to information security remains *internal* [6], [13], and [14]. Swartz [15] outlined several cases in which employees stole data while still working for their company, yet the majority of employee security breaches occur accidently or unintentionally [7] and [8]. In April 2011, Cyber-Ark® Software [4], substantiated this concern with the results of its "Snooping Survey" with respondents from Europe, the Middle East, Africa (EMEA), and the United States, with the upper echelon of managers of several companies as illustrated in Table 1.

Table 1. Have you accessed any cases on insider sabotage or IT security fraud conducted at your workplace?

	EMEA	%	US	%	C-Level	%
Yes	121	21%	137	16%	11	16%
No	303	54%	452	53%	44	63%
Don't Know	139	25%	269	31%	15	21%
Grand Total	563	100%	858	100%	70	100%

Source: Cyber-Ark Snooping Survey, April 11, 2011

This recent survey of 1,400 IT staff and C-level professionals (i.e., the CEO, CFO, COO) in both the EMEA and U.S. reveals a significant amount of these firms are aware of security breaches, or more alarmingly "don't know" if a problem exists [4]. There are currently many theories on the best way to combat these issues. These range from the importance of cultivating an information security policy to significance of employee training and awareness. Overall, just a few researchers have developed frameworks in order to help companies remain as secure as possible [14], [16], and [17].

2.1   Information Security Policy

An information security policy is the set of rules, standards, practices, and procedures that the company employs to maintain a secure IT system. This policy can contain items such as when and how an employee should access secure information and how often their passwords should be changed. It has been said that the "credibility of the entire information security program of an organization depends upon a well-drafted information security policy [18]." Also, many experts now think that the development of an information security policy is one of the most practical ways to preserve protected systems [17] and [19]. Knapp et al. [17] believe that "the development of an information security policy is the first step toward preparing an organization against attacks from internal and external sources." Sengupta et al. [20] affirms that ineffective implementation of security policy leads to weaknesses in enterprise information systems security.

One important factor that most researchers agree must be adhered to in policy development is the support of top level management [21] and [22]. The best way to get employees to comply with information security policies is to engrain the policy into the organizational culture of the company. The goal is to have employees follow and safeguard the policy as a second nature, not because the workers are being policed or audited [13]. Knapp et al. [17] actually developed an information security policy process that companies can use to develop and analyze their current programs. While security policies, procedures, and controls are the most implemented security measures, Hagen et al. [23] found through a survey of Norwegian organizations that they are not the most effective in information security.

2.2   Employee Awareness

"Creation and maintenance of security awareness include both individual and collective activities, i.e. education and awareness-raising initiatives, e.g. emails, pamphlets, mouse pads, formal presentations, and discussion groups" [23]. Many researchers now believe that employee awareness is one of the best ways to protect a company's data [16] and [24]. In fact, empirical research found that awareness creation is the most effective information security measure [23]. "Information security training and management support are possibly the most important components of an effective information security program. Training can increase security awareness, understanding, and thus, participation [25]." Systems are better protected by employees that have an enhanced understanding of the possible consequences of security breaches and are aware of ways to combat these breaches.
In addition, the extent to which employees' perceive that compliance with existing security policies are mandatory, is directly related to employees' motivation to take security precautions [6].

As illustrated in the recent Nasdaq and Sony PlayStation network cases, the increased security benefits are not only important to the sponsoring company, but its supplier and customer businesses as well [2] and [3]. Pollitt [26] actually reported a case in which a UK communications company offered free security training to customers to give them an understanding of the true risks of information security. Similar to the development and implementation of security policies, it is imperative for employee awareness to actually be an effective tool in combating poor security and top level management support is essential.

2.3   Access Control

Another commonly covered method to maintain information security is to limit employee access to certain information by roles. Access control is defined as the process a company takes to limit the access an employee has to various functions of the business; particularly functions not relevant to their position or containing more information than they should have access to [27]. She and Thuraisingham [27] stated that many companies now use Role Based Access Control (RBAC), which is a way to limit employee access by permissions, roles, users, and constraints. In the 2011 Cyber-Ark survey, an alarming 30% of their respondents identified as IT and C-professionals (n=514 managers from the U.S. and EMEA) admitted to accessing information from a system that was *not relevant to their role* in the firm [4].

D'Aubeterre et al. [16] developed a framework to generate higher security awareness in which RBAC is an integral function. By breaking employees into roles and profiles, it is easier to determine what employee has access to which information. For example, an Accounts Payable employee should only have access to processing invoices [28]. "Monitoring user access to mission-critical information and detecting unauthorized access to high-risk data are critical steps all companies should take to better protect their sensitive information [15]." In addition, because of organizational changes or modifications of security policy, access rules have to be frequently updated. This process needs to be controlled in an efficient, adaptable and secure manner [29].

2.4   Top Level Management Support

Michael Maccoby's book, *"The Leaders We Need: And What Makes Us Follow,"* further supports the old adage of "leading by example" that is increasingly important in today's environment and he states that, "the threats and opportunities facing us have never been greater. Rapid globalization and new technologies are transforming the economy and the way we work [30]." Although Maccoby's work is not directed to IT security leadership, it is apparent that employees must perceive that top level management believes that information system security is important to the success of the company and it is engrained into the corporate culture. The overarching objective of information security management is to convert the organization's security policy into a set of requirements that can be communicated to the organization, measured, and imposed [31]. Basically, the better the top management support of information security, the greater the preventative efforts a firm (and its employees) will make [14]. Overall, top management support is essential to security governance success [32].

2.5   Corporate Governance

The research of Weill and Ross [33] on IT governance in 300 companies found that "IT governance is a mystery to key decision-makers at most companies" and that only about one-third of the managers' surveyed understood how IT is governed at his or her company (p. 26). Engulfing all of these methods for security protection is the idea of corporate governance. "Corporate governance refers to organization controls such as reporting structure, authority, ownership, oversight, and policy enforcement [32]." For information security, this is the way top level management and the board decide to run the IT department, and in turn, information system security. This is where the true decisions on how to attack a possible weakness are made. These managerial decisions include items such as how to implement a security policy and where and how employee awareness trainings will be held. Solms [34] posits that "Information Security Governance is now accepted as an integral part of good IT and Corporate Governance (Information Security Governance)." Khoo et al. [35] stated that information security governance is a subset of corporate governance that relates to the security of information systems, and because the board of directors is ultimately in charge of corporate governance information security must start at the top [21]. To facilitate management in the governance of information security, Da Veiga and Eloff [32] developed a more comprehensive approach that combined key items from a few of the best current corporate governance frameworks.

3   Conceptual Framework

We have developed a conceptual model in Figure 1 for EIS security that encompasses the major themes found in our literature review. In its simplest form, we draw the analogy that the company's EIS security is the roof that protects four main pillars: security policy, security awareness, access control, and top level management support. The basic solid foundation of this 'house' is the company's corporate governance. As noted by Weill and Ross [33], the best performing firms in their study carefully planned their usage of IT. They further assert that, "60% to 80% of seniors executives in those companies have a clear understanding of and can describe their IT governance" (p. 26). The decisions that the leaders of the company make are the base of the entire system and will dictate the stability of it. Resting on the foundation, are the walls/pillars that support the roof. These four pillars are the processes that management and the board of directors can choose to implement to make the system as secure as possible. Having all four pillars is the best way to make the enterprise information system secure, however removing any one of these columns can truly diminish the stability/security of the entire system. Below is a pictorial representation of the model.

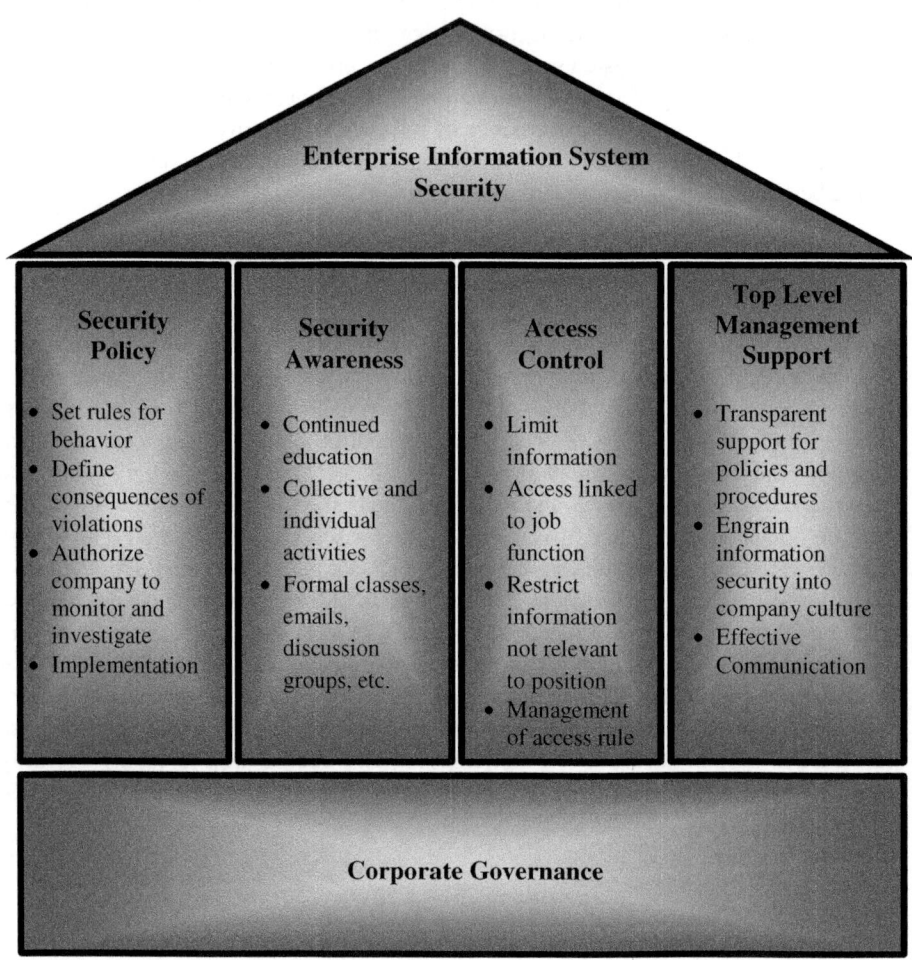

Fig. 1. Conceptual Model for Enterprise Information System Security

A summary of the research assertions in previous studies that led us to conceptualize the model in Figure 1 is provided below in Table 2.

Table 2. Constructs, Research Assertions, and Relevant Research Papers

Construct	Research Assertions	Relevant Research Papers
Security Policy	• An essential part of information security is the information security policy. • Senior level managers must plan policies in a broad and measurable way.	[13]: Vroom et al. (2004) [17]: Knapp et al. (2009) [18]: Kadam (2007) [19]: Myyry et al. (2009) [20]: Sengupta et al. (2011) [21]: von Solms and von Solms (2006) [22]: Doughty (2003) [23]: Hagen et al. (2008)
Security Awareness	• Employee awareness creation is the most effective measure for IS, but, it may be the least implemented. • Internal employees may be the biggest threat to data security. • IS training and management support are possibly the most important components of IS program. • Education is a powerful tool to ensure employees internalize IS policies. • Employees can underestimate the probability of security breaches. • Human error is important because employees may not even know they are exposing the company to information risks. • The biggest threat to intellectual property is internal, that may be either malicious or negligent employees. • Firms can give security training to their customers to educate them on the risks also.	[6]: Boss et al. (2009) [7]: Keller et al. (2005) [8]: Sumner (2009) [11]: Herath and Rao (2009) [13]: Vroom and von Solms (2004) [14]: Kankanhalli et al. (2003) [15]: Swartz (2007) [16]: D'Aubeterre et al. (2008) [19]: Myyry et al. (2009) [22]: Doughty (2003) [23]: Hagen et al. (2008) [24]: Chang and Yeh (2006) [25]: Ma et al. (2009) [26]: Pollitt (2005) [32]: Da Veiga and Eloff (2007)
Access Control	• Systems break employers into roles (essentially job titles), then into profiles (individuals in those roles), to determine who has access to what information, such as A/P employees access to processing invoices only. • Firms must develop a framework to analyze secure business processes that includes authorization and RBAC. • Companies need to monitor user access to critical information and effectively detect unauthorized access to high-risk data.	[15]: Swartz (2007) [16]: D'Aubeterre et al. (2008) [27]: She and Thuraisingham (2007) [28]: Allen (2008) [29]: Rinderle – Ma et al. (2009)
Top-Level Management Support	• Good information security governance is essential to combat human interaction risks. • The greater the top management support of IS; the greater the preventative efforts of the firm. • Information security must start at the upper echelon of the firm—the board of directors. • Top management must engrain the IS policy into the culture of the firm.	[13]: Vroom and von Solms (2004) [14]: Kankanhalli et al. (2003) [21]: von Solms and von Solms (2006) [25]: Ma et al. (2009) [32]: Da Veiga and Eloff (2007) [31]: Tracey (2007) [33]: Weill and Ross (2005) [35]: Khoo et al. (2007)

4   Conclusions and Future Research

The research in this paper has focused on how and what organizations execute to disseminate information related to security issues that evolve around the business processes with the enterprise information systems.   By analyzing the relevant literature, we identified four major themes that impact the security issues within organizations.   These four factors are identified as security policy documentation, access control, employee awareness, and top level management support.   Based on these four factors, a conceptual framework ingrained with the relevant literature was presented within the context of corporate governance for enterprise information systems.

It is the expectations of this research that the conceptual framework developed will assist businesses protect Enterprise Information System data that could potentially be breached through socio-organizational problems. To test the framework, two future phases of this research are planned. The next phase will consist of multiple in-depth interviews with IT officers using a cross-section of companies. The companies will be of different sizes and industry sectors to get a fully holistic view of actual practices in place. Finally, with the combination of the literature review conducted for this paper, the framework presented, and the information from the interviews, a survey instrument will be developed and distributed to a larger population of IT officers to further study the various issues that have been exposed in this research within the context of enterprise information systems security.

References

1. Davenport, T.: Putting the Enterprise into the Enterprise System. Harvard Business Review 76(4), 121–131 (1998)
2. Sherr, I.: Sony Faces Lawsuit Over PlayStation Network Breach (April 28, 2011), http://online.wsj.com/article/BT-CO-20110428-720452.html (accessed on April 30, 2011)
3. Barret, D.: NASDAQ Acknowledges Security Breach (February 6, 2011), http://online.wsj.com/article/SB100014240527487048433045761263 70179332758.html (accessed on April 30, 2011)
4. Cyber-Ark Snooping Survey (April 2011), http://www.cyber-ark.com/ downloads/pdf/2011-Snooping-Survey-data.pdf (accessed on April 30, 2011)
5. Kalish, B.: Security Breach of Employee Data at GSA (November 8, 2011), http://techinsider.nextgov.com/2010/11/work_at_gsa_your_ social_has_been_e-mailed.php (accessed on April 30, 2011)
6. Boss, S., Kirsch, L., Angermeier, I., Shingler, R., Boss, R.: If Someone is Watching, I'll Do What I'm Asked: Mandatoriness, Control, and Information Security. European Journal of Information Systems 18(2), 151–164 (2009)
7. Keller, S., Powell, A., Horstmann, B., Predmore, C., Crawford, C.: Information Security Threats and Practices in Small Businesses. Information Systems Management 22(2), 7–19 (2005)

8. Sumner, M.: Information Security Threats: A Comparative Analysis of Impact, Probability, and Preparedness. Information Systems Management 26(1), 2–12 (2009)
9. Walsh, K.: The ERP Security Challenge (January 8, 2008), http://www.cio.com/article/216940/The_ERP_Security_Challenge (accessed on April 30, 2011)
10. Siponen, M.T.: An Analysis of the Traditional IS Security Approaches: Implications for Research and Practice. European Journal of Information Systems 14(3), 303–315 (2005)
11. Herath, T., Rao, H.R.: Protection Motivation and Deterrence: A Framework for Security Policy Compliance in Organisations. European Journal of Information Systems 18(2), 106–125 (2009)
12. McNulty, E.: Boss, I Think Someone Stole Our Data. Harvard Business Review, 37–50 (September 2007)
13. Vroom, C., von Solms, R.: Towards Information Security Behavioural Compliance. Computers & Security 23(3), 191–198 (2004)
14. Kankanhalli, A., Teo, H.H., Tan, B.C.Y., Wei, K.K.: An Integrative Study of Information Systems Security Effectiveness. International Journal of Information Management 23(2), 139–154 (2003)
15. Swartz, N.: Protecting Information from Insiders. Information Management Journal 41(3), 20–24 (2007)
16. D'aubeterre, F., Singh, R., Iyer, L.: Secure Activity Resource Coordination: Empirical Evidence of Enhanced Security Awareness in Designing Secure Business Processes. European Journal of Information Systems 17(5), 528–542 (2008)
17. Knapp, K., Morris, R., Marshall, T., Byrd, T.: Information Security Policy: An Organizational-Level Process Model. Computers & Security 28(7), 493–508 (2009)
18. Kadam, A.W.: Information Security Policy Development and Implementation. Information Systems Security 16(5), 246–256 (2007)
19. Myyry, L., Siponen, M., Pahnila, S., Vartiainen, T., Vance, A.: What Levels of Moral Reasoning and Values Explain Adherence to Information Security Rules? An Empirical Study. European Journal of Information Systems 18(2), 126–139 (2009)
20. Sengupta, A., Mazumdar, C., Bagchi, A.: A Formal Methodology for Detecting Managerial Vulnerabilities and Threats in an Enterprise Information System. J. Netw. Syst. Manage. 19, 319–342 (2011)
21. von Solms, R., von Solms, S.H.B.: Information Security Governance: A Model Based on the Direct-Control Cycle. Computers & Security 25(6), 408–412 (2006)
22. Doughty, K.: Implementing Enterprise Security: A Case Study. Computers & Security 22(2), 99–114 (2003)
23. Hagen, J.M., Albrechtsen, E., Hovden, J.: Implementation and Effectiveness of Organizational Information Security Measures. Information Management & Computer Security 16(4), 377–397 (2008)
24. Chang, A.J.T., Yeh, Q.J.: On Security Preparations Against Possible IS Threats Across Industries. Information Management & Computer Security 14(4), 343–360 (2006)
25. Ma, Q., Schmidt, M., Pearson, J.: An Integrated Framework for Information Security Management. Review of Business 30(1), 58–69 (2009)
26. Pollitt, D.: Energis Trains Employees and Customers in IT Security. Human Resource Management International Digest 13(2), 25–28 (2005)
27. She, W., Thuraisingham, B.: Security for Enterprise Resource Planning Systems. Information Systems Security 16, 152–163 (2007)
28. Allen, V.: ERP Security Tools. The Internal Auditor 65(1), 25–27 (2008)

29. Rinderle Ma, S., Reichert, M.: Comprehensive life cycle support for access rules in information systems: the CEOSIS project. Enterprise Information Systems 3(3), 219–251 (2009)
30. Maccoby, M.: The Leaders We Need: And What Makes Us Follow. Harvard Business School Press, Boston (2007)
31. Tracey, R.P.: IT Security Management and Business Process Automation: Challenges, Approaches, and Rewards. Information Systems Security 16, 114–122 (2007)
32. Da Veiga, A., Eloff, J.: An Information Security Governance Framework. Information Systems Management 24(4), 361–372 (2007)
33. Weill, P., Ross, J.: A Matrixed Approach to Designing IT Governance. Sloan Management Review 46(2), 26–34 (2005)
34. von Solms, S.H.B.: Information Security Governance: Compliance management vs. operational management. Computers & Security 24, 443–447 (2005)
35. Khoo, B., Harris, P., Hartman, S.: Information Security Governance of Enterprise Information Systems: An Approach to Legislative Compliant. International Journal of Management and Information Systems 14(3), 49–55 (2010)

Implications of ERP as Service

Gustaf Juell-Skielse[1] and Håkan Enquist[2]

[1] Stockholm University
gjs@dsv.su.se
[2] School of Business, Economics and Law, University of Gothenburg
hakan.enquist@handels.gu.se

Abstract. In this paper we present implications for using and delivering Enterprise Resource Planning as services (ERP-as-a-service). The objective is to construct a framework of opportunities and challenges for users and suppliers of ERP-as-a-service. The framework is based on a combination of literature study and field study and includes approximately 80 implications. New implications, not found in literature, were identified in the field study. Examples of new implications include: more focus on IT-value; simplified phasing of implementation and improved supplier brand. For future research it is suggested that the framework is tested in a larger setting and that implications are prioritized for certain industries and types of business models.

Keywords: ERP-as-a-service, Implication, Software-as-a-service, Enterprise resource planning, Service orientation, Cloud computing.

1 Introduction

Recently, service orientation has emerged as an important change driver in private and public sector organizations. Service orientation offers means to radically improve customer service, business processes and sourcing of information systems. Suppliers begin to offer information systems according to service based business models, such as Software as a Service and Cloud Computing, rather than standard application packages. Service based business models challenge conventional payment models, on-premise installations and monolithic designs of standard application packages and have vast implications for both users and suppliers of information systems. Through service based business models, suppliers can expand their potential customer base and offer more choices that enable customers to focus on core competencies and reduce initial investments in standard applications [1].

So far, research in service oriented software has concentrated on user and supplier implications on limited application areas such as Customer Relationship Management [2]. However, a great challenge for service oriented software is the migration of Enterprise Resource Planning (ERP) from locally installed systems to ERP-as-a-Service. ERP systems are complex standard application packages that include a large variety of application areas and are configurable to satisfy needs from many users

C. Møller and S. Chaudhry (Eds.): CONFENIS 2011, LNBIP 105, pp. 129–151, 2012.

with high demands on integration with legacy systems. Due to its profound impact on user organizations, ERP is challenging to implement [3]. There are numerous examples of companies that have suffered severely from poorly conducted ERP implementations where the bankruptcy of Foxmeyer Drug in 1996 [4] represents an early example.

ERP represents a significant portion of the global software industry and suppliers are beginning to offer ERP-as-a-service. In 2008 the size of the ERP market corresponded to 34.4 billion USD in software licenses and 103 billion USD in ERP related services [5]. New suppliers, such as Netsuite and 24Sevenoffice, appear on the ERP market offering service based ERP alongside with established suppliers, such as Lawson. Lawson has migrated its Enterprise Management System to a service and use the Amazon Elastic Computer Cloud infrastructure for service delivery [6].

ERP is a large, complex and business critical investment and it is necessary to understand the organizational impact of ERP-as-a-service to make rational investment decisions. ERP-as-a-service represents a major shift in what is delivered, how and by whom. For example, ERP-as-a-service has the potential to decrease up-front investments and reduce implementation costs and risks for ERP [7, 8, 9]. But it could also reduce the possibilities to configure and integrate the software to specific user needs [10]. Furthermore, ERP-as-a-service can serve as an interesting case for service orientation. The conventional ERP business model is product centric and revolves around the ERP system which is implemented on the premises of the using organization, while ERP-as-a-service follows a service dominant logic [11] where users consume services bundled as offerings delivered over the Internet by a supply chain of service providers.

In this paper we investigate implications for organizations that use Enterprise Resource Planning as a service (ERP-as-a-service) rather than the conventional ERP business model. The objective is to establish a framework of implications for ERP-as-a-service. The framework includes opportunities and challenges for users and suppliers of ERP-as-a-service. It is constructed using a combination of literature study and a cross-sectional field study involving user and supplier organizations. This paper provides a case of service orientation for a large portion of the software industry and a framework for implications of ERP-as-a-service. By implications we mean opportunities and challenges for users and suppliers of ERP-as-a-service. The framework includes implications not earlier identified in literature as well as additional evidence for implications found in literature. Several field studies of ERP-as-a-service are used to collect data, including small and large public sector and private sector organizations, users as well as native and migrant ERP-as-a-service suppliers. The framework provides practice with a basis for evaluating sourcing alternatives to conventional ERP and as a guide to risk management when implementing ERP-as-a-service.

The article is organized as follows. In the next chapter implications are defined followed by a discussion on the characteristics of ERP-as-a-service. In chapter four the methodology is presented, including a presentation of the field study participants and a methodological discussion. In chapter five, the framework is presented followed by a discussion in chapter six. In the final chapter, conclusions are made together with suggestions for future research. A complete framework with references to literature and field study cases is found in the appendix.

2   Implications

In this paper, we use implication, when we refer to effects that are consequences of adopting ERP-as-a-service. Authors use different terms when discussing implications. For example [1] use the terms benefit and risk while [12] uses the terms opportunity and challenge. Authors also use terms like advantage [8], disadvantage [9] and uncertainty [13].

In this paper we follow Cusumano [12] and specify implication in terms of opportunity and challenge. By opportunities we mean implications that may have positive effects on the effectiveness of the ERP-as-a-service user or the ERP-as-a-service supplier. An example of an opportunity is reduced operating costs. By challenges we mean implications that may have negative effects on the effectiveness of the service user or the service supplier. An example of challenge is increased demands for technical skills.

3   Enterprise Resource Planning

Enterprise Resource Planning (ERP) represents a significant market for suppliers and consultants providing ERP related services to using organizations. In 2008 the size of the ERP market corresponded to 34.4 billion USD in software licences and 103 billion USD in ERP related services [5]. ERP systems are standard application packages designed to meet demands from different users [14]. ERP systems are enterprise wide and include administrative functions for finance, human resources, production, logistics and sales and marketing. The various components or modules are integrated across an enterprise through a central database [3]. ERP provides support to coordinate the work along business processes and to monitor activities spanning large organizational and geographical distance [15]. ERP-systems also provide embedded knowledge, often referred to as best practices [16], that supports using organizations to enhance their business processes [16, 17] within the company and between the company and its partners [17]. ERP has been extended to include more advanced planning functions such as supply chain management and customer relationship management and improved support for e-business [17].

ERP systems are standard applications and represent economies of scale in development since development costs can be shared among several customers [18, 19, 20]. Standard applications aggregate knowledge and experiences from earlier development and represent fewer risks compared to software developed in-house. However, ERP implementations are associated with several risks for user organizations [21]. For example, there is a risk that a company's organizational strategy, structure and processes are not aligned with the chosen ERP system. In order to increase alignment it is often suggested that organizations adjust their operational processes to fit the processes embedded in the software. Another risk is that ERP projects escalate and lack control which is caused by decentralized decision making and subsequent ineffective ratification of decisions.

The conventional business model of ERP involves three actors: using organization, ERP vendor and consultant [22, 23]. In brief, the using organization selects and implements packaged software from an ERP vendor. The vendor has designed the software taking into account current best practices for processes and business domains. The vendor upgrades the software in new releases regularly. ERP vendors partner with consulting firms that help using organizations to select, implement and use the ERP software. Partnerships with the major ERP vendors are usually offered based on a certification procedure. The revenue model for ERP vendors is based on the number of licenses needed by the using organization. Services provided by consulting firms are essentially paid for on a resource basis, i.e. per hour. Interaction between user organizations, consultants and ERP suppliers vary between phases of the ERP lifecycle. From a using organization's perspective, the ERP lifecycle consists of several phases: analysis, selection, set-up, deployment, operation, improvement and settlement [24, 25, 26]. Consultants are normally more involved in the earlier phases of the ERP life cycle, while ERP vendors become more actively involved from the set-up phase and onwards.

3.1   ERP-as-a-Service

ERP-as-a-service is ERP delivered through a SaaS model [27]. SaaS (Software-as-a-Service) is a business model where customers access business functionality remotely, usually over the internet [28]. The main characteristics that distinguish ERP-as-a-service from other types of SaaS models are related to the content of the service. In ERP-as-a-service, the service includes elementary offerings for enterprise-wide, integrated and standardized business functions and support for business processes which are characteristic to ERP. Essentially it is an ERP application delivered as a service [29] accessed through a web browser [30]. In addition to business functionality, the technical infrastructure, the right to use the service, hosting, maintenance and support services are bundled into a single service [28]. The ownership of the software is separated from its use [28, 31]. However, the possibilities to customize the service are limited due to the multi-tenant infrastructure [32, 33].

Users of ERP-as-a-service include most types of companies, regardless of size or industry [2]. The primary channel is the internet [28]. However, there are concerns regarding the organizational size. Gartner Group claims that ERP as-a-service is only a viable business model for small and medium sized organizations [34] while Benlian et al. [35] found no correlation between size and benefits. Due to the scalability of services, organizations can make limited deployments to test reliability and then scale up their solutions [36].

The infrastructure of ERP-as-a-service consists of service providers that remotely operates and maintains the software on their own hardware or hardware provided by third-parties [8]. Service providers use a one-to-many distribution model where the infrastructure most often has been prepared for multi-tenancy [37]. The application is delivered from one instance with a single source code and configurable metadata for each tenant have several advantages [38]. There could also be several service providers co-operating to deliver a joint service consisting of several smaller services. The interface to the customer could be managed by an intermediary who coordinates supply chains of service providers [39] or the customer may combine several services into a coherent service on his own. The development of the software is continuous and delivered to the customer through incremental updates [8] and version free software [1]. The solution is modularized according to SOA principles [40].

The financial aspects of the ERP-as-a-service business model include usage based payment models [28, 1] and cost models that are unconnected to the investment costs for developing the software [1].

4   Method

A cross-sectional field study [41, 42] was performed in order to gather information about implications. 17 firms are included in the sample which includes eight pairs of users and suppliers of ERP-as-a-service and one additional supplier where the user organization was undefined, see table 1. By pairs of users and suppliers we mean that they represent the consumer side and provider side of the same ERP service. Sample organizations were selected based on the following criteria:

- Service content should be similar to the functionality of a conventional ERP system. The object of study is ERP-as-a-service and not merely Software-as-a-service since ERP is a type of software with specific characteristics, see section "Enterprise Resource Planning", above.
- User organizations of different size since smaller organizations are thought to adopt ERP-as-a-service more easily than large organizations [34].
- User organizations from different industries since ERP adoption vary between industries [43].
- Supplier organizations with different backgrounds: suppliers new to the ERP market (native); established ERP suppliers (migrant) and established consulting firms which offer ERP-as-a-service complementary to consulting services (also migrant).

Data has been collected using an open form without confronting participants with implications found in literature. The participants have been directed to focus on the business models of the case companies before and after using ERP-as-a-service and the implications of these changes. Hereby it is believed that participants have been less biased when reporting implications than if they would have had to respond to a number of statements about implications. The form was tested on two pilot organizations and discussed with a reference group of ERP-as-a-service suppliers, consultants and organizations using ERP-as-a-service. The cases were selected in cooperation with the members of the reference group and are either implemented business models or business model designs for service oriented ERP. The field studies were documented during 2009-2011. Field study write ups were provided by key personnel with support from the authors of this paper. Key personnel included managers at ERP suppliers, project managers at consultants and managers from using organizations. The authors provided support in the form of written guidelines for the use of the form, individual and group meetings to discuss cases and in some situations also documentation support.

Table 1. Field study organizations

Field Study	User	Size of Customer Organization	Supplier	Case Provider
A	Real estate management firm	Small	Hogia	Hogia
B	Travel agency	Small to medium	Scandisys	Microsoft
C	Manufacturing company	Medium	Systeam	Systeam
D	Service company	Medium	Agresso	Agresso
E	Local business unit	Large	Stena Metall IT	Stena Metall AB
F	Manufacturing company	Small	24SevenOffice	24SevenOffice
G	Accounting firm	Small	Acando	Acando
H	Media company	Medium	Netsuite	Alterview
I	N/A	Medium to large	Lawson	Lawson

A structured literature review was performed in parallel with the field study. The search process was a digitally aided search for journal articles, conference proceedings and white papers since 2000. The main concepts used in the search process were enterprise resource planning, service orientation and implication. The aim of the search process was to identify work that discusses the implications of service orientation on enterprise resource planning. Several keywords for the three concepts were included in the search:

- Enterprise resource planning, ERP
- Service Orientation, ERP-as-a-service, Software as a service, SaaS, Cloud computing, Application Service Provider
- Implication, benefit, advantage, opportunity, risk, challenge, disadvantage, uncertainty

The initial search resulted in approximately 800 identified articles. These articles were reviewed by the authors and articles that discussed implications for users or suppliers were included in the literature review. A total of 32 articles were selected.

Statements regarding implications were collected from the field study write-ups. To relate the results to previous research, statements were interpreted, and mapped onto implications found in literature. Some implications found in the field studies map well onto implications found in literature while other implications are only found in the field studies, see appendix.

5   Framework of ERP-as-a-Service Implications

In this section, a framework of implications is presented from the perspective of the user and the perspective of the supplier. The framework is created from the results of the literature study and the results of the field study. The implications are divided into opportunities and challenges. New implications not found in literature are marked with an asterisk (*) and further described below, see section "New Implications". The implications with references to literature and field studies are found in appendix.

5.1   User Perspective

The user opportunities with ERP-as-a-service are primarily related to financial advantages infrastructural changes, see table 3. The financial opportunities come from reduced investment and implementation costs as well as productivity improvements and reductions in stock and personnel. Infrastructure opportunities lie in improved business processes and in sourcing software and IT infrastructure as services from third parties. In addition there are opportunities to improve customer responsiveness and to focus more on core processes.

The user challenges of ERP-as-a-service are primarily related to infrastructural and organizational changes, see table 2. The infrastructure challenges concern the implementation project and the dependency on third parties for service delivery. The organizational challenges relate to changes in organizational responsibility between users and suppliers where suppliers take over responsibility from users' IT departments.

Table 2. User implications

User Opportunities	User Challenges
UO1. Reduced up-front investments	UC1. An ERP project must be a business initiative
UO2. Decreased implementation costs and risks	UC2. Lack of senior management involvement
UO3. Predictable and lower costs	UC3. Lack of detailed systems implementation plan
UO4. Productivity improvements	
UO5. Stock reductions	UC4. Project escalation and lack of control
UO6. Personnel reductions	UC5. Lack of policies and laws
UO7. More focus on IT-value*	UC6. Lack of involvement of internal audit
UO8. Customer responsiveness	
UO9. Complete service offerings from several vendors	UC7. Poor use of consultants
	UC8. ERP-as-a-service requires local software*
UO10. Increased bargaining power	
UO11. Access to and flexibility to choose between state of the art technologies	UC9. Less customization and integration possibilities
UO12. Access to reliable, secure and scalable infrastructure	UC10. Large dependency on vendor
	UC11. Less availability, reliability and performance
UO13. Up-to-date software	
UO14. Remote access from anywhere at anytime	UC12. Increased security risks
	UC13. More rigid organizations*
UO15. Easier access to technical expertise	UC14. Structural changes
UO16. Easier version management	UC15. Redistribution of responsibility
UO17. Improved processes	UC16. Lack of alignment
UO18. Order cycle improvements	UC17. Lack of project team expertise
UO19. Improved financial close cycle	UC18. User resistance
UO20. Improved information and transparency	UC19. High demands on process orientation*
UO21. Increased integration of information	
UO22. Increased standardization	
UO23. More proactive purchasing behavior*	
UO24. Simplified phasing of implementation*	
UO25. Single Point of Contact*	
UO26. Increased focus on core competencies	
*) New implication not found in literature.	

5.2   Supplier Perspective

Supplier opportunities are related financial advantages, but also to the possibilities to expand the customer base and to build new skills, see table 3. The financial opportunities come from more predictable revenue flows at a potentially greater profit. From a customer perspective there are opportunities to expand the customer base and to offer more choices to customers. There are also opportunities to build economies of scale in distribution and operation as well as leverage domain knowledge and build application expertise.

Supplier challenges are related to finance but also to service development and organizational changes, see table 3. Financial challenges come from high initial investments and turnover reductions when migrating to services. From a service development perspective there are challenges related to serviticizing software products and to changes in contractual agreements. Infrastructure wise there are great challenges in developing multi-tenant effective applications and to manage networks of suppliers. From a learning and growth perspective, the challenge is to establish new sales processes and sales competence.

Table 3. Supplier implications

Supplier Opportunities	Supplier Challenges
SO1. More predictable revenue flows	SC1. High initial investments for starting a
SO2. Potentially greater profit	SaaS business
SO3. A need for standard applications in	SC2. Initial reduction in turnover
the market	SC3. Anticipate customer requirements
SO4. Expansion of potential customer	SC4. Serviticize software products
base	SC5. Offer customizable services
SO5. Improved supplier brand*	SC6. Contractual Changes*
SO6. Increased ability to offer more	SC7. Increased demands on fast updates
choices to customers	SC8. Manage service transitions
SO7. Shorter sales cycle	SC9. Increased responsibility for customer
SO8. More focus on IT-value*	operations
SO9. Improved transparency in pricing*	SC10. Difficult to manage complex
SO10. Strong lock-in effect of customers*	networks of SaaS suppliers
SO11. Lowered risk of pirated software	SC11. Address end-user prosumption in
SO12. Economy of scale in development	service architecture
SO13. Improved economy of scale in	SC12. Manage development effectively
distribution and operation	SC13. Develop for flexibility
SO14. Increased flexibility	SC14. Manage complexity of enterprise
SO15. Decreased risk	applications
SO16. Leverage domain area knowledge	SC15. Manage service operation and
SO17. Knowledge aggregation	maintenance effectively
SO18. Improved possibilities to build	SC16. Manage security effectively
application expertise	SC17. High requirements on service
SO19. Increased technological capabilities	availability, performance and
	scalability
	SC18. Balance over- and under capacity
	SC19. Support several versions of software
	SC20. New sales processes
*) New implication not found in literature.	

5.3   New Implications

The field studies revealed some new implications not found in literature, see table 4. New implications are identified for both users and suppliers.

Table 4. Summary of new implications

User	Supplier
Opportunities	*Opportunities*
UO7. More focus on IT-value	SO5. Improved supplier brand
UO23. More proactive purchasing behavior	SO8. More focus on IT-value
UO24. Simplified phasing of implementation	SO9. Improved transparency in pricing
UO25. Single point of contact	SO10. Strong lock-in effect of customers
Challenges	*Challenges*
UC8. ERP-as-a-service requires local software	SC6. Contractual Changes
	SC8. Manage service transitions
UC13. More rigid organizations	SC9. Increased responsibility for customer operations
UC19. High demands on process orientation	
	SC20. New sales processes

5.4   More Focus on IT-Value (UO7 and SO8)

ERP-as-a-service improves users' focus on IT-value since it becomes easier to define costs related to specific service functions or service modules. Customers can get a better picture of the total cost for the value created by the service. There are no hidden costs. Customers understand better what drives costs and can more easily identify where to make improvements.

SaaS refines the roles and you get a clear model of cooperation. It becomes easier to justify integrated value creation involving both users and suppliers. The relationship between business needs and delivery of service becomes clearer and there is a shift from charging consulting hours to improving organizational performance. (Case C – Systeam)

5.5   More Proactive Purchasing Behavior (UO23)

ERP-as-a-service can affect the working relationship between users and consultants. One of the suppliers notes that their customers become more proactive in how they purchase consulting services, from a needs-based purchasing behavior to a standing order with a fixed amount of hours per week.

There is a shift in how customers buy consulting hours, from reactive purchasing behavior to proactive. An example is when customers purchase a certain number of hours per week instead of purchasing hours when there is a problem. (Case C – Systeam)

5.6   Simplified Phasing of Implementation (UO24)

Historically, most companies have preferred Big-Bang strategies when implementing ERP [44] in order to shorten implementation time and cost for consultants. Service based enterprise systems make it easier for users to phase implementations.

It is easy for the customer to add new functionality, for example start with finance and then continue with supply chain management. (Case G – Acando)

5.7   Single Point of Contact (UO25)

With ERP-as-a-service it becomes clearer for users how to get support. Support organizations for conventional ERP tend to have several lines of support and different contact persons for different types of problems.

[Customers have] one support organization to turn to whether the problem is related to systems usage, program error or operational issues. (Case D – Agresso)

5.8   ERP-as-a-Service Requires Local Software (UC8)

In order to be able to use enterprise software services organizations may have to install additional software locally. This is software, such as integration engines or software for user administration, which is required by the service to function properly. Additional software may come as a surprise to the using organization and be considered a hidden cost if the user is not informed in advance.

User administration and single sign-on need a new technical solution when buying ERP-as-a-service. (Case D – Agresso)

5.9   More Rigid Organizations (UC13)

There is a risk that organizations that orient their IT towards services, such as ERP-as-a-service, become more rigid since they attract a different type of employees. Service oriented organizations tend to be more structured and less agile.

We see a risk that individuals and organizations change to become more structured and less agile. This is both positive and negative. Other types of individuals are attracted ... (Case C – Systeam)

5.10   High Demands on Process Orientation (UC19)

Suppliers experience a difficulty in selling service oriented ERP to customers that are not process oriented, for example organizations that apply an application centric maintenance model find it hard to adopt a service oriented delivery model.

The [user] organizations are not process oriented; it is difficult to be service oriented if you are not process oriented. This is a challenge for the customer. (Case C – Systeam)

5.11   Improved Supplier Brand (SO5)

Suppliers brand image can be improved since they take full responsibility for the delivery of the enterprise system. Suppliers invest more in technical expertise and will no longer be affected by poorly installed and operated software at their customers' sites. Often, suppliers can be blamed for delivering a poor system when customers lack the technical proficiency to install and operate the software well.

Hogia can take responsibility for the entire deployment; there will be no problems related to that customers' technology do not function properly. Today it is complex to operate [ERP] solutions which many times have a negative effect on Hogia's [conventional ERP] solution. (Case A – Hogia)

5.12   Improved Transparency in Pricing (SO9)

ERP-as-a-service can improve transparency in pricing since costs for infrastructure, operation and maintenance are included in the service price. There are no or minor additional costs for using the service. From a user perspective it becomes clearer what the total price for ERP is and how much extra costs additional services, such as separate modules, incur.

Business units understand better and accept easier the basis for charging costs. Before, costs were often questioned when business units did not understand what caused them. This led to that some business units required to buy IT-services from third parties, which decreased the possibilities to coordinate and share IT resources among business units. (Case E – Stena Metall)

5.13   Strong Lock-in Effect of Customers (SO10)

A great advantage of service orientation is the possibility of changing from one service supplier to another. However, this may not be the case for ERP-as-a-service since ERP is a complex type of application. ERP suppliers still believe that customers will stay long once they have started to use an ERP service due to the complexity of changing from one ERP service to another ERP service.

Customers stay around 7-10 years due to satisfaction with services and complexity in changing services. This means that we dare to offer services without long terms. (Case C – Systeam)

5.14   Contractual Changes (SC6)

Suppliers that migrate from conventional ERP to ERP-as-a-service there is a need to re-define service delivery which affects how contracts are written.

We have to re-define fulfillment of delivery, when have you done what you promised in the sales process? (Case C- Systeam)

5.15   Manage Service Transitions (SC8)

In conventional ERP, ERP systems are often operated side by side with legacy systems during long transition periods. Suppliers of ERP-as-a-service anticipate the same situation when customers decide to change from one ERP service supplier to another. There are few models and little experience available for this type of transition. Today, some suppliers of ERP-as-a-service offer migration functions to make it easier for customers to migrate data to new services.

... there is a lot of export possibilities to export data so if you like to stop the subscription, you can do it yourself by pressing a button. (Case H – Alterview)

5.16   Increased Responsibility for Customer Operations (SC9)

Service orientation makes ERP more of a utility which requires that suppliers take greater responsibility for their customers' businesses. Suppliers cannot just switch off utility services even if customers neglect to pay for them, it would hurt customers' operations too much.

Although there is a three months mutual termination of contract, we cannot [just] terminate the contract. If we terminate the contract it will cause too much harm to our customers' businesses. (Case C – Systeam)

5.17   New Sales Processes (SC20)

Suppliers migrating from offering conventional ERP to offering ERP-as-a-service need to establish new sales processes. Sales cycles become shorter and sales remuneration change from being based on license sales to being based on usage, subscription and time period. Sales personnel can also bypass conventional purchasing routines and start to sell to end-users.

[ERP-as-a-service] represents a great shift for a company where the entire remuneration system is based on license sales per sales person. Today you don't get a raise based on customer value created. The whole [remuneration] system must be re-designed in order to enable ... sales bonus based on service agreements, for example by calculating the net present value of the sales price over a five year period. (Case C – Systeam)

6   Discussion

In the discussion we highlight some aspects of the framework for implications of ERP-as-a-service. We will elaborate on some of the more interesting new implications and discuss some contradictions found in the framework. We will also discuss the relevance of implications for companies migrating from conventional ERP to ERP-as-a-service. In addition, the service orientation of the ERP market will be discussed followed by a methodological discussion.

6.1   More Focus on IT Value

An interesting finding among the new implications is the increased focus on IT value, both from the user perspective (UO7) and from the supplier perspective (SO8). ERP-as-a-service makes it easier to link business opportunities enabled by ERP and the costs for these opportunities. Also, ERP-as-a-service makes it easier for companies to focus on their core competences and not spend time and resources on building in-house application competence required for conventional ERP. This should mean that the sales process for ERP-as-a-service will become different from the sales process for conventional ERP. As a consequence sales personnel needs to build a better understanding of how ERP services contribute to improved IT value in different industry domains. Hence, sales roles become more consultative.

6.2   Simplified Phasing of Implementation

Simplified phasing of implementation (UO24) refers to the complex and long implementation processes of ERP spanning several years (Sumner 2005). Service orientation seems to simplify this for two reasons. First it becomes easier to add new functionality which means that the using organization can start with a core of functionality and then easily add new functionality over time. The second reason is that the roll-out of the solution to different business units becomes simpler when you do not need to install and maintain the system locally.

6.3   Lock-in of Customers

Another interesting result is the lock-in of customers. A great advantage of service orientation is the increased possibility to change service supplier. But this seems not to be the case for ERP-as-a-service. Suppliers of ERP-as-a-service believe that customers will stay long once they have started to use an ERP service due to the difficulty of changing from one ERP service to another ERP service. ERP is a complex type of information system and the process- and structural adjustments made by an organization to effectively adopt and use ERP appear to still make it difficult for a company to quickly change from one ERP service to another. This hampers the user opportunities related to increased bargaining power and increased flexibility (UO10, UO11).

6.4   Improved Supplier Brand

ERP-as-a-service appear to be a viable strategy for suppliers who suffer from poor on-premise installations. Their brand image (SO5) can be improved since they can take full responsibility for the delivery of the enterprise system. Hereby they will no longer be blamed for delivering a poor system when customers lack the technical proficiency to install and operate the software well on their own premises. ERP-as-a-service extends suppliers' control over their products when they are made available to the customer's own value creating activities, the so called *representative* knowledge process [45].

6.5   More Rigid Organizations

A surprising result is that service orientation may lead to using organizations become more rigid (UC13). The argumentation is that organizations that source IT as services tend to attract different types of employees with a more administrative profile than organizations that invest more in in-house development. This finding challenges what we have learned so far about how service oriented software enables organizational flexibility (UO11).

6.6   More or Less Secure Solutions

One of the more interesting discussion illustrated by the framework is the question of whether ERP-as-a-service is a more secure IT solution than on-premise installations of ERP systems or a less secure solution. ERP-as-a-service can offer access to a reliable, secure and scalable infrastructure (UO12) due to the specialized IT-skills developed by the provider. But ERP-as-a-service could also increase the risk of lowered reliability and performance since vendors deliver services over the Internet and share application and server capacity (UC11). Moreover, ERP-as-a-service increases the security risk of losing data to third party since vendors share application and server capacity (UC12).

For a small or medium sized company the supplier of an ERP service may provide a better infrastructure than the company itself may be able to do while a large company may have both higher security requirements and internal capabilities to operate a more secure and reliable infrastructure. Several suppliers included in the field study claim that they are able to offer a better infrastructure to than their customers are able to establish on their own. The suppliers have also found that the question about security is moving from being a drawback to becoming a strength when selling ERP-as-a-service. Although one can claim that Internet delivery increases vulnerability of company data, one can also claim that most companies, even though they are operating their own infrastructure, open up their infrastructure to the Internet.

6.7   Previous Use of ERP

The framework of implications is based on literature on both SaaS implications and ERP implications, as discussed above in the Methodology section. As a consequence, the framework includes opportunities and challenges for companies new to ERP as well as companies new to service oriented ERP. For example, ERP enables companies to increase customer responsiveness through the use of ERP (UO8). This opportunity should be equally relevant to companies that begin to use ERP through a service and to companies that use conventional ERP. However, companies that migrate from conventional ERP to ERP-as-a-service, this opportunity is no longer relevant. They have already benefitted from this implication when they started to use ERP, although they were using conventional ERP at the time.

Therefore, an important variable hidden in the framework is companies' *previous use of ERP*. Users could be new to ERP when they start to use ERP-as-a-service or they could be migrants from conventional ERP. For users new to ERP most of the implications in the framework are relevant while for users migrating from conventional ERP to ERP-as-a-service only parts of the framework are relevant. The same goes for suppliers, that could be new entrants to the ERP market by offering ERP-as-a-service or they could be established on the ERP market through conventional ERP packages which they replace or complement by ERP-as-a-service. For example, the implication initial reduction of turnover (SC2) is only relevant to migrant suppliers.

6.8   Service Orientation of the ERP Market

ERP-as-a-service is a case of transformation of the software industry. ERP is a significant portion of the software industry and represent complex applications which are of vital importance to most organizations today. ERP-as-a-service shows how a new business model, enabled by technological development, opens up for new entrants to the ERP market and creates opportunities for established suppliers to gain competitive advantage by offering new services according to new business logic.

Since ERP is complex and has a great impact on the using organization it puts a lot of pressure on suppliers. The framework shows that suppliers need to invest in developing multi-tenant effective solutions that offers the same or better configuration and integration features as conventional ERP systems. This is a major investment for suppliers when migrating conventional ERP systems to ERP-as-a-service. For example, Lawson migrates the M3 system to a service where they still have to maintain multiple instances of the solution and possibly several versions in parallel. Netsuite, who doesn't carry the ballast of an old ERP system, started out in the late 90's with a small standardized service which has grown into an ERP service that challenges both SAP and Oracle in many user organizations.

ERP-as-a-service may be an indication of that the ERP industry is taking a first step from a fluid phase to a transitional phase where the focus is on process innovation rather than product innovation [1, 46]. Suppliers of ERP-as-a-service challenge user organizations' internal processes for installing and operating ERP systems by offering more robust and secure processes as services. Also, this extends suppliers' control over their products at customers' sites. However, there are great restraining forces to the migration of conventional ERP to ERP-as-a-service in terms of the large installed base of conventional ERP systems that still needs to be maintained and the huge investments made by consultants in building ERP implementation competence. In addition, conventional sales processes and remuneration practices of sales staff also restrain both users and suppliers to adopt a service oriented business model for ERP.

6.9   Methodological Discussion

Quality in qualitative research, such as field studies, depends on how data is collected and how the analysis of collected data is conducted. To judge the quality of research presented in this paper, the following criteria [47] are discussed: credibility, dependability, transferability and confirmability. Credibility refers to that the results of the inquiry is believable and understandable from the eyes of the particpants. Dependability means that the reseracher shows that the process of research is logical and clearly documented. Transferability to which degree results can be generalized and transferred to other contexts. Confirmability relates to how well the results can be confirmed by others.

6.10   Credibility

The framework of implications is developed using a combination of literature review and cross-sectional field study. The implications derived from literature are based on different types of investigations. A few of them have been tested using statistical methods while others have been observed in case studies and some have only been argued for. Therefore the empirical grounding of implications derived from literature is only partially trustworthy. Hence, the field study provides additional support for some of these implications.

In order to ensure credibility of the framework, separate meetings have been held with representatives from the organizations included in the field study to judge the credibility of the results. Since the statements collected from the participants in the field studies were translated into English and then mapped onto implications derived from literature it was important to verify the credibility of the implications. Some clarifications were made as well as a few changes to implications and descriptions.

6.11   Transferability

The field study includes organizations which use or supply ERP-as-a-service. The organizations cover both public and private organizations including native and migrant suppliers. Therefore, there is no reason to believe that the framework could not be applicable to other users or suppliers of ERP-as-a-service. However, there are some concerns regarding the localization and size of these organizations that may restrict the transferability of the framework. First, although some of the participants are global organizations and the services are distributed over the Internet, they are all active on the Scandinavian market. Hence, the transferability could be limited to Scandinavian market conditions. Second, although there are small, medium and large organizations represented in the field study, there is by international standards a focus on medium sized organizations. There are no multinational companies among the users. Therefore the contribution by the field study is somewhat limited to Scandinavian market conditions and small to medium sized organizations.

6.12   Dependability

Data has been collected since the start of the research project in 2008. At that point in time, ERP-as-a-service was a fairly unknown phenomenon. Since then, the concept of Software-as-a-service has become more established and we have seen the advent of Cloud Computing. The knowledge about these concepts and their implications have grown in general and among field study participants due to the learning taking place as an effect of the investigation. In parallel, the technology has been developed to become more secure, stable and multi-tenant effective. This means that today some implications are less relevant and new implications appear. For example, today security is less of an issue than three years ago. Therefore we can hardly expect to get the same results from a similar study if we were to conduct one.

6.13   Confirmability

The method is described above, see section Methodology, and the authors are willing to share readers with documents showing how statements have been translated and mapped onto implications found in literature.

7   Conclusion

In this paper we have presented a general business model for ERP-as-a-service and a framework for its implications. The framework is based on a combination of literature study and field study. ERP-as-a-service is primarily viewed as a process innovation and indicates that the ERP industry is leaving the fluid phase and slowly moves into the transitional phase. The framework can be used to further investigate types of service oriented business models for ERP.

Users can benefit from the framework in their IT and business planning short-term and long-term. For example users can adopt new sourcing strategies for ERP and plan the transition from conventional ERP to ERP-as-a-service. The framework supports the development of investment analysis by providing potential benefits, costs and risks for moving from conventional ERP to ERP-as-a-service. It can also be used to formulate strategic objectives, operational targets and key performance indicators to measure the fulfillment of these objectives and targets.

The framework can be use by ERP suppliers to plan for new business relationships with current customers and also identify potential new customers. The framework also supports suppliers in identifying important challenges with service orientation in general and specifically ERP-as-a-service.

Future research is suggested to include prioritization of implications for certain industries and types of organizations.

References

1. Sääksjärvi, M., Lassila, A., Nordström, H.: Evaluating the software as a service business model: From CPU time-sharing to online innovation sharing. In: Isaisas, P., Kommers, P., Mc-Pherson, M. (eds.) IADIS International Conference e-Society 2005, Qawra, Malta, June 27-30, pp. 177–186 (2005)
2. Dubey, A., Wagle, D.: Delivering Software as Services. The McKinsey Quarterly, Web Exclusive, 1–12 (May 2007)
3. Davenport, T.H.: Putting the enterprise into the enterprise system. Harvard Business Review, 121–131 (July-August 1998)
4. Scott, J.E.: The FoxMeyer Drugs' bankruptcy: was it a failure of ERP? In: 5th Americas Conference on Information Systems, Milwaukee, WI, August 13-15 (1999)
5. Jacobson, S., Shepherd, J., D'Aquilla, M., Carter, K.: The ERP Market Sizing Report 2007-2012. AMR Research (2008)
6. Thornton, J.: Lawson Announces Full-Function ERP on Amazon Web Services Infrastructure, Lawson (March 2010), http://www.lawson.com/about-lawson/news-room/news-releases/english/2010/lawson-announces-full-function-erp-on-amazon-web-services-infrastructure (last accessed April 15, 2011)
7. Chong, F., Carraro, G.: Architecture Strategies for Catching the Long Tail. Microsoft Corporation (April 2006), http://msdn.microsoft.com/en-us/library/aa479069.aspx (last accessed June 6, 2011)
8. Choudhary, V.: Comparison of software quality under perpetual licensing and software as a service. Journal of Management Information Systems 24(2), 141–165 (2007)
9. Fan, M., Kumar, S., Whinston, A.B.: Short-term and long-term competition between providers of shrink-wrap software and software as a service. European Journal of Operational Research 196(2), 661–671 (2009)
10. Fuller, S., McLaren, T.: Analyzing Enterprise Systems Delivery Modes for Small and Medium Enterprises. In: AMCIS 2010 Proceedings. Paper 380 (2010)
11. Vargo, S.L., Lusch, R.F.: Service–dominant logic: continuing the evolution. Journal of the Academy of Marketing Science 36(1), 1–10 (2008)
12. Cusumano, M.A.: The changing software business: Moving from products to services. Computer 41(1), 20–27 (2008)
13. Vassiliadis, B., Stefani, A., Tsaknakis, J., Tsakalidis, A.: From application service provision to service-oriented computing: a study of the IT outsourcing evolution. Telematics & Informatics 23(4), 271–293 (2006)
14. Nilsson, A.G.: Using Standard Application Packages in Organisations - Critical Success Factors. In: Nilsson, A.G., Pettersson, J.S. (eds.) On Methods for Systems Development in Professional Organisations, Studentlitteratur, Lund, pp. 208–230 (2001)
15. Al-Mashari, M.: Enterprise Resource Planning Systems: A Research Agenda. Industrial Management and Data Systems 102(3), 165–170 (2002)
16. Kumar, K., van Hillegersberg, J.: ERP experiences and evolution. Communications of the ACM 43(4), 23–26 (2000)
17. Möller, C.: ERP II: a conceptual framework for next-generation enterprise systems? Journal of Enterprise Information Management 18(4), 483–497 (2005)
18. Sawyer, S.: Packaged software: Implications of the differences from custom approaches to software development. European Journal of Information Systems 9, 47–58 (2000)

19. Carmel, E., Becker, S.: A process model for packaged software development. IEEE Transactions on Engineering Management 41(5), 50–61 (1995)
20. Hedman, J., Lind, M.: Is There Only One Systems Development Life Cycle? In: Barry, C., et al. (eds.) Information Systems Development: Challenges in Practice, Theory, and Education, vol. 1, pp. 105–116. Springer, Heidelberg (2009)
21. Grabski, S.V., Leech, S.A.: Complementary controls and ERP implementation success. International Journal of Accounting Information Systems 8(1), 17–39 (2007)
22. Brockmann, C., Gronau, N.: Business Models of ERP System Providers. In: AMCIS 2009 Proceedings. Paper 582 (2009)
23. Johansson, B., Newman, M.: Competitive advantage in the ERP system's value-chain and its influence on future development. Enterprise Information Systems 4(1), 79–93 (2010)
24. Brandt, P., Carlsson, R., Nilsson, A.G.: Välja och Förvalta Standardsystem, Studentlitteratur, Lund (1998)
25. Sumner, M.: Enterprise Resource Planning. Prentice Hall, Upper Saddle River (2004)
26. Parr, A., Shanks, G.: A Model of ERP Project Implementation. Journal of Information Technology 15(4), 289–304 (2000)
27. Papazoglou, M.P.: Service-oriented computing: Concepts, characteristics and directions. In: Fourth International Conference on Web Information Systems Engineering, Rome, Italy (2003)
28. Sun, W., Zhang, K., Chen, S., Zhang, X., Liang, H.: Software as a Service: An integration perspective. In: Krämer, B., Lin, K., Narasimhan, P. (eds.) Service-Oriented Computing – ICSIC 2007, Vienna, Austria, September 17-20, pp. 558–569. Springer, Heidelberg (2007)
29. Hoch, F., Kerr M., Griffith A.: Software as a Service: Strategic Backgrounder. Software and Information Industry Association (2001), http://www.siia.net/estore/pubs/SSB-01.pdf (last accessed April 15, 2011)
30. Mäkilä, T., Järvi, A., Rönkkö, M., Nissilä, J.: How to Define Software-as-a-Service – An Empirical Study of Finnish Saas Providers. In: Tyrväinen, P., Jansen, S., Cusumano, M.A. (eds.) ICSOB 2010. LNBIP, vol. 51, pp. 115–124. Springer, Heidelberg (2010)
31. Turner, M., Budgen, D., Brereton, P.: Turning software into a service. Computer 36(10), 38–44 (2003)
32. Lassila, A.: Taking a service-oriented perspective on software business: How to move from product business to online service business. IADIS International Journal on WWW/Internet 4(1), 70–82 (2006)
33. Xin, M., Levina, N.: Software-as-a-Service model: Elaborating client-side adoption factors. In: Boland, R., Limayem, M., Pentland, B. (eds.) Proceedings of the 29th International Conference on Information Systems, Paris, France, December 14-17 (2008)
34. Wailgum, T.: Impact of SaaS on the enterprise ERP Market. Infoworld (August 2008), http://www.infoworld.com/t/applications/impact-saas-enterprise-erp-market-090 (last accessed April 15, 2011)
35. Benlian, A., Hess, T., Buxmann, P.: Drivers of SaaS-Adoption – An Empirical Study of Different Application Types. Business & Information Systems Engineering 1(5), 357–369 (2009)
36. Kaplan, J.: Software-as-a-Service Myths. BusinessWeek Online (April 17, 2006)
37. Bezemer, C.P., Zaidman, A.: Multi-tenant SaaS Applications: Maintenance Dream or Nightmare? In: Proceedings of the 4th International Joint ERCIM/IWPSE Symposium on Software Evolution (IWPSE-EVOL). ACM (2010)

38. Kwok, T., Mohindra, A.: Resource Calculations with Constraints, and Placement of Tenants and Instances for Multi-tenant SaaS Applications. In: Bouguettaya, A., Krueger, I., Margaria, T. (eds.) ICSOC 2008. LNCS, vol. 5364, pp. 633–648. Springer, Heidelberg (2008)

39. Demirkan, H., Cheng, H.K., Bandyopadhyay, S.: Coordination Strategies in anSaaS Supply Chain. Journal of Management Information Systems 26(4), 119–143 (2010)

40. Stuckenberg, S., Heinzl, A.: The Impact of the Software-as-a-Service Concept on the Underlying Software and Service Development Processes. In: PACIS 2010 Proceedings. Paper 125 (2010)

41. Lillis, A.M., Mundy, J.: Cross-sectional field studies in management accounting research—closing the gaps between surveys and case studies. Journal of Management Accounting Research 17, 119–141 (2005)

42. Eisenhardt, K.M.: Building theories from case study research. Academy of Management Review 14(4), 532–550 (1989)

43. Juell-Skielse, G.: Adoption of Extended ERP Among Small and Medium Sized Companies in Kista Science City. In: Proceedings of the 3rd International Conference on Enterprise Systems and Accounting (ICESAcc 2006), Santorini Island, Greece, June 26-27 (2006)

44. Olhager, J., Selldin, E.: Enterprise resource planning survey of Swedish manufacturing firms. European Journal of Operational Research 146, 365–373 (2003)

45. Wikström, S., Norman, R.: Knowledge and value: a new perspective on corporate transformation. Routledge, London (1994)

46. Utterback, J.: Mastering the dynamics of innovation. Harvard Business School Press, Cambridge (1994)

47. Guba, E.G., Lincoln, Y.S.: Effective Evaluation: Improving the Usefulness of Evaluation Results Through Responsive and Naturalistic Approaches. Jossy-Bass, San Francisco (1981)

48. Bennett, K., Layzell, P.J., Budgen, D., Brereton, P., Macaulay, L., Munro, M.: Service-based software: The future for flexible software. In: Proceedings of the Asia-Pacific Software Engineering Conference, Singapore, December 5-8, pp. 214–222. IEEE CS Press (2000)

49. Dörner, C., Draxler, S., Pipek, V., Wulf, V.: End Users at the Bazaar: Designing Next-Generation Enterprise Resource Planning Systems. IEEE Software 26(5), 45–51 (2009)

50. Demirkan, H., Chen, H.K.: The risk and information sharing of application services supply chain. European Journal of Operational Research 187(3), 765–784 (2008)

51. Hofmann, P.: ERP is dead, Long live ERP. Internet Computing. IEEE Publication 12(4), 84–88 (2008)

52. Jacobs, D.: Enterprise Software as Service. Queue, 36–42 (July/August 2005)

53. Rettig, C.: The Trouble with Enterprise Software. MIT Sloan Management Review 49(1), 21–27 (2007)

54. Rochwerger, B., Breitgand, D., Levy, E., Galis, A., Nagin, K.: The reservoir model and architecture for open federated cloud computing. IBM Systems Journal (October 2008)

55. Saeed, M., Jaffar-Ur-Rehman, M.: Enhancement of software engineering by shifting from software product to software service. In: Khan, W., Ahmed, F. (eds.) First International Conference on Information and Communication Technologies (ICICT 2005), Karachi, Pakistan, August 27-28, pp. 302–308 (2005)

56. Sharif, A.M.: It's written in the cloud: the hype and promise of cloud computing. Journal of Enterprise Information Management 23(2), 131–134 (2010)

57. Susarla, A., Barua, A., Whinston, A.: A transaction cost perspective of the "software as a service" business model. Journal of Management Information Systems 26(2), 205–240 (2009)
58. Torbacki, W.: SaaS-direction of technology development in ERP/MRP systems. International Scientific Journal 32(1), 57–60 (2008)
59. Armbrust, M., Fox, A., Griffith, R., Joseph, A.D., Katz, R., Konwinski, A., Lee, G., Patterson, D., Rabkin, A., Stoica, I., Zaharia, M.: A view of cloud computing. Communications of the ACM 53(4), 50–58 (2010)

Appendix

User Opportunities			User Challenges		
Impl.	References	Cases	Impl.	References	Cases
UO01	[7, 8, 39, 32, 1, 58]	D, F	UC01	[21]	
UO02	[8, 9, 53, 57, 1, 58]	F, G, H, I	UC02	[21]	
UO03	[8, 52, 55, 58]	A, B, C, D, E, G	UC03	[21]	
UO04	[25]		UC04	[21]	
UO05	[25]		UC05	[13]	
UO06	[25]	A, C	UC06	[21]	
UO07		D	UC07	[21]	
UO08	[25]	A	UC08		H
UO09	[1]	D, I	UC09	[35, 10, 55, 1, 13]	D, G, H, I
UO10	[8, 55]		UC10	[1, 13]	C, I
UO11	[35, 1, 58]	C	UC11	[35, 1, 13]	H
UO12	[1]	C, D, F, G, H, I	UC12	[35, 1, 58, 13]	G, H, I
UO13	[8, 55, 58]		UC13		C
UO14	[8, 32, 1, 58]	C, H	UC14	[13]	C, I
UO15	[35, 32, 1]	B	UC15	[13]	C
UO16	[1, 58]	H	UC16	[21, 24]	C
UO17	[25]		UC17	[21]	
UO18	[25]		UC18	[21]	
UO19	[25]	A, D	UC19		C
UO20	[25]	A			
UO21	[25]	A			
UO22	[25]	G			
UO23		C			
UO24		G			
UO25		D			
UO26	[8, 35, 32, 1]	B, F, H, I			
Supplier Opportunities			Supplier Challenges		
Impl.	References	Cases	Impl.	References	Cases
SO01	[32, 1]	D, I	SC01	[1, 36, 32, 58, 9, 12]	
SO02	[12]	D	SC02	[1, 32]	I
SO03	[18, 19, 20]		SC03	[20]	

SO04	[32, 56, 1]	A, G	SC04	[12]	
SO05		A	SC05	[1, 7, 52, 32, 13, 9]	H
SO06	[12, 9, 55]	A, B, D, I	SC06		C
SO07	[1]	A, D	SC07	[1, 48, 32]	
SO08		A, C	SC08		C
SO09		E	SC09		C
SO10		A	SC10	[1, 39, 54, 40, 13, 32]	A
SO11	[55]		SC11	[49]	
SO12	[18, 19, 20, 1, 37, 52]	A	SC12	[40, 9]	
SO13	[35, 37, 8, 51, 52, 32, 54, 1]	B	SC13	[20]	
SO14	[48, 8, 54]		SC14	[53]	I
SO15	[19, 20, 18]		SC15	[13, 37]	
SO16	[32]		SC16	[52, 27, 37]	
SO17	[19, 20, 18]		SC17	[1, 7, 12, 32, 27, 37, 52]	C
SO18	[8]	I	SC18	[59, 50]	
SO19	[54]		SC19	[20]	
			SC20		A, C

ERP Software as Service (SaaS): Factors Affecting Adoption in South Africa

Motheo Lechesa[1], Lisa Seymour[1], and Joachim Schuler[2]

[1] Information Systems Department, University of Cape Town, Private Bag,
Rondebosch 7700, South Africa
[2] Pforzheim University, Tiefenbronnerstrasse 65,
75175 Pforzheim, Germany
Lisa.Seymour@uct.ac.za, Joachim.Schuler@hs-pforzheim.de

Abstract. Within the cloud computing hype, ERP SaaS is receiving more focus from ERP vendors such as ERP market leader SAP announcing SAP by Design, their new ERP SaaS solution. SaaS is a new approach to deliver software and has had proven success with CRM systems such as Salesforce.com. The appeal of SaaS is driven by amongst other things, lower Total Cost of Ownership and faster implementation periods. However, the rate at which ERP SaaS is being adopted is low in comparison to other SaaS applications such as CRM or Human Resource systems. Hence the need to establish the reasons for this low adoption. Consequently the purpose of this research was to determine barriers that affect the adoption of ERP SaaS in South Africa. Using interviews and qualitative data analysis, this study developed a model that explains the factors that affect the adoption of ERP SaaS. Network limitations, customisation, security and cost concerns were raised as dominant factors affecting the adoption of ERP SaaS. The research concludes by suggesting that over time the adoption of ERP SaaS should increase as the technology matures.

Keywords: ERP adoption, SaaS, South Africa, cloud computing.

1 Introduction

Enterprise Resource Planning (ERP) Systems have been adopted by many organisations as a way to improve efficiency and to achieve strategic goals set by management [1]. The major benefit associated with ERP systems is their ability to integrate organisational data and processes to achieve improved efficiency and productivity levels [2]. Despite their usefulness, ERP system implementations are associated with high implementation costs driven by the cost of hardware, software and consultancy as well as high maintenance costs [1],[2].

As organisations continue to seek ways to reduce costs and utilise available technology to achieve desired objectives, alternative ways of implementing ERP systems have had to be explored [3]. In particular, the Software as a Service (SaaS) model has emerged as a real alternative to implementing in-house ERP systems. ERP

C. Møller and S. Chaudhry (Eds.): CONFENIS 2011, LNBIP 105, pp. 152–167, 2012.
© IFIP International Federation for Information Processing 2012

SaaS has been implemented successfully in Europe, some parts of North America and in Asia Pacific Countries [4].

The major benefit of ERP SaaS is low implementation costs and a flexible pricing model that does not require a major capital outlay. However, in comparison to other SaaS applications, the rate at which ERP SaaS is being adopted is low [5]. The reason for slow adoption of ERP SaaS varies from issues around security and customisation to integration and other concerns [6].

The purpose of this paper is to determine factors that affect the adoption of ERP SaaS in South Africa. This paper should be useful to potential clients of ERP SaaS, to assess the factors that they should consider in deciding whether to adopt ERP SaaS or not. For Vendors, this paper shall provide an understanding of the factors that their clients consider in making decisions about whether to adopt ERP SaaS or not. This work also contributes to the research domain by providing issues central to ERP SaaS adoption.

2   Literature Review

2.1   Software as a Service

Software as a Service (SaaS) is explained as a business model that allows the vendor to manage software and deliver it as a service over the internet [7]. SaaS first came into the scene in the late 1990s when discussions about turning software into a service emerged and Salesforce.com launched CRM SaaS [8]. The SaaS architecture is multi-tenant based with SaaS application vendors owning and maintaining it [9],[7]. Contrary to the ASP model, SaaS provides a much better value creation through resource sharing, standardisation of processes and centralised data.

The National Institute of Standards and Technology (NIST) and Cloud Security Alliance (CSA) have described cloud computing as "a model for enabling convenient, on demand network access to a shared pool of configurable computing resources that can be rapidly provisioned and released with minimal management effort or service vendor interaction" [10]. The cloud model incorporates Software as a Service (SaaS), Platform as a Service (PaaS) and Infrastructure as a Service (IaaS) [10],[11].

As technology involved in cloud computing matures, SaaS continues to attract interest across a broad spectrum of stakeholders and is gaining momentum across a spectrum of applications. The vendor and the user alike benefit from the adoption of SaaS [12]. On the part of the vendor, SaaS reduces the maintenance and upgrading costs of the system [13]. In addition, SaaS vendors gain competitive edge over other software vendors since they provide faster upgrades and patches [13].

On the part of the Clients, a SaaS application allows a software implementation project to be started on a pay-as-you go basis, scaling on business needs. This saves in upfront costs because payments for software and hardware are paid over a period of time [14]. So, SaaS helps to focus on the core areas of the business without too much concern on information technology issues [8]. SaaS implementations are also shorter compared to installed applications [13].

2.2   ERP SaaS

ERP SaaS means, to deliver an ERP system "as a service", not as in the past, where ERP systems had been implemented "on premise" as products bought by clients. The most important disparities between ERP SaaS and installed in-house ERP applications are, that ERP SaaS is accessed through the internet, the application and data are under control of the service provider while installed applications are offered as a product and accessed and controlled from the customer's location. Moreover, the payment for the software services is provided through subscriptions that have to be paid e.g. per user on a monthly basis [14].

Although ERP SaaS has been implemented in Europe and in the United States of America (USA), the rate at which it is being adopted is lower in comparison to other software applications such as CRM and Human capital management (HCM) [15]. The reason for this slow adoption is the fact that most organisations are not yet ready to trust the SaaS model with business, critical or core applications.

An Aberdeen Group survey [16]carried out on over 1200 companies operating mainly in Europe found ERP SaaS deployments to be less prevalent compared to other SaaS deployments. Although ERP is lagging behind other applications in terms of SaaS based applications there seems to be a general consensus that ERP SaaS is gaining momentum [17]. To increase the adoption rate of ERP SaaS, issues impeding its adoption need be addressed.

2.3   Barriers to Adoption of ERP SaaS

In general the issues that negatively impact on the adoption of ERP SaaS model are similar to concerns raised for adopting cloud computing. These issues include security and privacy, support, interoperability and compliance as well as loss of control over data and other computing resources [18].

Customisation. Although SaaS is implemented in a quicker and easier manner than "on-premise", in most cases, it does so at the expense of configuration and customisation, thereby losing flexibility [19],[7]. A balance needs to be maintained when it comes to customisation and configuration of SaaS products for both the vendor and the client. Flexibility is necessary as an ERP SaaS system or any system for that matter may require some kind of configuration or customisation in order to address or cater for the unique aspects of the adopting organisation [4]. Hence, the SaaS architecture should support configurability because it is a crucial requirement for clients in order to differentiate their business from competition [20]. Otherwise, the SaaS model may experience a low adoption rate [20]. Hence there is a challenge for vendors to offer ERP SaaS solutions capable of delivering customisable source code for more complex ERP systems [4].

Security and Privacy. Security is always an issue when it comes to any software implementation [10]. Concerns over security have been raised as a concern with the SaaS model with many potential clients reticent to trust third parties with their data, especially sensitive corporate data [21]. Yet, [21] argue that there is no reason why services over the cloud can't be as secure as those provided by in-house IT.

Cost. The issue of ERP SaaS cost is twofold, being the once off implementation cost and the annual subscription [22]. The implementation cost of ERP SaaS may include initial consulting and configuration costs, while on-going subscriptions costs includes hardware, software and support personnel [22]. The most appealing SaaS feature is the lower total cost of ownership (TCO), with the majority of articles referring to SaaS benefits mentioning the lower TCO. Burrel [6] mentioned that "SaaS has been touted to major organisations as the new cure-all that solves the CIO's cost enigma at a stroke by significantly reducing implementation costs, outsourcing developments, slashing consultancy costs and devolving infrastructure maintenance and servicing".

Regulation. The legal framework in the form of legislation and standards within which organisations operate has become very stringent [23]. In this respect legal issues about data protection, confidentiality, copyright, audit and controls should be considered by both the potential user and vendors alike [24]. In particular the enterprise clients need to ensure that the technology they adopt satisfies the legal requirements in terms of the data it provides [18]. An example is legal requirements in many countries prohibiting SaaS vendors from keeping customer data and copyright material outside the national boundaries within which those clients reside, such as the USA Patriot Act [21].

Network Limitations. Linked with the network limitation is the availability of system concern. Often organisations would require a 100% availability of systems especially those such as ERP systems that are considered critical [18]. To ensure that the ERP system itself and the network provides 100% availability or very close to that, it is vitally important that service level agreements (SLA) are entered into between the vendors and the clients [18].

Application and Organisation Specific Issues. Drivers of SaaS vary depending on the characteristics of the application that is considered for SaaS outsourcing. Since ERP systems possess strategic significance for organisations and are not highly standardised, they rank among the applications with the lowest SaaS adoption rates [5]. Furthermore, there are some organisations for which, because of their nature, SaaS is not well suited [25]. For instance, organisations which base their survival on maintaining secret or confidential data are more likely not to adapt SaaS. Therefore the speed at which ERP SaaS is adopted may differ depending on the nature of the organisation or industry.

Integration. The integration of SaaS applications with other in-house application or other SaaS vendors is still a big challenge to the extent that the cost of integration can be 30-45% of the overall SaaS implementation [12]. Another aspect of the issue around integration relates to the fact there are no interoperability standards within the cloud computing arena which creates a possible lock-in scenario for the clients [26] where they are not able to use integrated SaaS applications provided and supported by distinctive vendors, as the two solutions would not be interoperable [4]. This emphasises the importance for vendors to design and develop SaaS integration by first reviewing business processes, integration design and implementation, data migration, testing, production and monitoring; and then figuring areas where integration may be a concern with the aim of addressing deficiencies[12],[19]. Integration as a service solutions are beginning to find ways of simplifying integration issue on a cloud-to-cloud platform while SaaS vendors are addressing in house integration issues by pre-building integration within the SaaS solution with the aim of reducing complexity and cost [12].

Summary of Barriers. The reviewed literature suggests that ERP SaaS is an attractive solution for organisations that have insufficient resources to consider on-premise ERP adoption. Yet there is limited research into SAAS ERP and adoption has been slow. A review of the literature identified that the major barriers to adoption of SaaS applications include concerns around security and privacy; regulatory compliance; limited customisation; network limitations; cost clarity; integration concerns; and application and organisation specific issues. However, due to a lack of empirical research it is not known whether these adoption concerns are valid for SaaS ERP. Also there seems to be a lack of frameworks or theory supporting these concerns. Hence, the need for more understanding and this research.

2.4   Research Framework

The purpose of this research was to study the factors that affect adoption. The Technology-Environment-Organisation (TOE) framework was considered as the most appropriate theoretical model for the purpose of this research. The framework is an institutional theory that has been widely used for the adoption of complex innovations such as e.g. e-businesses [27]. It focuses on three main characteristics associated with technology innovation namely technology, organisation and environment. The use of TOE is suitable for technology innovations that are associated with uncertainties regarding the current and future status of that technology innovation [28].

3   The Context: SaaS in South Africa

ERP adoption is arguably more of a challenge for organisations in developing countries such as South Africa, given the high cost of capital and the shortages of IT skills. Hence the SaaS model does appear to address many adoption barriers. While a number of articles has been written in South Africa about cloud computing and ERP SaaS, there is limited literature from credible sources about it. There are articles that are intermittently posted on web sites about cloud computing, in particular ITweb has a number of articles. A survey was carried out in 2009 by Fujutsi Technology

Solutions that revealed that organisations in South Africa are aware of cloud computing [29]. The survey revealed that in South Africa, the value of cloud computing is not clear, and where the value was clear it was by hampered by the required networking infrastructure [29].

4   Research Method

The research followed an interpretive philosophy [30] to gain a deep understanding of factors affecting ERP SaaS adoption in South Africa. Qualitative primary interview data was collected from individuals with the required knowledge and experience. Purposive sampling was used to select participants from five South African organisations. All participants had experience of a minimum of 10 years in the Information, Communication and Technology (ICT) industry. Ethical clearance for the research was obtained from the university, participants signed to indicate interview consent and their anonymity was assured. Table 1 summarises the participant's details, their experience, type of industry and other relevant information.

Table 1. Research Participants

Interviewee Position	ICT Experience in IT-Years	Industry Sector	Size in terms of # employees	Code-Participants
IT Director	10	Health-Clinical Research	750	Participant A
CIO	15	Mining	50,000	Participant B
CIO	20	Energy-Petroleum	3,500	Participant C
Business Development Manager (Retail)	26	Retail	49,000	Participant D
Deputy Director, IT	25	Education-University	900	Participant E

Semi-structured interviews with open-ended questions were chosen to probe for answers because of their flexibility and ability to obtain rich data from interviews [31]. Face to face interviews were carried out and tape-recorded. In some instances, follow up questions through telephone were carried out to seek clarity.

The Thomas general inductive approach [32] of thematic data analysis employed allows "research findings to emerge from the frequent, dominant or significant themes inherent in raw data, without the restraint imposed by structured methodologies" [32]. To increase dependability of analysis [33] audit trails for three iterations of coding were kept and transcribed notes were sent back to respondents for verification.

5   Findings and Implications

Based on the findings of the research, a theoretical model (based on the TOE framework) was developed to explain the relationships between established categories and concepts (Figure 1). The underlying construct of the model is that all three factors affects one another, where the decision to adopt technology innovation is concerned. Hence, the outer link has been made to indicate that any of the technology, organisation and environment factors may affect one another.

For each of the three pillars of the model, three key themes emerged from the data analysis, namely, Business Benefits, Organisation Readiness and System Trust. These three main issues within the TOE aspects influence the decision whether to adopt ERP SaaS or not and are now discussed, supported by quotes from the participants and literature evidence.

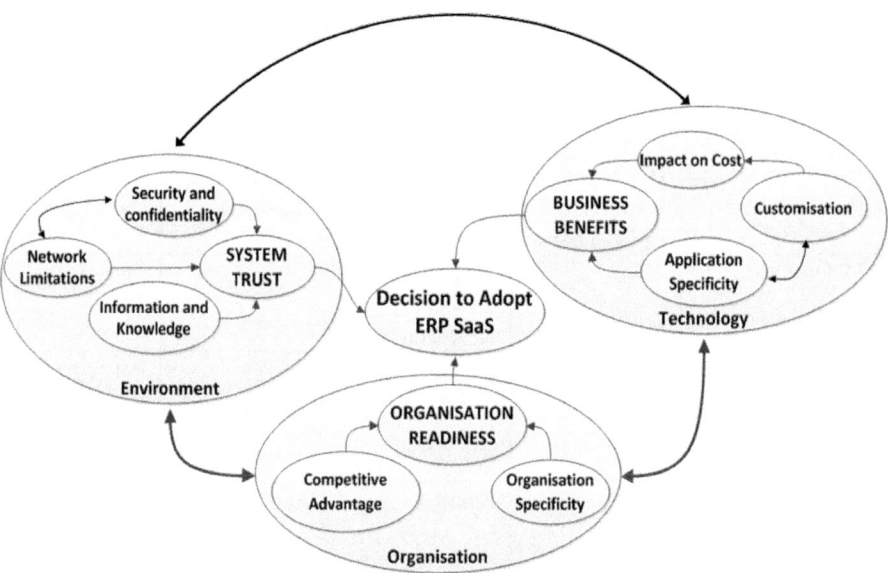

Fig. 1. ERP SaaS adoption model

5.1   Business Benefits

Under the technological characteristics of the adoption of ERP SaaS, the perceived business benefits that the clients associate with ERP SaaS have an impact on the overall decision whether to adopt ERP SaaS or not. In regard to business benefits, three main issues emerged from the study.

Cost. The main benefits associated with the adoption of the SaaS model are: low TCO, the subscription pay-as-you go model and ease of implementation [14]. On the other hand ERP systems are associated with high costs of implementation and maintenance [1]. The expectation therefore is that the adoption of the ERP implemented on the SaaS model shall neutralise the huge upfront costs associated with ERP systems, and shall also lower the overall cost of ERP systems.

In agreement with findings by Burrel [6] participants perceived that savings in the required upfront implementation costs are seen as a benefit mostly associated with small businesses. Smaller businesses do not have sufficient resources in terms of the technical manpower and funding to manage installed software and therefore could benefit from SaaS without the need to acquire the personnel with requisite skills. *"I personally think it could help smaller companies maybe more" (Participant A).* Participant D mentioned that ERP-SaaS offered by one prominent ERP software vendor in South Africa targets smaller operations that want to get some elements of ERP running.

The investment in ERP SaaS needs to be justified like any other investment through a clear decision making tool. The clients are of the opinion that they do not have a tool or a yardstick that can be used as a basis for decision making. This uncertainty makes it difficult for the decision makers such as the participants to determine whether ERP SaaS is beneficial in terms of return on investment. Costs and benefits involved in SaaS have been noted as hard to determine [34]. Most importantly, the research participants were very critical of the cost reduction benefits of SaaS, especially for certain organisations with their need for rapid customisation. Yet, the fact that in-house ERP systems are seen as expensive by the participants means that there is an opportunity for ERP SaaS to make headway in any type of organisation regardless of size. That said, the issue of SaaS cost reduction can't be looked at in isolation because of the participant's view that ERP systems demand flexibility that in turn impacts the cost.

Customisation. According to Guo [4], the perceived lack of customisation of ERP SaaS negatively impacts on the adoption of ERP SaaS. This is not only in terms of possible cost increases but also in terms of the flexibility to meet business requirements. ERP systems are not static as rapid customisations are often needed to meet business requirements [1]. In contrast, ERP SaaS is perceived as rigid. The high level of customisation in a rapidly changing environment impacts negatively on the cost reduction benefit, which in turn negatively affects the perceived benefit of ERP SaaS technology.

Yet, SaaS applications are purported to be loosely coupled with configurable components. Clients are able to customise their applications through on-screen clicks without code modifications [12]. This implies that to meet unique requirements of the customers, there may be a need to increase the configurable limit as far as possible towards the client's unique requirements [4].

The view that the respondents hold is that, SaaS is more appropriate for standardised applications that requires little or no customisation. The issue of customisation came out as very important because it is seen as a way to differentiate from the competitors; hence, it was rated highly by the participants.

"Now, the economies of scale and scope, provided the scope is the same, are fantastic in terms of reducing cost. Right? But those services can't give you....,

there's no differentiating between businesses. You know, it doesn't give you any competitive edge" (Participant B).

Another issue raised about customisation is that which relates to the presence of organisations in different regions or parts of the world. One participant was concerned that the customisation requirements for different regions could complicate ERP SaaS. On analysis, the issue of customisation is seen as a very important inhibiting factor of adopting ERP SaaS. The clients perceive it as being an issue that makes the SaaS model expensive, especially for ERP systems that need to be agile to facilitate a faster response to the changing environment, as well as for facilitating unique processes that gives a company a competitive edge over other competing firms. However, none of the respondents seemed to be aware of the configurability of the SaaS applications, which to some extent addresses the issue of customisation.

Application Specificity. The main issue about application specificity is the fact that ERP is considered too important to run on a SaaS model. The general feeling amongst the research participants is that, although some parts of ERP could be run as ERP SaaS, the model is more appropriate for applications such as Business Intelligence (BI) and Customer Relationship Management (CRM).

Since ERP is seen as a core application, it not considered as appropriate for SaaS model, especially in relation to modules that are considered core. "If you look at ERP systems, you can't just leave it out in the Internet, in a cloud somewhere. It needs to be very secure" (Participant B).

On addressing the question about which applications are more suitable for the SaaS Model, Participant D was of the opinion that the CRM is more suitable for SaaS. *"That is very different to the complexity of an integrated ERP environment...the peripheral functionality that needs quick scaling, quick flexibility, you could probably go and say, let's get that out of the cloud" (Participant D).*

Two of the organisations that took part in the study are already using cloud computing, for Spam and Virus filtering and the other one for e-mail. This supports the view that at least for now, the SaaS model is seen as appropriate for standardised and peripheral applications.

The important role ERP system plays in organisations today makes it difficult to hand control over to third parties. One can conclude that the extent to which an application is perceived as being core to the business operations has a negative impact on the adoption of SaaS, and hence ERP SaaS.

5.2   Organisation Readiness

The extent to which the business is ready to adopt technological innovation covers organisational factors that influence the adoption or non-adoption decision. Two main issues that were found to affect the organisation's readiness to adopt ERP SaaS are competitive advantage and organisation specificity.

Competitive Advantage. The competitive advantage here refers to the actual enterprise functions or the processes, and not the type of application itself. The participants were of the opinion that organisation readiness is influenced by the perceived importance of a process/function. If the process is seen as being something that is so important to the organisation in that it provides a competitive edge over other competitors, then such a process/function may negatively influence the decision to adopt. On the other hand processes/functionalise that are not considered core can be readily accepted for adoption of SaaS. Thus ERP modules that are considered less important or not mission critical to the organisation could be easily adopted by such organisations.

"Services that are differentiating to your business, probably software as a service may not work, or maybe it will work but you won't get the economies of scope because it's your specific processes that you don't want to share with other customers or other competitors" (Participant B).

Core processes and functionalities are currently considered as being appropriate only for running in-house because of the reluctance to share the differentiating functionalities with competing firms. It is not so much about the issue of trust as it is the case in application specificity, but rather about the possibility of losing unique identity which is so crucial for businesses to compete successfully.

Organisation Specificity. In addition, the participants view of the size or nature of the organisation influences the adoption of ERP SaaS. The analysis revealed that some of the participants felt that the type of organisation they are in may not be suitable for ERP SaaS adoption. On the other hand, Participant C asserted that the vendors are probably not looking into ERP SaaS for large organisations.

With regard to the nature of the organisation, there are two main issues raised concerning customisation and confidentiality [28]. As indicated above, organisation with rapid customisation requirements are seen as not being appropriate for ERP SaaS adoption. On the other hand the literature points to certain types of organisations such as those with requirements for confidentiality not readily accepting the adoption of ERP SaaS [25]. This was confirmed by participants:

"How are you going to ensure confidentiality of client's information? We deal with very sensitive information about client's information you know. Medical condition and research issues. How are you just going to leave that in the cloud somewhere?" (Participant A).

Adoption of ERP SaaS amongst big enterprises is impeded by the view that ERP SaaS is appropriate for small operations rather than large corporate. The issue about the need for rapid customisation for enterprises that requires agility and flexibility is also seen as being inappropriate for those organisations. In addition, the nature of organisation with high requirements for confidentiality may negatively impact the decision to adopt ERP SaaS.

5.3   System Trust

System Trust in the context of this paper is the extent to which the organisation expects to benefit from the adoption of ERP SaaS within acceptable levels of security and guarantees in terms of structural assurances and third party guarantees. The structural assurance refers to internet reliability and bandwidth issues. Third party guarantees refer mainly to the assurances that the risk of adopting ERP SaaS shall be mitigated and managed by the vendor. There are three main issues that emerged under the system trust theme: network limitations, security and knowledge.

Network Limitations. The participants felt that the reliability and cost of bandwidth negatively affect the adoption of ERP SaaS in South Africa. The issue of bandwidth did not only apply to the South African environment but in Africa as a whole. SaaS requires a stable and reliable internet connection to access web-based service [9]. Since there are still challenges about broadband access and cost in South Africa and Africa [35],[36] the adoption of ERP SaaS shall be slow compared to other developed countries such as in America and Europe.

Security and Confidentiality. Security and confidentiality strongly influences the trust that the organisation is willing to place on the system [10]. Security was raised as a concern by almost all participants. *"Where's the security? How are you going to guarantee security?" (Participant B).*

The participants suggested that ERP SaaS vendors have a vested interest in ensuring the security and confidentiality of client's information. But as Participant A mentioned: *"What happens when the vendor goes out of business?"*

Moreover, since none of the participant organisations use ERP SaaS the concern about security seems to have been caused by the uncertainty about the way in which ERP SaaS operates. This lack of understanding or knowledge about aspects of SaaS could impacts the level of security trust that the users are willing to place on ERP SaaS. In addition, since the vendors have a vested interest in security as it impacts their integrity and reputation, they would probably have more stronger security controls in place than many clients [8].

While maintenance and upgrades were seen by the participants as a benefit of adopting ERP SaaS, others are of the view that it is problematic for the organisation in question. Xin & Levina [7] have noted that vendors drive future developments of the ERP SaaS system, which makes the users powerless over the control of their upgrades and therefore heavily reliant on the clients on the vendors. This was confirmed by participants: *"You lose the ownership and lose the control that you have over the system and you are more manipulated or forced into the direction by the system as when you actually hosting it yourself" (Participant E).*

Information and Knowledge. Although the participants seemed to understand what SaaS is and how it works, there is an apparent lack of information about the specifics of ERP SaaS. Information about ERP SaaS may also impact on the organisation readiness, since decision making becomes difficult if there is not enough knowledge about the issue at hand.

In addition, there are still "grey areas" in terms of ERP SaaS functionality such as how security works. Participant C summarised it nicely: *"The issue with culture, obviously, needs to be addressed on two levels because there needs to be a clear understanding by everybody in the business, if we were to propose this change, on exactly what Software as a Service entails in the modern business environment today, because I doubt that there is a clear understanding of how it works."*

5.4   Summary of Findings

Table 2 below highlights factors that affect the adoption of ERP SaaS as well as their impact on the decision to adopt.The environment factors emerged as key in impacting the decision to adopt ERP SaaS in South Africa. Network limitation, security and confidentiality, and the extent of information available to the organisations about ERP SaaS affect the level of trust the clients could place on the system itself. The level of trust placed by the clients on the system as a whole affects the decision whether to adopt ERP SaaS or not. Second to environment issue, are the technology factors, about cost, customisation and application specificity. The current cost of ERP implementation and maintenance positively affect the adoption of ERP SaaS. Yet big organisations do not perceive the SaaS model as being appropriate, especially with respect to their customisation requirements to deliver differentiating products or services. ERP are seen as core applications that are not appropriate for SaaS delivery. On the other hand, the peripheral modules of ERP seem to be favoured with clients for adoption as SaaS.

Surprisingly, the participants did not mention the integration aspects of ERP Software as a Service (SaaS) in determining ERP SaaS. This is despite being one of the most complex and expensive component of SaaS implementation, especially in the enterprise space [12] and with several studies raising integration as one of the factors where SaaS needs to improve [4].

The SaaS model is an emerging business model that completely changes the way software is being delivered to participants [3]. Where ERP SaaS is adopted as opposed to in-house ERP the technology support landscape changes tremendously. This is not restricted to the ICT departments and includes the whole organisation, in terms of culture and required structural readjustments [3]. This implies that ERP SaaS potential clients should consider the likely impact of ERP SaaS adoption on the organisational strategy, Information Technology strategy and governance processes.

The issue of change management and culture was raised by one participant in this research. Another issue that has not been addressed much by empirical research literature is the potential gains in terms of environmental impact of SaaS adoption.

Table 2. Summary Findings for ERP SaaS Adoption

TOE	Factor	Impact on Decision to Adopt – Positive or Negative
Technology Main Theme	**Business Benefit – Perceived business benefits shall influence decision to adopt**	
Technology	Cost	Negative for large companies due to customisation
		Positive for small companies
		Negative for ERP core applications
Technology	Customisation	Negative for rapidly changing enterprises
Technology	Application Specifity	Negative for ERP core applications
Organisation Main Theme	**Organisation Readiness – Organisation´s preparedness to adopt ERP**	
Organisation	Competitive Advantage	Negative for processes seen as offering competitive advantages
Organisation	Organisation Specifity	Negative for large enterprises
Environment Main Theme	**System Trust – The level of trust influences the decision to adopt**	
Environment	Network Limitation	Negative for immature
Environment	Information and Knowledge	Negative for system trust
Environment	Security	Negative and indifferent
Environment	Regulation	Indifferent (not included in the theoretical model)

6   Conclusion

The objective of this research was to determine factors that affect the adoption of ERP SaaS in South Africa. Using the TOE framework as a theoretical lens, factors affecting the adoption of ERP SaaS were determined from qualitative data collection and analysis.

In particular, factors relating to the environment emerged as key in deciding on the adoption or non-adoption of ERP SaaS in South Africa with issues around network limitations and security concerns strongly impacting potential adoption. However, as internet technology improves and the cost of bandwidth begins to drop in Africa and South Africa the network issues shall be of a lesser concern.

In regard to issues around the technology, the main factor inhibiting the adoption of ERP SaaS is a concern around customisation and possible costs associated with it. The SaaS model is perceived to be rigid and not allowing for the flexibility required for systems such as ERP.

Seemingly the evolution has began, with clients starting to adopt peripheral applications through cloud computing. As one participant put it, a transition will occur. *"So that's why I'm saying, very excited, think that it's an opportunity and a possibility, but it's going to have to be planned properly and the migration is probably going to be over time. So, what I see here is that there's a transition that will take place from where we are now, to eventually procuring all the services in the cloud."*

In general there is a lack of empirical research about Software as a Service (SaaS) in South Africa. This paper has made a first attempt. The research on the same subject focusing on certain industry or type of organisation could also be useful. For instance, the research could focus on the factors affecting adoption of ERP SaaS in Small and Medium Enterprises in South Africa. The results of such research could be consistent and more concrete without generalising amongst participants operating in different industries.

References

1. Helo, P.: Expectation and reality in ERP implementation: consultant and solution provider perspective. Industrial Management & Data Systems 108(8), 1045–1059 (2008)
2. Verduyn, M.: Drive Business performance with ERP (2009), `http://www.pastel.co.za/Downloads/Newsroom/Enterpreneur August2009.pdf?relid=3657`
3. Hofmann, P.: ERP is Dead, Long Live ERP (2008), `http://www.computer.org/portal/web/csdl/doi/10.1109/MIC.2008.78`
4. Guo, P.: A survey of Software as a Service Delivery Paradigm (2009), `http://www.cse.tkk.fi/en/publications/B/5/papers/guo_final.pdf`
5. Benlian, A., Hess, T., Buxmann, P.: Drivers of SaaS- Adoption- An empirical study of different application types. Business & Information Systems Engineering 1(5), 357–369 (2009)
6. Burrel, C.: New engagement approach in Europe by Fujitsu Services. Fujitsu Science and Technology Journal 45(3) (2009)
7. Xin, M., Levina, N.: Software-as-a-Service Model: Elaborating Client-Side Adoption Factors. In: Boland, R., Limayem, M., Pentland, B. (eds.) Proceedings of the 29th International Conference on Information Systems, Paris, France, December 14-17 (2008)
8. Clair, G.: Software-as-a-Service (SaaS). Put the Focus on the KM/Knowledge Services Core Function. EOS International (2008), `http://smr-knowledge.com/wp-content/uploads/2010/01/EOS-SaaS-White-Paper-2008.pdf`
9. Kaplan, J.: SaaS: Friend or Foe? (2007), `http://smrknowledge.com/wp-content/uploads/2010/01/EOS-SaaS`
10. ISACA: Cloud Computing: Business Benefits with Security, governance and assurance perspectives (2009), `http://www.isaca.org/Knowledge-Center/Research/Documents/Cloud-Computing-28Oct09-Research.pdf`
11. Vaquero, L.M., Cáceres, J., Morán, D.: The Challenge of Service Level Scalability for the Cloud. International Journal of Cloud Applications and Computing 1(1), 34–44 (2011)

12. Hai, H., Sakoda, S.: SaaS and Integration best practices. Fujutsi Science Technology Journal 45(3), 257–264 (2009)
13. Liao, H., Tao, C.: An anatomy to SaaS Business Mode Based on Internet. International Conference on Management of e-Commerce and e-Government (2008), http://ieeexplore.ieee.org/Xplore/guesthome.jsp
14. Dubey, A., Wagle, D.: Delivering Software as a Service (2007), http://www.mckinsey.de/downloads/publikation/mck_on_bt/2007/mobt_12_Delivering_Software_as_a_Service.pdf
15. Lucas, K.: The State of Enterprise Software Adoption in Europe (2007), http://www50.sap.com.ezproxy.uct.ac.za/m1/images/global_data/ERP%20Lead/UK/Full_Doc_Forrester_012907.pdf
16. AberdeenGroup: Trends and Observations (2009), http://www.abeerdeen.com
17. Montgomery, N.: Magic Quadrant for ERP for Product-centric midmarket companies. Gartner G00205542 (2010), http://sme.news-sap.com/files/2011/01/SAP-vol2art5.pdf
18. Kim, W.: Cloud Computing: Today and Tomorrow. Journal of Object Technology 8(1) (January-February 2009)
19. Sahoo, M.: IT Innovations: Evaluate, Strategize, and Invest. IT Professional 11(6), 16–22 (2009)
20. Nitu, M.: Configurability in SaaS (Software as a Service) Applications. In: Proceedings of the 2nd India Software Engineering Conference, Pune, India, February 23-26 (2009)
21. Armbrust, M., Fox, A., Gritthin, R., Joseph, A.D., Katz, R., Konwiski, A., Lee, G., Patterson D., Rabkin, A., Stoica, I., Zaharia, M.: Above the clouds: A Berkeley View of Cloud Computing (2009), http://radlab.cs.berkerley.edu
22. Godse, M., Mulik, S.: An approach to selecting Software as a Service (SaaS) Product (2009), http://doi.ieeecomputersociety.org/10.1109/CLOUD.2009.74
23. Jaekel, M., Bronnert, K., Mewaldt, M.: Software as a Service (SaaS) with Sample Applications (2010), http://www.it-solutions.siemens.com/country/cee/en/Documents/Publications/at-cc-softwar_PDF_e.pdf
24. Yang, H., Tate, M.: Where are we at with cloud computing? In: Proceedings of the 20th Australasian Conference on Information Systems, ACIS 2009, pp. 807–819 (2009)
25. Mangiuc, D.: Software: From product to service the evolution of a model (2009), http://oeconomica.uab.ro/upload/lucrari/1120091/08.pdf
26. Krishnan, K., Vin, H., Raghavan, V.: TCS and Cloud Computing (2009), http://www.indiainfoline.com/Markets/Company/Fundamentals
27. Heart, T., Pliskin, N., Tractinsky, N.: Explaining adoption of remote hosting: A case Study (2008), http://is2.lse.ac.uk/GlobalSourcing/papers2008/ITP0871.pdf
28. Heart, T.: Empirically Testing a Model for The Intention of Firms to Use Remote Application hosting (2007), http://is2.lse.ac.uk/asp/aspecis/20070065.pdf
29. Nthoiwa, J.: Jumping into the cloud (2010), http://www.itweb.co.za/survey/fujitsusurvey/2009/
30. Klein, H.K., Myers, M.D.: A Set of Principles for Conducting and Evaluating Interpretive Field Studies in Information Systems. MIS Quarterly 23(1), 67–93 (1999)
31. Frankel, R., Devers, K.: Study Design in Qualitative Research – 1: Developing Questions and Assessing Resource Needs (2000), http://www.nova.edu/ssss/QR/Quality.pdf

32. Thomas, D.R.: A general inductive approach for qualitative data analysis. School of Population Health, University of Auckland, NewZealand (2003)
33. Anfara, V.A., Brown, K.M., Mangione, T.L.: Qualitative Analysis on Stage: Making the Research Process More Public. Educational Researcher, 28–38 (2002)
34. Measuring the return on investment of web application acceleration managed services. IDC, http://www.essextec.com/assets/cloud/akamai/idc-waa-roi-wp.pdf
35. Bernabé, F.: Broadband Quality Score III – A global study of broadband quality. Oxford SAID Business School, CISCO (September 2010)
36. Lopez, A.L., Rey, P.: Foreclosing competition through access charges and price discrimination. IESE business school working paper WP – 801 (2009), http://papers.ssrn.com/sol3/papers.cfm?abstract_id=1440157

Process Support of Business and IT Management in Czech Companies

Renáta Kunstová

University of Economics, Faculty of Informatics and Statistics
W. Churchill sq. 4, Prague 3, Czech Republic
kunstova@vse.cz

Abstract. Defined, monitored and measured processes are significant preconditions for a well process-managed company. They are also important conditions for delivering information technology resources as services. The model, which is based on service management, is described at the beginning of this paper. The main part of this paper focuses on the results of an extensive survey. This survey dealt with an investigation into whether companies operating on the Czech market have defined business and IT processes, and if these processes are monitored, measured and continuously optimized.

Keywords: Model of management, business processes, IT processes, IT services.

1   Introduction

Information systems, and information and communication technologies (IS/ICT, or in short IT) are important factor for successful companies. Their purpose is to support business activities. The alignment between business needs and IT capabilities became a main area of top management concern because if IT supports business strategies and processes, then IT brings competitive advantage. The business/IT alignment depends on many factors, such as the level of communication between business and IT managers, their cooperation in strategic planning, definition of IT and business metrics, which are monitored etc. [12, 16] The business/IT alignment is also influenced by a current trend to solve everything through services. Software as a Service, Infrastructure as a Service, Platform as a Service etc. are new business models, which changed the usual approaches to the management of enterprise IS/ICT. Service-oriented approaches increase commitment to process orientation, and put emphasis on managing the relationship between business and IT [17]. Companies need to satisfy the following preconditions to take full advantage of new service-oriented models:

- management of business processes,
- management of IT processes,
- delivering IS/ICT resources through IT services.

The members of the Department of Information Technology at the University of Economics in Prague deal with the management of enterprise IT. The service-oriented

C. Møller and S. Chaudhry (Eds.): CONFENIS 2011, LNBIP 105, pp. 168–181, 2012.

approach to IT and business management is illustrated in the SPSPR model, see Fig. 1. The acronym "SPSPR" is formed from the first letters of key words: Strategy – Process – Service – Process – Resource. These words refer to layers of the model. The layers of this model can be assigned to appropriate levels of management. The strategic management layer and the business processes layer belong to the strategic level of management. The IT Services layer corresponds to the tactical level of management. The IT processes layer and IT Resources layer relate to the operational level of management.

The SPSPR model was first published in 2001 [21]. On the basis of our experiences with its implementation, the model was continuously updated from that time. The implementation of IT services, according to the SPSPR model, includes the following phases:

- definition of processes, services and resources and their metrics,
- operational management of processes, services and resources,
- monitoring and measuring of processes, services and resources,
- optimization of processes and services according to the business strategy, and to the consumption of resources.

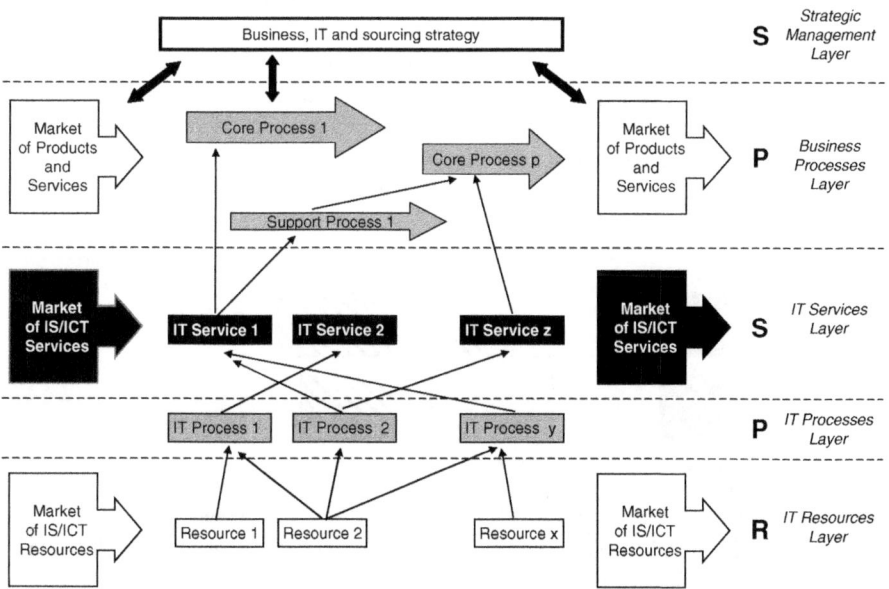

Fig. 1. The SPSPR model

The basic principle of the SPSPR model is a linking of business processes and IT processes through IT services. The other principle is that business and IT processes are measured and monitored. This allows the quick identification of emerging issues and allows management the opportunity to react immediately and to change the performance of processes. From a top down view it is seen that business strategy is realized through business processes, business processes are executed by IT services,

IT services are managed by IT processes and IT processes use IT resources. The SPSPR model contributes to business/IT alignment.

Within our current grant project, "Advanced Principles and Models for Enterprise ICT Management", we are working on the proposal of the overall conceptual model for corporate performance management. The SPSPR model is one of the fundamental elements. The conceptual model follows on our previous work (for instance 1, 2, 3, 9, 10, 13, 14, 15, 19, 20 and 22), current business requirements and the results of our surveys.

As mentioned above, the important precondition of a well managed service-oriented company is a process-oriented management of business and IT processes. Within the survey we verified if companies operating on the Czech market have implemented process management. The results of this survey are discussed in this paper.

2   Using of IT to Support Business

As the implementation of process-oriented management relies on the use of IT in companies [5, 18], we checked the status of IT in Czech companies on the basis of statistical data. We used the data which is freely available on the website of the Czech Statistical Office [4]. We found that although the trend of the use of IT is growing long-term in Czech companies, only two thirds had a corporate computer network, less then a quarter of companies use the electronic exchange of structured data within business processes between companies and fifteen percent of companies regularly share business information electronically with suppliers or customers. In comparison with EU27 data, also published at [4], the Czech Republic is below the EU27 average in most indicators (see Fig. 2).

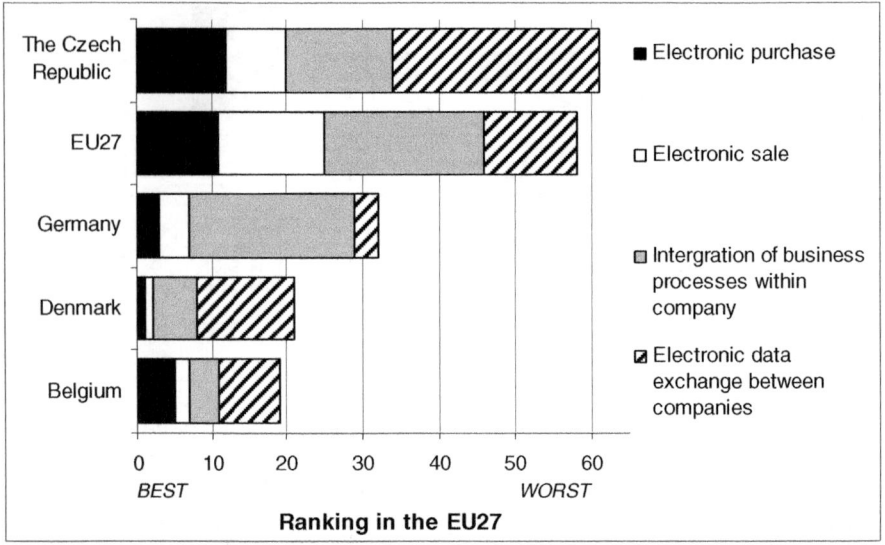

Fig. 2. Countries according to the sum of the rank position in the selected indicators

The indicators published above reflect the percentage of the total number of companies in the country. Indicator values were ranked in descending order. This means that the shorter the column on the graph, the better the ranking. Belgian companies present the most extensive use of IT in business. Denmark ranks first in electronic purchases and sales. Third place is occupied by Germany. The Czech Republic ranks nineteenth. It is below the EU27 whose position is 14. Further details about the ranking of the Czech Republic in comparison to other European countries are in [6, 7 and 8].

From this comparison it is evident that the Czech Republic does not have a good standing among other countries of the European Union. On the other hand, the realization of electronic purchases, electronic sales, electronic data exchange and the integration of business processes demonstrates the existence of processes in companies. Therefore, we decided to realize our own survey which will provide information about features of processes such as monitoring, measurement, managing and optimization.

3   Survey Methodology

As the management of business and IT processes is a one of the conditions for successful management of services, our survey focused on processes. The goal of our survey was to investigate, if companies operating on the Czech market are interested in their processes, if they have their processes described and implemented in day-to-day operations and if these processes are managed, measured and optimized.

The basic structure of our investigation is shown in Fig. 3. In accordance with the basic principles of the SPSPR model, we differentiated between business processes (the main processes supporting the business goals of the company) and IT processes (the processes of the company's own management of IS/ICT). A company which would agree with these statements for business and IT processes meets the assumptions for providing IT as a service and business/IT alignment.

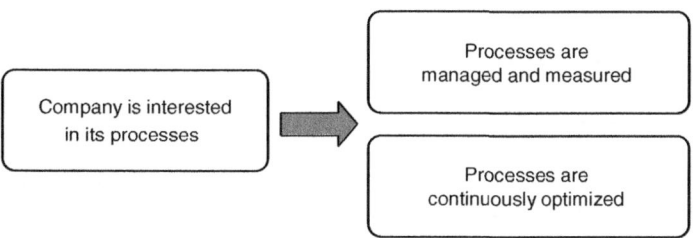

Fig. 3. Basic structure of investigation

The survey hypotheses were as follows:

1. Hypothesis: If a company has specified business processes, then it has specified IT processes too.
2. Hypothesis: If a company has specified business processes, then it manages, measures and optimizes them.
3. Hypothesis: If a company has specified IT processes, then it manages, measures and optimizes them.

4   Survey Realization

The survey was a starting the point of our following work so it had to extensive and national in nature. We chose a professional company to receive a large sample of quality data. The questionnaire contained questions to verify the hypotheses related to our work on a conceptual model for corporate performance management. Hence, this paper focuses only on a part of the survey. The survey was realized in October 2010 and the survey data was analyzed in 2011.

4.1   Data Collection

On the basis of the offers submitted by several professional companies, we contacted Ipsos Tambor, s.r.o. (http://www.ipsos.cz). This company is a part of an independent international company (http://www.ipsos.com), which has offices in 66 countries and ranks fifth among global research companies.

The company chosen recommended using the CATI (Computer–Assisted Telephone Interviewing) method for data collection. This method increases the accuracy and comparability of data collected, and the speed and efficiency of their collection. All interviews are recorded and a research company can listen to these interviews.

The company ensures the highest quality of interviewing through control mechanisms and practices. The operators of the professional company first contacted every respondent and asked them for their consent to participate in the survey. Then respondents received a questionnaire and answered the questions in a controlled phone call. The operators had the questionnaire available with detailed instructions.

4.2   Data Sample

The data sample was based on statistical data published by the Czech Statistical Office with the following demands.

1. The survey had to cover all industry sectors, except for companies operating in the IT industry. Among the industry sectors, in which the company operates, the following should be preferred: banking and insurance, telecommunications, utilities, government and public services. These companies, highly dependent on IT, should be about a third of all surveyed companies.
2. The survey has to involve only companies with the following number of employees: 10 – 49, 50 – 249, 250 and more. According to the expected use of our work, we preferred companies with 50 – 249 employees.

Companies were selected by quota sampling. The total number of surveyed companies was limited by the purchase price of the professional data collection. The survey involved respondents from 600 companies operating on the Czech market. The basic characteristics of these companies were very different.

4.3   Questionnaire Structure

The questionnaire was divided into six sections. The author focuses only on the first and the third section, which are related to this paper. The first section of the questionnaire contained questions designed to detect essential characteristics of the company and its respondent. Respondents always marked one item from the list.

We discovered the following characteristics:

- How many employees does your company have?
- In which industry sector does your company operate?
- What is your company's establishment?
- What is your job position?

The third section of the questionnaire contained the main research questions. The first set of questions related to business processes, the second set of questions related to IT processes. The questions and possible answers are shown in Table 1.

Table 1. Research questions and possible answers

	1st set of questions	**2nd set of questions**
Question 1	**How are business processes specified (i.e. defined and described) within a company?**	**How are IT processes specified within a company?**
Answer 1.1	Processes are not specified.	Processes are not specified.
Answer 1.2	Parts of processes are specified.	Parts of processes are specified.
Answer 1.3	Processes are fully specified.	Processes are fully specified.
Question 2	**Are business processes managed and measured?**	**Are IT processes managed and measured?**
Answer 2.1	Yes	Yes
Answer 2.2	No	No
Question 3	**Are business processes continuously optimized?**	**Are IT processes continuously optimized?**
Answer 3.1	Yes	Yes
Answer 3.2	No	No

The respondents received Question 2 and 3 only if they had chosen the second or third answer on Question 1.

5   Survey Results

We received the data collected in the form of a Microsoft Excel table. The analysis was performed using statistical functions. Data was analyzed in several phases. At first, the absolute and relative frequency of individual characteristics was measured. Then the analysis of processes according to basic characteristics was performed. At the end dependences were examined by contingency tables. The strength of the correlation between the features analyzed was calculated by C-Pearson, V-Cramer and Cohen's "kappa" coefficients.

5.1   Analysis by Company Size

The total number of participating companies was 600. The largest group of respondents, 63% (in absolute numbers it was 380 companies), was from mid-size companies with 50 – 249 employees. Twenty percent of respondents (120 companies) were from companies with 250 and more employees. The remaining 17% of respondents were from small companies with 10 – 49 employees (100 companies).

Ninety six respondents (16%) answered that their company has no specified business processes and 134 respondents (22%) answered that their company has no specified IT processes. The largest group were companies with partly defined processes (business processes – 282 companies, 47%; IT processes – 318 companies, 53%). Two hundred and twenty two companies (37%) have fully specified business processes, 25% (148) of companies have fully specified IT processes.

With the increasing number of employees (see Fig. 4), the probability that the processes are not specified significantly decreases. This trend appeared for business and IT processes too.

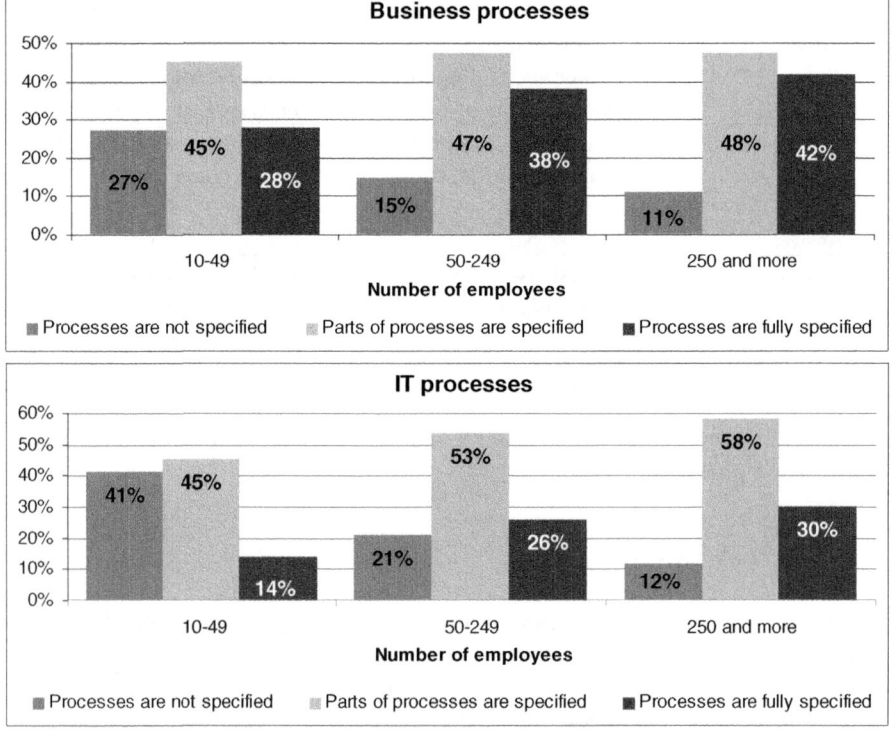

Fig. 4. Processes specification according to number of employees

5.2   Analysis by Industry Sector

Due to the fragmentation of companies in different industry sectors, the numbers of companies from various industry sectors were accumulated according to their dependence on IT. The number of companies which are highly dependent on IT (banking, insurance, utilities, telecommunication services, government and public services) was 204 (34%). The number of companies with medium dependence on IT (manufacturing, retailing, accommodation and catering, real estate, healthcare, wholesale business) was 202 (34%). The number of low dependence on IT companies (construction, education, culture and recreation, mining industry, forestry and fishing, agriculture) was 194 (32%).

The survey did not establish a link between the level of a company's dependence on IT and whether the company has specified processes and / or their parts. The number of companies in each group was almost the same, the percentage distribution was very similar too – see Fig. 5.

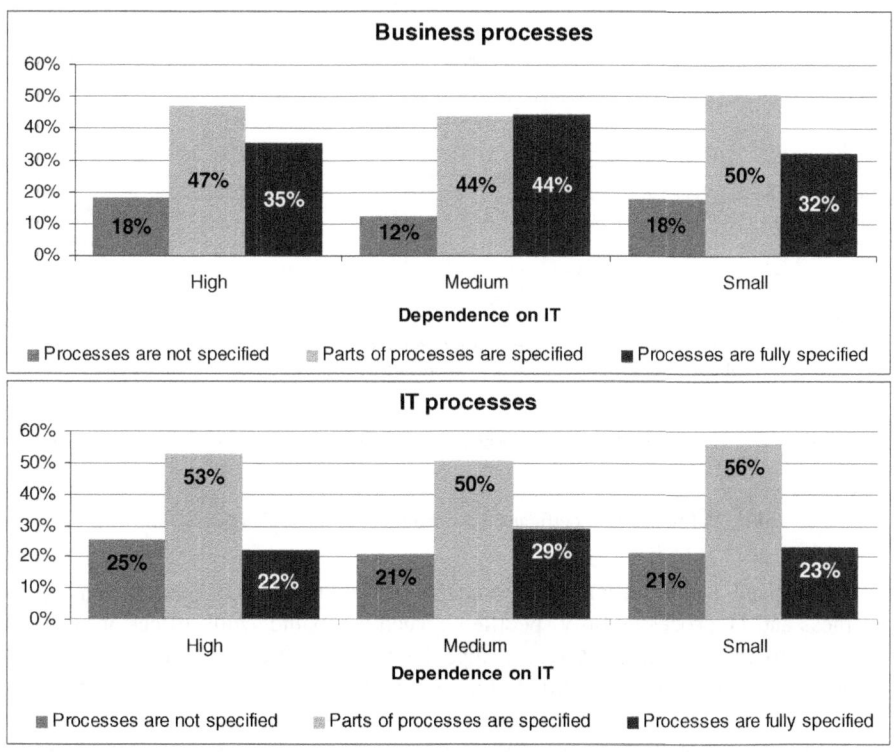

Fig. 5. Processes specification according to industry sector – dependence on IT

5.3   Analysis by Company's Establishment

The largest group of companies were companies founded in the Czech Republic without offices abroad – 488 (81%), affiliates of multinational companies presented 79 (13%) of companies and the remaining 33 (6%) companies were Czech companies now with offices abroad – see Fig. 6.

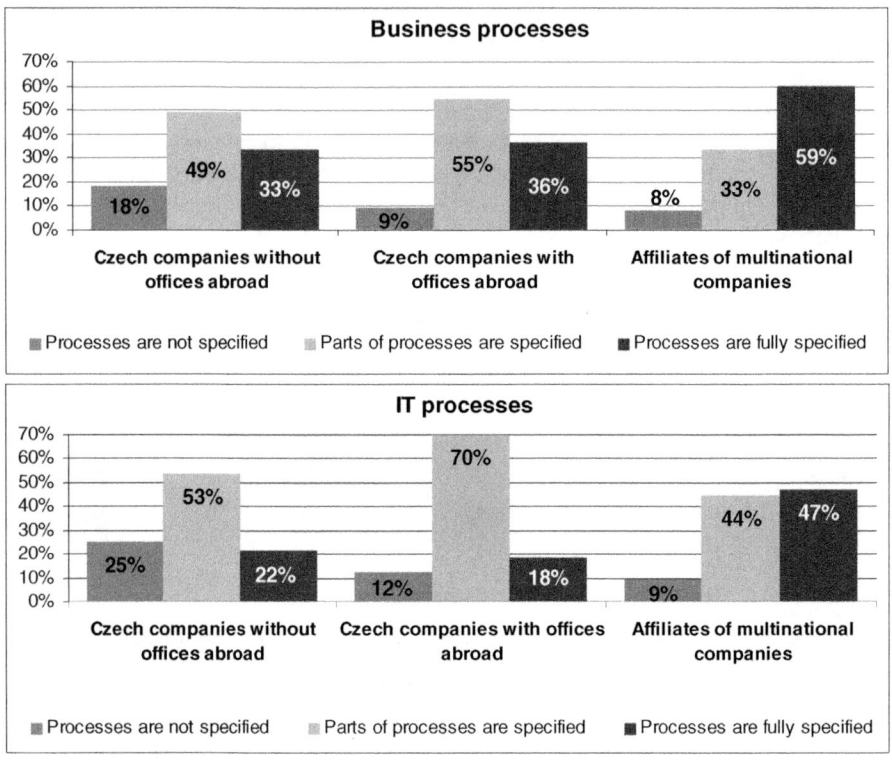

Fig. 6. Processes specification according to company's establishment

Respondents from multinational companies often answered that their company has business and IT processes fully specified. Czech companies with offices abroad have parts of processes specified. Czech companies without offices abroad also have most often parts of processes specified, but the percentage distribution is lower. The comparison of business processes against IT processes within each group by company establishment show that business processes are more often fully specified and IT processes are more often specified in parts. The worst situation was in Czech companies without offices abroad.

5.4   Analysis by Management Level of Processes

Eighty four percent of all companies surveyed (47 % of companies which have defined parts of the business processes, and 37 % companies with fully defined business processes, i.e. 504 companies) were also examined to find whether their processes are measurable, managed and continuously optimized. Twelve percent of these answered that they have defined business processes and / or their parts, but nobody measures, manages or optimizes them. The companies more often continuously optimize business processes than they measure and manage them (see Fig. 7).

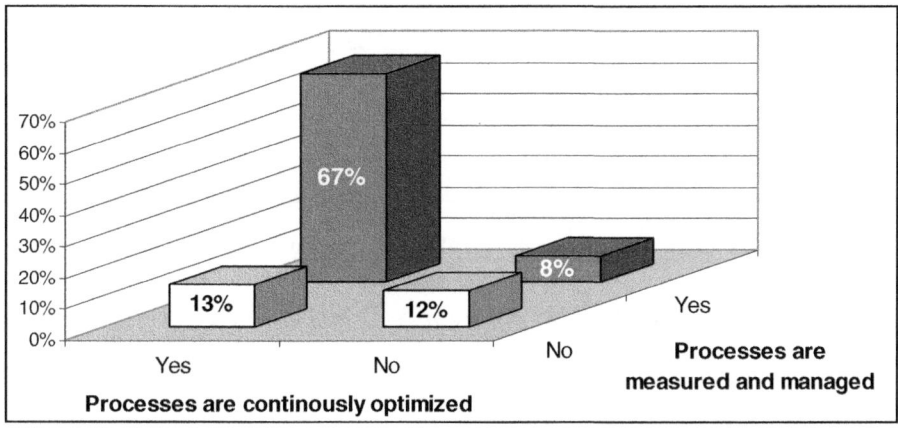

Fig. 7. Division of companies according to the conducting of business processes

Questions relating to the measurement and optimization of IT processes were referred only to 466 respondents (53% of companies which have defined parts of the IT processes and 25% of companies with fully defined IT processes) – see Fig. 8. The percentage of continuously optimized, measured and managed IT processes is lower than business processes. The IT processes are three times more often continuously optimized than measured and managed.

It could be assumed that the measured, managed and continuously optimized processes will be applied mainly by those companies in which the sector is highly dependent on IT, but the survey results did not support that implication. No significant dependences were found upon investigation of the relationship between the characteristics of the companies and the conducting of the company's processes. The number of employees in the company, and the company's dependence on IT, was distributed uniformly.

An increasing trend was seen depending on the company's dislocation. Companies with offices abroad have a higher percentage of measured, managed and optimized processes, and companies which are a part of a multinational company have an even higher percentage.

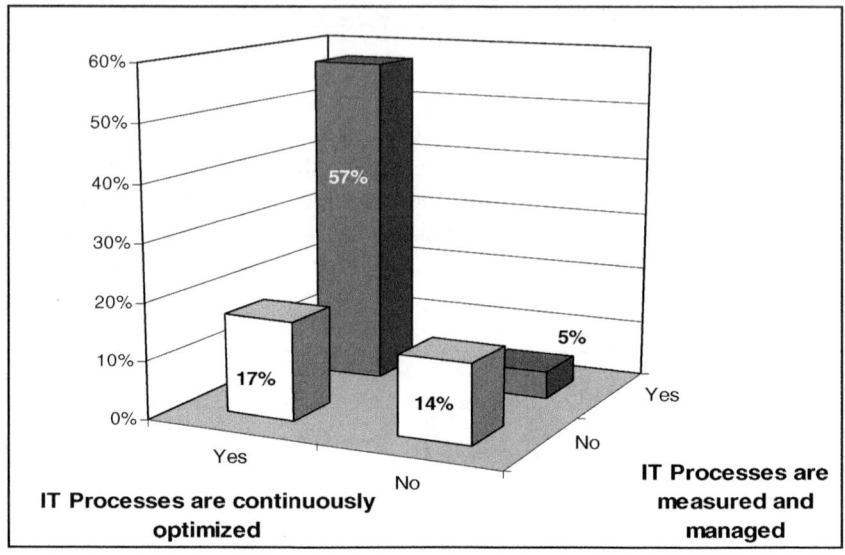

Fig. 8. Division of companies according to the conducting of IT processes

5.5   Analysis of Relations between Business Processes and IT Processes

This phase of the analysis was started by comparing the relative frequency, of the characteristics of business and IT processes observed. The co-occurrence of single characteristics is demonstrated in Table. 2. The largest percentage of all combinations is partially specified business and IT processes (35%). The smallest percentage (1%) is the combination of fully specified business processes and unspecified IT processes.

Table 2. Percentage distribution observed characteristics of business and IT processes

	IT Processes are not specified	Parts of IT processes are specified	IT Processes are fully specified
Business processes are not specified	12%	4%	1%
Parts of business processes are specified	7%	35%	5%
Business processes are fully specified	3%	14%	19%

Inter-rater reliability was determined by Cohen's kappa coefficient. The results investigated are in Table 3. The most significant agreement is in the relation between the managing and measuring of business and IT processes. If business processes are managed and measured, IT processes are managed and measured too. This dependency was confirmed by the chi-square test with Pearson's contingency coefficient, 0.53 (the maximum value is 0.707), and Cramer's V coefficient, 0.62.

Table 3. Reliability determined by Cohen's kappa coefficients

Validated addiction	kappa
Defining, partially defining or non defining of business and IT processes	0.46
Managing and measuring of business and IT processes	0.61
Optimizing of business and IT processes	0.56
Managing / measuring and optimizing of business processes	0.38
Managing / measuring and optimizing of IT processes	0.41

The weak rate agreement is within the conducting of business processes (0.38 kappa). The survey had the following finding: if the company manages and measures business processes, it does not mean that business processes are also optimized. Other measures of dependence are in the range of kappa, 0.41 – 0.56. It is interpreted as moderate agreement [11].

6   Discussion

The hypotheses were tested on the data sample from six hundred respondents. We investigated the probability of confirming these hypotheses, and a relationship with external factors arising from the characteristics of companies and respondents.

The first hypothesis, "If a company has specified business processes, then it has specified IT processes too", was proved with Cramer's V coefficient, 0.50 and Pearson's coefficient, 0.58 (the maximum value is 0.82). The dependence was reduced by the factors that companies usually have fully or partially specified business processes rather than IT processes. A significant difference is shown between the Czech companies and affiliates of foreign corporations. Multinational companies had specified business and IT processes rather than Czech companies.

The second hypothesis, "If a company has specified business processes, then it manages, measures and optimizes them", was confirmed by 336 (i.e. 56%) of the companies. The third hypothesis, "If a company has specified IT processes, then it manages, measures and optimizes them", was confirmed by 266 (i.e. 48%) of the companies.

Companies which confirmed all three hypotheses have, with a high probability, implemented process management and therefore they are prepared to provide IT as a service, or they already do it this way. The number of these companies was 259 (i.e. 43%). These companies were Czech company without offices abroad, with 50 – 250 employees, operating in different industry sectors.

7   Conclusion

Current trends in the business environment give attention to services. A service-oriented approach emphasises on the management of processes. Our research focused on the level of process-oriented approaches in Czech companies. We realized an extensive national survey for this purpose.

Although this study was limited to the Czech market, the research provides sufficient data to show that Czech companies converge slowly on process management. The implementation of the SPSPR model is possible but on the basis of the results of the described survey, we should focus on the specified group of companies.

An important conclusion arising from the survey is that the systematic management, measurement and optimization of business processes are far from usual in Czech companies. If a company is engaged in business processes, it does not mean that it has implemented process management in the area of IT. The implementation of IT services will require these companies to change their approach to the management of the business and IT processes.

Acknowledgments. This paper was supported by the "Advanced Principles and Models for Enterprise ICT Management" grant, from the Czech Science Foundation under the number P403/10/0092.

References

1. Basl, J., Gála, L.: The Role of ICT in Business Innovation. In: IDIMT-2009 System and Humans – A Complex Relationship, pp. 67–76. Trauner, Linz (2009)
2. Bruckner, T.: Who is responsible for requirements definition for ICT services and which SLAs are defined in Czech businesses (survey results). Systémová Integrace 17(4), 125–147 (2010)
3. Buchalcevová, A.: Research of the Use of Agile Methodologies in the Czech Republic. In: Barry, C., Conboy, K., Lang, M., Wojtkowski, G., Wojtkowski, W. (eds.) Information Systems Development - Challenges in Practice, Theory, and Education, vol. 1, pp. 51–64. Springer, New York (2009)
4. Czech Statistical Office. Public database,
   http://www.czso.cz/eng/redakce.nsf/i/information_society
5. Doucek, P.: Dynamic Modelling of the Software Development Process. Cybernetics and Systems 27(4), 403–410 (1996) ISSN 0196-9722
6. Doucek, P.: Resources in ICT – ICT Effects on GDP. Jindřichův Hradec 08.09.2010 – 10.09.2010. In: IDIMT-2010 Information Technology – Human Values, Innovation and Economy, pp. 97–105. Trauner, Linz (2010)
7. Doucek, P., Nedomová, L.: ICT and Economy – Slovenia and Czech Republic Experience. Portorož 23.03.2011 – 25.03.2011. In: Organizacija prihodnosti – Future Organization (CD-ROM), pp. 268–278. Univerzita v Mariboru, Maribo (2011)
8. Doucek, P., Nedomová, L., Novotný, O.: How ICT Affect the Czech Economy? ECON 19(1), 106–116 (2011)
9. Kunstová, R.: Barriers and Benefits of Investments into Enterprise Content Management Systems. Organizacija 43(5), 205–213 (2010)
10. Kunstová, R.: Enterprise Content Management and Innovation. In: IDIMT-2010 Information Technology – Human Values, Innovation and Economy, Linz, Trauner, pp. 49–56 (2010)
11. Landis, J.R., Koch, G.G.: The measurement of observer agreement for categorical data. Biometrics 33(1), 159–174 (1977), http://jstor.org/stable/2529310

12. Luftman, J.: Assessing Business-IT Alignment Maturity. Communications of the Association for Information Systems 4, Article 14, 1–50 (2000)
13. Maryška, M.: Model for Measuring and Analysing Costs in Business Informatics. In: The Eighth Wuhan International Conference on E-Business (CD-ROM), pp. 1–5. Alfred University Press, Sigillum (2009)
14. Novotný, O.: ICT Performance Reference Model in the Context of Corporate Performance Management. In: IDIMT-2009 System and Humans – A Complex Relationship, pp. 13–16. Trauner, Linz (2009)
15. Pour, J., Voříšek, J.: Results of the survey of IS/ICT management in the Czech Republic. Systémová Integrace 18(1), 15–34 (2011)
16. Řepa, V.: Building the Process-managed Organization by Means of Services. Journal of Systems Integration 2(2), 1–6 (2011) ISSN 1804-2724, http://si-journal.org/index.php/JSI/article/view/87
17. Řepa, V.: Service-oriented Business Process Management. Funchal 06.10.2009 – 08.10.2009. In: IC3K 2009 (CD-ROM). INSTICC, Funchal, pp. 284–287 (2009) ISBN 978-989-674-013-9
18. Shen, C.W., Chou, C.C.: Business process re-engineering in the logistics industry: a study of implementation, success factors, and performance. Enterprise Information Systems 4(1), 61–78 (2010)
19. Voříšek, J. et al.: Principles and Models of Enterprise IT Management, p. 446. Oeconomica, Prague (2008)
20. Voříšek, J., Feuerlicht, G.: The Impact of New Trends in the Delivery and Utilization of Enterprise ICT on Supplier and User Organizations. In: Amant, K. (ed.) IT Outsourcing: Concepts, Methodologies, Tools, and Application. Infromation Science Reference, pp. 2303–2316 (2009)
21. Voříšek, J., Dunn, D.: Management of Business Informatics – Opportunities, Threats, Solutions. In: Systems Integration 2001, Prague, pp. 665–677 (2001), http://si.vse.cz/archive/index.asp?volume=2001
22. Voříšek, J., Jandoš, J., Feuerlicht, G.: SPSPR Model – Framework for ICT Services Management. Journal of Systems Integration 2(2), 3–10 (2011), http://www.si-journal.org/index.php/JSI/article/viewFile/85/58

Towards Diversity in ERP Education – The Example of an ERP Curriculum

Christian Leyh[1], Susanne Strahringer[1], and Axel Winkelmann[2]

[1] Technische Universität Dresden,
Chair of Information Systems, esp. IS in Manufacturing and Commerce
[2] University of Muenster,
European Research Center for Information Systems
{christian.leyh,susanne.strahringer}@tu-dresden.de,
{axel.winkelmann}@ercis.uni-muenster.de

Abstract. The need for providing ERP knowledge by teaching the concepts of ERP systems in university courses and, above all, the possibilities of using these systems themselves in courses are frequently discussed in literature. There are many ERP systems with different technologies and philosophies available on the market. Here, the universities face the challenge of choosing the "right" number of ERP systems, how to include them in the curriculum and to what extent / how deep each of the systems should be taught. Within this paper, as a curriculum example, we will describe the ERP curriculum at the / Dresden University of Technology / Technische Universität Dresden, its different ERP courses, and how the ERP systems are provided and taught.

Keywords: ERP systems, curriculum, course descriptions, teaching, diversity, problem-oriented learning, education.

1 Introduction

Today, standardized enterprise resource planning (ERP) systems are being used in a majority of enterprises. For example, more than 92 percent of all German industrial enterprises use ERP systems [1]. Due to this strong demand, there are many ERP systems with different technologies and philosophies available on the market [2]. Therefore, the ERP market is strongly fragmented, especially when focusing on systems targeting small and medium-sized enterprises (SMEs) [3]. The growing multitude of software manufacturers and systems is making it more and more difficult for enterprises that use or want to use ERP systems to find the "right" software and then to hire the appropriate specialists for the selected system. Also, for future investment decisions concerning the adoption, upgrade, or alteration of ERP systems, it is important to possess the appropriate specialized knowledge and skills in the enterprise [2], [4]. This is essential since errors during the selection, implementation, or maintenance of ERP systems can cause financial disadvantages or disasters, leading to insolvencies of the affected enterprises (e.g., [5], [6]). In order to prevent this from happening, it is necessary to strive for a sound education on ERP systems.

C. Møller and S. Chaudhry (Eds.): CONFENIS 2011, LNBIP 105, pp. 182–200, 2012.

This places the responsibility of transferring the specialized knowledge to their students and graduates on universities, in particular on university courses in the field of information systems [7].

Because of the increasing importance of ERP systems and their educational value, many universities use or want to apply ERP systems in university courses [8] to teach and demonstrate different concepts and processes [9]. To support these courses, some ERP manufacturers co-operate closely with universities and offer their systems and resources for academic teaching [10]. One of the goals of using ERP systems in courses is to prepare students for their career by giving them at least an introduction to ERP systems. A further goal, promoted by ERP manufacturers themselves (especially by making their systems available for university courses), is for students to learn about the products as early as possible since they, later as graduates, will work with these systems or will hold enterprise positions that influence ERP investment decisions. Therefore, it is necessary for universities to offer the appropriate systems, processes, and suitable courses for their students [11], [12], [13].

The need for providing this knowledge through university courses and, above all, the possibilities of using these actual systems in courses are frequently discussed in literature (e.g., [12], [14], [15], [16], [17], [18]). These discussions clearly point out that ERP systems are or should be an important component of university curricula in information system-related subjects and courses. However, this is not a trivial task, as Noguera and Watson [19] discuss. Because there is no standardized approach, the choice of systems and their number, as well as the structure and number of ERP courses, differ from university to university [8]. For example, for teaching the respective systems, the lecturer has to be familiar with the system's concepts and its practical usage. Thus, the choice of one or more ERP system for a course strongly depends on the knowledge and experience of the lecturers. Additionally, the variety of ERP systems used in courses is limited by the manufacturers' willingness to provide their systems. This results in a situation in which only a small variety of systems and software manufacturers are represented at universities in spite of the heterogeneous ERP market.

In particular, the software manufacturer SAP is represented in numerous universities through its University Alliance program. With more than 400 partner universities participating in this program, SAP is probably the most widely used system in study courses worldwide [16], [20]. Smaller systems are rarely used in teaching; yet, a more diversified integration of ERP systems into education is advisable, especially from the viewpoint of SMEs [13], [21]. In addition, by including more than one ERP system in the curriculum, the students gain a broader overview of different ERP systems, the ERP market itself, and different ERP concepts and architectures. Furthermore, by teaching a diverse set of ERP systems, the students' awareness of functional approaches, process support, and interface ergonomics will increase. Additionally, by including ERP systems for smaller companies, the differences between SMEs and large-scale companies [22] will be illustrated to students because they are reflected in the appropriate design of the respective systems [3]. All these are reasons to strive for more diversity in ERP education.

However, at this point it is difficult to decide how many systems should be part of the curriculum and to what extent they should be taught. Of course, ERP systems and their concepts can also be described theoretically without direct system access. However, the learning experience and understanding are much better promoted through the use of real systems [23]. Yet, choosing the "right" number of ERP systems is difficult since too many systems can lead to student confusion or misunderstandings. Also, in-depth insights in selected systems are mandatory to ensure a deeper understanding of the concepts and constructs. Hence, it is not advisable to provide deep insights into too many ERP systems. Again, this would lead to student confusion or misunderstandings. Here, the universities face the challenge of how to include a couple of ERP systems in the curriculum and to what extent / how deep each of the systems should be taught.

The Dresden University of Technology / Technische Universität Dresden (TUD) – especially the Chair of Information Systems (IS in Manufacturing and Commerce) – has gained much experience with including a diverse set of ERP systems in its curriculum for students in Information Systems. Within this paper, we will describe the different courses and how the ERP systems are provided and taught. Therefore, the paper is structured as follows. Following this introduction, we provide the general design of the curriculum. The different IS programs are briefly described and a state of the art of teaching ERP systems at German universities is given. Afterwards, the respective ERP courses (lectures, projects, and seminars) are described in detail before an evaluation of the courses is given. Finally, we address limitations and summarize the overall curriculum design and major aspects.

2   Background and General Design of the Curriculum

2.1   Teaching ERP Systems at German Universities

For gaining an insight into the current ERP teaching at German universities, we conducted a survey among 92 university chairs [10]. Among those 92 respondents, 59 are teaching ERP topics. Our investigation resulted in a large variety of teaching methods, which are used to familiarize students with ERP knowledge and skills. The question on the employed teaching methods was mostly answered with "Lectures". Eighty-five percent of all the participants who are involved in ERP topics use ERP at least in their lectures. Practical exercises and case studies were mentioned by 36 and 29 participants (cp. Table 1). Therefore, lectures and practical exercises can be seen as the typical methods employed, whereas the other methods mentioned allow for a deeper learning experience. For example, case studies help students to not only understand enhanced ERP system functionality but also to strengthen their individual soft skills like problem-solving or teamwork. However, despite this variety of teaching methods, out of these 59 participants only 38 (64%) are using ERP systems practically (e.g., in computer lab exercises, projects, independent teaching formats, etc.). A majority of the participants who are teaching ERP systems practically are using SAP (35 out of 38; 92%) [10].

Table 1. Teaching methods (multiple answers allowed, n=59)

Teaching methods	Absolute frequency	Relative frequency (n= 59)
Lectures	50	85%
Practical exercises	36	61%
Case studies	29	49%
Projects	23	39%
Seminars	20	34%
Assignment paper	14	24%
Simulation games	4	7%
Other teaching methods	4	7%

Other ERP systems used are Microsoft Dynamics NAV and AX (39%), Semiramis (10%), and ProAlpha (10%). Mostly, more than one ERP system is used. Thus, many participants who use ERP systems in teaching employ different systems. This fact supports the demand mentioned in our introduction [10].

2.2   Aim of the ERP Curriculum at the Technische Universität Dresden

The role of knowledge as a strategic resource is well understood in the business world. However, the question of how to teach and to make best use of it still remains insufficiently answered [24]. For universities, there is always a small degree between academic "truth" (in terms of general, but too broad domain knowledge or theories) and practical skills (that may be outdated in a few months) [4]. Therefore, our ERP curriculum is based on the idea of providing theoretical knowledge about ERP systems and their concepts as well as practical abilities in using these systems for bachelor students and later on for master students.

In general, people pass several competence stages when they acquire knowledge. For example, in the Dreyfus model of skill acquisition, five stages of knowledge acquisition from novice to expert are distinguished [25]. Researchers agree that reflective practice is necessary in order to go through different stages of learning. It involves considering personal experiences in applying gained knowledge to practice while being coached by professional tutors [26]. According to the stages of maturity on the competence ladder [27], students have to go through different levels of competence acquisition in order to achieve sufficient knowledge and hence competency within their focused field of study. The views of North and Hornung [27] differ from learning about incoherent symbols and data without meaning to information that becomes knowledge in combination with certain experiences and in a specific context. Furthermore, the actual application of knowledge to know-how and its critical reflection, in terms of gaining competency, allows for the final goal of individually applying different methods, instruments, and experiences in a unique and hence competitive way (cp. Figure 1). This complements Kolb's experiential learning theory model that outlines four approaches towards grasping experience, namely

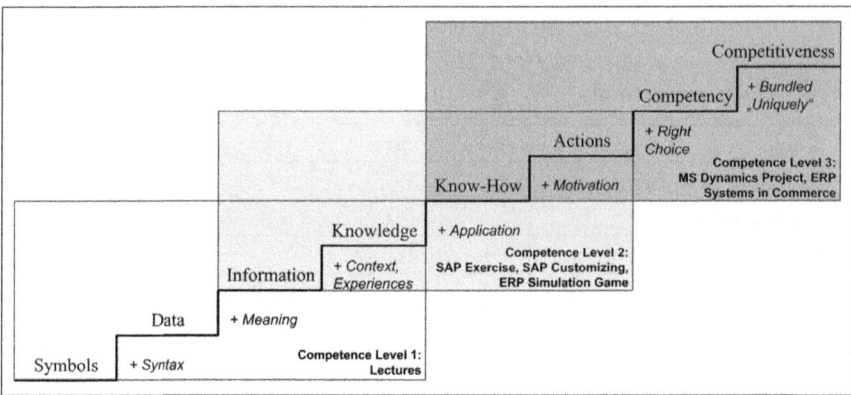

Fig. 1. Stages of maturity on the competence ladder with regard to the ERP curriculum (cp. [28], [29])

abstract conceptualization, reflective observation, active experimentation, and concrete experience [28].

Competence Level 1 consists of theoretical lectures on IS development and the usage of managerial IS, especially ERP systems. Aim of Competence Level 2 is the application of theoretical background based on SAP ERP 6.0 exercises, business processes, and customizing as well as on an SAP simulation game. Competence Level 3 seeks to transfer knowledge of various systems in depth (e.g., implementation of Microsoft Dynamics) and breadth (e.g., overview case studies on various medium-sized ERP systems).

Thus, in order to allow for a broad education combined with several deep insights, we decided on setting up an ERP curriculum with lectures, seminars, and projects in the Bachelor IS program and in the Master IS program at TUD.

It consists of different lectures where especially ERP topics are focused in the third and fourth semester as mandatory parts of the bachelor program. In combination with the lecture of the third semester, a mandatory hands-on exercise (SAP Exercise) is provided as well as an optional project seminar (MS Dynamics Project) in the second half of the third semester. Following the lectures of the fourth semester, in semester five another hands-on exercise is given (SAP Customizing). Within the master program two practical courses are included in the curriculum. Both courses take place in the first half of the first semester of the master program. The first course is a project seminar (ERP Systems in Commerce) that lasts the whole semester. The second course is an SAP-based simulation game (ERP Simulation Game), which takes place in the second half of the first semester.

Before the different courses and lectures are described in detail, a short overview of the mentioned bachelor and master programs is given in the following sections.

2.3   Bachelor IS Program at the Technische Universität Dresden

The Bachelor program in Information Systems at Dresden University of Technology / Technische Universität Dresden (TUD) is a six-semester program comprising 180 ECTS that lead to a "Bachelor of Science" degree. It is one of four bachelor programs the TUD faculty of business & economics offers. The IS program combines classes in Information Systems, Informatics, Mathematics, Business Administration, and Economics. Each area has to be attended and offers different types of classes such as lectures, exercises, seminars. In addition there is a module specifically intended to acquire soft skills during a mentoring program and two projects. In the fourth and fifth semester, students have to select two specialization modules (minor) from offerings in business and economics. However, there are electives within many of the other mandatory modules as well where students choose from a well-defined catalog of offerings. The program ends with the writing of a research-oriented bachelor thesis.

The ERP curriculum is integrated into two of the four information systems modules (IS track) that build on an introductory IS class in semester 1, which is an integral part of the four bachelor programs the faculty offers. The logic of the IS track is to reverse the order of a system lifecycle by starting with the intended outcome of information systems and then proceeding backwards step-by-step to what is required in order to achieve this outcome. Thus, there are three modules reversing the lifecycle logic that structure the IS track as follows:,

- Module 1 in semester 2: Adding value through information systems
  (6 credits, 2 lectures, 1 project)
- Module 2 in semester 3: Using information systems
  (9 credits, 1 lecture, 2 hands-on exercises, 1 project)
- Module 3 in semesters 4 & 5: Providing information systems
  (12 credits, 2 lectures, 1 hands-on exercise, 2 projects)
and one additional module with IS electives, that is
- Module 4 in semesters 5 & 6: Selected topics in information systems
  (6 credits, 2 courses from a catalog of offerings).

The ERP curriculum is mainly included in modules 2 and 3 and encompasses one of the hands-on exercises (SAP Exercise) and the project (MS Dynamics Project) in module 2 and parts of the lectures and one of the exercises (SAP Customizing) in module 3.

2.4   Master IS Program at the Technische Universität Dresden

The Master IS program is one of five master programs the TUD Faculty of Business & Economics offers. It provides students with the ability to identify and frame problems related to using and providing information systems and information technology in private and public companies and organizations, to analyze these problems by applying scientific methods, and to work out feasible solutions. The integration of Management and Informatics in the program allows students to identify, illustrate, and consider interdisciplinary coherences.

During the studies courses in Research Methodology, Additional Qualifications, an internship and a research seminar have to be attended. Students specialize in different fields by choosing six specializations, two from the field of information systems, two from informatics and two from any specialization the school offers (including IS). Thus students can either go for a broader range of areas by choosing two IS specializations only or heavily concentrate on information systems by choosing four IS specializations. Each specialization consists of two modules with 6 and 9 credits. The IS specializations are:

- Application Systems in Business and Administration
- Business Intelligence
- Information Management
- Systems Development

The ERP curriculum is mainly included in the first specialization which is the one chosen by most of the IS students. Within this, "ERP Simulation Game" and "ERP Systems in Commerce" take place.

The study program ends with the writing of the research-oriented master thesis.

3   Description of the ERP Curriculum's Elements

In this section we will describe the respective ERP courses. We will focus on the practical parts of the ERP curriculum – the hands-on exercises, the project seminars, and the ERP simulation game. Additionally, we will refer each course to the competence ladder and its different competence levels (cp. Figure 1). We will not describe the lectures, since within the lectures "common" ERP topics (e.g., packaged vs. home-grown applications, ERP architecture, ERP selection and implementation, license models, etc.) are taught.

3.1   SAP Exercise – Competence Level 2 (Bachelor IS Program)

SAP Exercise is a hands-on exercise. It takes place within the third semester of the Bachelor IS program and is a mandatory course.

For this exercise, we chose SAP as one of the big players because our university was already a member of the SAP University Alliance Program. The access to the system (SAP ECC 6.0) was easy to establish. Also, detailed instruction materials and click-by-click process descriptions needed for the course were provided through SAP´s University Competence Centers (UCC). Furthermore, the lecturers were already familiar with this kind of course and with the corresponding system.

Since the students learned some theoretical basic knowledge about ERP systems within the lectures, the students got a first practical hands-on understanding of one ERP system while attending SAP Exercise. The scenario for SAP Exercise is part of the materials and therefore, it was predetermined because of the click-by-click instructions provided by the UCC. In order to gain access to the detailed instructions, one has to be a member of the SAP University Alliance Program. Table 2 shows a short compendium of the scenario.

The three parts (production, controlling, and retail) of this course were performed in three separate sessions, which took place in the computer lab of the university. For every session a time slot of three hours was scheduled. This was enough time to let the students perform the processes at their own pace.

Table 2. Scenario for SAP Exercise (compendium)

Generic production process	Create a stock of materials Create bill of materials Create routings Generate a production order Assembly of the individual parts Assembly of the whole product
Controlling Case Study	Create Cost Centers Plan the Number of Employees Plan Primary Cost Inputs Plan Internal Activity Inputs Automatic Price Calculation Create Work Centre Integrate Work Centre in Routing Perform New Product Cost Estimate
Generic retail process	Create master data for customers and vendors Enter a framework contract Create Sales Order Create Production Order Create Purchase Order Outbound Delivery with Order Reference Create Transfer Order for Delivery Note

Before the beginning of each session a lecturer gave a short overview of the process which should be performed during the session. Additionally, one or two lecturers (depending on the number of students) stayed in the lab during the whole session to provide helpful advice or solve problems if the students had done a wrong click, forgot to enter some data, etc. Furthermore, before the three sessions took place a "navigation-session" was offered to the students during which they could learn how to work with an SAP system. This was optional, but the majority of the students who did not have any experience with SAP participated. For example, students who had worked with SAP during internships did not attend this "pre-session".

A more detailed description of the course and the approach of setting up this course can be found in [21].

3.2   MS Dynamics Project – Competence Level 3 (Bachelor IS Program)

MS Dynamics Project is an optional project seminar in the third semester of the Bachelor IS program. Students who attended SAP Exercise can take on this project seminar to deepen their gained ERP knowledge. For this seminar, we chose Microsoft as manufacturer of ERP systems for small and medium-sized enterprises. Even though Microsoft has a university program, too – the so-called Microsoft Business Solutions Academic Alliance (MBSAA) – detailed instruction materials are not provided. Instead, access to the ERP systems of Microsoft (Microsoft Dynamics NAV and Microsoft Dynamics AX) as well as to other Microsoft Business Solutions are provided without fees. Therefore, in this course the participating students had to evaluate the functionalities of Microsoft Dynamics NAV 5.0 (winter semester 2009 / 2010). By repeating this course in winter semester 2010 / 2011 we changed the system to Microsoft Dynamics AX 2009. There is no need for changing the system within this course from a learner perspective. However, from a lecturer's perspective this allows for gaining more experience with different systems (see for a more detailed argumentation why we chose to change the system in [21]).

For MS Dynamics Project, the chosen scenario contains a generic retail process that has to be examined by the students. Additionally, a generic production process that contains the assembly of a product consisting of individual parts was added to the scenario. Table 3 gives an overview of the scenario. The complete scenario for MS Dynamics Project in English and German can be requested from the first author.

Table 3. Scenario for MS Dynamics Project (compendium)

Generic production process	Create a stock of materials Create bill of materials Generate a production order Assembly of the individual parts Assembly of the whole product
Generic retail process	Create master data for customers and vendors Enter a framework contract (1,000 motorcycle helmets for 299 Euro each) Normal purchase price 349 Euro each Order 150 motorcycle helmets for next month for 299 Euro each Supplier sends a delivery notification Supplier delivers 150 motorcycle helmets that have to be checked and stored A customer asks for an offer for 10 motorcycle helmets The customer orders 8 motorcycle helmets relating to the initial offer Take order amount from the warehouse and ship to the customer

By providing the scenario, the students should be able to identify the processes that have to be performed within the ERP system and therefore to define the necessary work packages. This enables them to organize their teams for themselves. Furthermore, additional literature is helpful to compensate possible gaps in the students' knowledge (e.g., for retail literature, [30], [31], [32]). During a kick-off meeting we described the organizational basics and general conditions of the course as well as the idea of the scenario and the tasks that had to be fulfilled.

During the course, participants worked independently in small groups on the given processes with their ERP system. The students were given two months (until the beginning of the fourth semester) to evaluate the ERP system and to write the required documentations. There was no training for the students by the ERP manufacturers. Once they had access to the system, the students independently performed the initial skill adaptation training. The mentoring of the lecturers was only required for individual group meetings, during which the teams could ask questions concerning technical aspects or problems with regard to the content of the scenario. Students had to evaluate the ERP systems based on the requirements of the scenario. They had to enter all necessary data in order to properly document the functionality later and had to reproduce the processes based on the functionalities of their ERP systems. If some aspects of the scenario were not supported by the system because of missing functions, students mentioned this in their written documentation. Access to the systems was granted during the kick-off meeting. There, the students had to install the system on their own laptops (Microsoft Dynamics NAV 5.0). For Microsoft Dynamics AX 2009, we provided access to the system through the computer labs with an installation on faculty servers. Afterwards, the students had to organize themselves to fulfill the tasks.

A more detailed description of the course and the approach of setting up this course can be found in [21].

3.3   SAP Customizing – Competence Level 2 (Bachelor IS Program)

SAP Customizing is a hands-on exercise, too. It takes place during the second half of the fifth semester of the Bachelor IS program and is a mandatory course.

For this exercise, we chose SAP, too, since all of the students in this semester as well as the lecturers were familiar with this system.

Since the students learned some theoretical basic knowledge about tailoring ERP systems within the lectures of the fourth semester, this course gives a hands-on understanding of how to configure / customize a specific ERP system. The scenario for SAP Customizing, again, is part of the materials provided from the UCC and therefore, it was predetermined because we referred mainly to the provided click-by-click instructions.

Contrary to SAP Exercise, this course also consists of some theoretical parts. In general, three different components are part of this course. The scenario deals with a smaller company that is inherited from a large multi-national enterprise. Therefore, the first part of the course is to understand the different organizational structures of the two companies. Additionally, the students have to identify the different organizational units of the SAP system that refer to the companies' structures. Afterwards, the students have to perform the configuration of the companies within the SAP system practically by using a click-by-click instruction.

The third part of this course sums up both previous parts. Here, the students get another (shorter) scenario similar to the previous scenario. Again, they have to identify the necessary organizational units and perform the configuration within the SAP system. However, for this part, we do not provide any detailed instruction materials. The students have to "use" the knowledge learned during the other parts and have to work on their own.

The parts of this course were performed in three separate sessions (3 hours each), which took place in the computer lab of the university. Within the first session a strong interaction between the students and the lecturers is necessary, to ensure that the students understand the scenario correctly and that they identify the "right" organizational units. Students complete parts two and three at their own pace. Additionally, one or two lecturers (depending on the number of students) stayed in the lab during the whole session to provide helpful advice or solve problems if the students had done a wrong click, forgot to enter some data, etc.

3.4   ERP Simulation Game – Competence Level 2 (Master IS Program)

This course takes place in the first semester of the master program. As the course title indicates, this course is based on a simulation game, originally designed by academics of the HEC Montreal. Contrary to other simulation games, this game includes SAP as ERP system to handle the business activities and processes [33], [34].

Using a continuous-time simulation, students have to run their business with a real-life ERP (SAP ECC 6.0) system. The students are divided in teams of 3 to 4 members. They have to operate a firm in a make-to-stock manufacturing supply chain (manufacturing game) and must interact with suppliers and customers by sending and receiving orders, delivering their products, and completing the whole cash-to-cash cycle. [35]. Additionally, for German universities, a "distribution game" was developed that incorporates reduced functionality of the make-to-stock manufacturing game. We use this "light" version of the game for introductory purposes. The students have to play this game before playing the extended version.

A simulation program was developed to automate some of the processes to reduce the game's complexity and the effort required of the students. For example, the sales process, parts of the production process, and parts of the procurement process are automated. Automation is especially applied to steps where no business decisions are involved. Using standard and customized reports in SAP, students must analyze their transactional data to make business decisions and ensure the profitability of their operations [34], [35].

To get access to the game, the university has to be a member of the UCC program of SAP. Then again, detailed instruction materials as well as training for the lecturers are provided.

In winter semester 2010 / 2011 we included this game in the curriculum for the first time. The students had to play the game three times. For every session a time slot of three hours was scheduled. Within the first session, the distribution game was played to allow the students to "get in touch" with the game. Afterwards, the students continued to play the manufacturing game with reduced complexity and functionality within the second session, before playing the manufacturing game with full functionality in the third session. Before the games started, a lecture was given as introduction to the respective game and to its processes in order to ensure an overview for the students. After the introduction one or two lecturers (depending on the number of students) stayed in the lab during the whole session to provide helpful advice or solve problems.

A more detailed description of the course and the approach of setting up this course can be found in [33], [34], [35].

3.5   ERP Systems in Commerce – Competence Level 3 (Master IS Program)

This course is based on a project seminar described by Winkelmann and Matzner [4] and its enhancement in Winkelmann and Leyh [13]. It takes place in the first semester of the master program. Similar to MS Dynamics Project, a problem-oriented, learner-centered approach [18], [36] is used. With case studies, the students train themselves independently in small groups to use different ERP systems and present their findings and experiences through live demos of the respective system, for example. The seminar participants can increase their knowledge through investigating different ERP systems. We have enhanced the original concept [4] and simultaneously applied their model to three different universities [13].

We chose a scenario of existing processes from enterprises that served as a starting point for the students' evaluation. At the end of the semester, after the analysis of the respective systems, students had to present their results. We divided the students into groups of 2-6 each. Every group had to fully explore one ERP system and take a look at the other systems in order to derive questions for the final presentations. Each team had to present its ERP system in a similar, structured way, but the detailed focus and design of the presentation was incumbent upon each team.

This project has been part of the curriculum for three years. It is taking place each winter semester at the universities of Dresden, Koblenz-Landau, and Muenster. During a kick-off meeting, at the beginning of the seminar, we described the organizational basics and general conditions of the seminar as well as the idea of the scenario and the tasks that had to be fulfilled. In analogy to MS Dynamics Project, during the seminar, participants worked independently in small groups on the given processes with their respective ERP system. At the end of the semester, they provided a written evaluation of "their" ERP system. Additionally, a presentation of the systems had to be done. Presentations in a two-day block meeting were considered practical, since the ERP systems and their functionality were presented in a condensed way during a short period of time and allowed immediate comparison of the different systems. Therefore, each team had 60 minutes for the presentation and an additional 30 minutes for a discussion and questions. For the presentations, the participation of all students was mandatory. This guaranteed that learning outcomes did not remain limited to one system but were extended to the other ERP systems.

Again, there was no training for the students by the ERP manufacturers. The students independently performed initial skill adaptation training after they got access to the systems. Contact with the manufacturers was only necessary if a technical problem evolved and prevented further processing of the scenario (e.g., missing access rights, running out of the license). The mentoring of the lecturers was only required for individual group meetings. Since we offered the e-mail addresses of the teams from the other universities to each ERP team, they were able to solve most technical and economic questions among themselves. However, we also had to send questions to the ERP vendors. During the different semesters, we changed the set of ERP systems used. Therefore, Figure 2 shows the different systems per winter semester (WS) with the access possibilities.

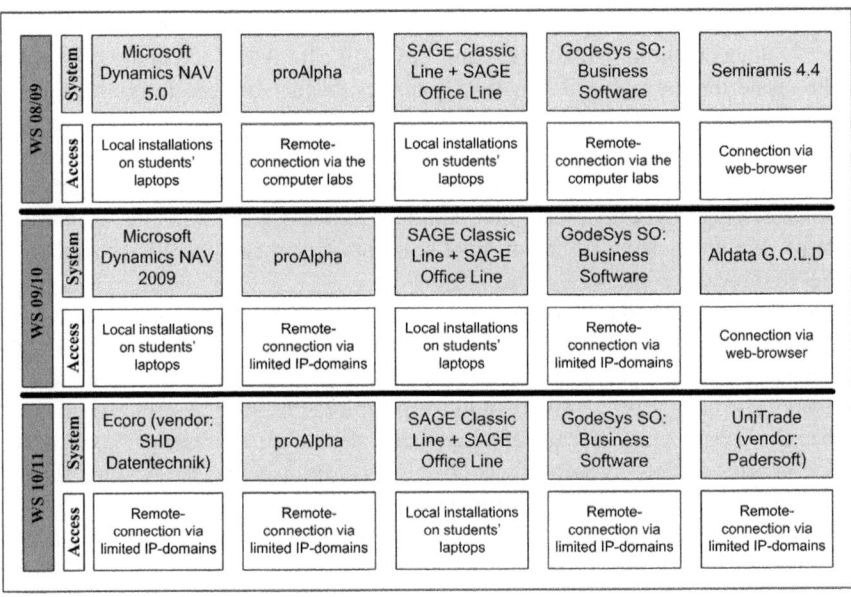

Fig. 2. Overview of the ERP systems per semester

The ERP manufacturers were asked for remote access to their system and most of the manufacturers provided this access. The Microsoft Dynamics and SAGE systems were made available locally on computers at the universities or were installed on the students' notebooks. The appropriate licenses and full versions of the ERP systems were released free of charge for the period of the seminar.

The scenario chosen contained generic and specific retail processes that were examined by the students. Additionally, a generic production process that contained the assembly of a product consisting of individual parts was added to the scenario. Table 4 gives a general overview of the processes and tasks that make up the scenario.

Table 4. Scenario for ERP Systems in Commerce (compendium)

Generic retail process	Enter a framework contract (1,000 PCs / 299 Euro each) Normal purchase price 349 Euro each Order 150 PCs for next month for 299 Euro each Supplier sends a delivery notification Supplier delivers 150 PCs that must be checked / stored A customer asks for an offer for 10 PCs The customer orders 8 PCs relating to the initial offer Take order amount from the warehouse and ship to the customer
Specific retail process	Check for basic price conditions, transaction-based conditions, and subsequent price conditions for purchase and sales (conditions such as basic bonuses, market share increase bonuses, listing bonuses, allowance adjustment bonuses, etc., are given in the scenario) Check if the system is capable of conditions depending on specifics such as regions, customer loyalty, etc. Check for calculation possibilities in purchase (different gross and net costs, etc.) Evaluate warehouse structures in terms of organization, areas, and attributes such as restrictions in weight or article characters (explosives, chemicals, etc.) Check whether it is possible to split sales offers into orders Check whether it is possible to deliver to different stores with different prices but send all bills once a month
Generic production process	Create a stock of materials Create bill of materials Generate a production order Assembly of the individual parts Assembly of the whole product

A more detailed description of the course and the approach of setting up this course can be found in [13].

4   Course Evaluation

4.1   Students' Perspective

Since an evaluation of seminars and/or courses in general is of high importance for the improvement of teaching concepts [8], the same questionnaires were handed out to the students at all practical courses. Within the lectures we did an evaluation, too. But these evaluation results will not be part of this chapter. We will focus on the evaluation of the practical ERP courses and the competence levels 2 and 3 only.

The questionnaires were filled out anonymously. This questionnaire served to identify possible weaknesses and opportunities for improvements with respect to the courses' realizations, the scenarios, and the support from the lecturers as well as the adequateness of the respective ERP systems. Also, the positive aspects that should be repeated in the next cycles could be emphasized. The questionnaire consisted of 21 questions based on scale evaluations (grades 1-5), yes/no, and free text answers. Some selected evaluation results are shown in Table 5. The presented results are from the evaluation of the course in winter semester 2010 / 2011. Additionally, feedback discussions were conducted with some of the teams separately to gather further suggestions from the students. This was especially done at the end of MS Dynamics Project and ERP Systems in Commerce.

Table 5. Results of the course evaluations of winter semester 2010 / 2011

	Average grade per course (1=very high, 5=very low)				
	SAP Exercise Level 2 (n=30)	MS Dynamics Project Level 3 (n=12)	SAP Customizing Level 2 (n=26)	ERP Simulation Game Level 2 (n=10)	ERP Systems in Commerce Level 3 (n=12)
Knowledge **before** course	3.90	3.5	2.65	2.70	2.67
Interest in ERP issues **before** course	2.47	2.17	2.46	2.50	2.50
Interest in ERP issues **after** course	2.47	1.83	2.62	2.40	2.17
Motivation for thoughts and opinion building	3.37	2.17	3.24	2.10	2.58
Increase of ERP knowledge in general	2.43	3.17	2.35	2.20	1.92
Increase of knowledge regarding the respective ERP system	2.63	2.33	2.35	2.20	2.08
Increase of knowledge in comparison to other seminars	2.92	2.67	2.72	1.90	2.45
Usefulness of the scenario	2.50	2.00	2.24	2.10	2.18
Adequateness of the respective ERP system	2.27	1.83	2.09	1.78	2.00

Table 5. (*continued*)

Level of difficulty (2=**much too high**, 0=**reasonable**, -2=**much too low**)	-0.37	0.17	-0,08	-0.10	0.42
Effort needed (2=**much too high**, 0=**reasonable**, -2=**much too low**)	0.13	0.00	0.00	0.00	0.58
Effort needed in comparison to other courses (2=**much too high, 0=reasonable,** -2=**much too low**)	-0.50	-0.50	-0.08	-0.40	0.67

Instead of a detailed empirical evaluation that would not be statistically relevant because of the small seminar sizes, our goal is to report on students' and lecturers' experiences in order to make this knowledge available for other universities. As seen in Table 5, the students emphasize an increase in interest in ERP issues. Only, the hands-on exercises do not lead to such an increase. The level of difficulty is seen as quite reasonable for all courses within Competence Level 2 (cp. Figure 2). For the two courses of Competence Level 3, the students feel the level of difficulty a little bit too high. Contrary to that fact, the effort for these courses in comparison to other courses is seen as quite reasonable. Only the effort for ERP Systems in Commerce is seen as too high.

Especially MS Dynamics Project and ERP Systems in Commerce turned out to be very popular among students. However for ERP Systems in Commerce (since this was not mandatory), we always feared attracting too few students, which would imply skipping some of the systems. This would have meant disappointing some of the ERP manufacturers who had invested time in advance to our seminar

4.2   Lecturer's Perspective

The inclusion of the different lectures and hands-on exercises with the addition of "self-learning" ERP courses (MS Dynamics Project and ERP Systems in Commerce) was a good opportunity to enhance the information systems curriculum at the TUD. For the students, this not only enabled a deeper insight in specific ERP systems for large-scaled enterprises but for small and medium-sized enterprises as well.

A further benefit of MS Dynamics Project lies in the documentation of the respective ERP system produced by the students. Thereby, the lecturers obtained click-by-click instructions that can be used for further course enhancements or additional hands-on exercises. If the teams perform well in MS Dynamics Project, these documentations can be used without considerable effort for adjustment of the materials.

For ERP Systems in Commerce, the expansion of the seminar to three universities was a good opportunity for the lecturers to foster the exchange with colleagues in the same research area. They could explore and discuss in which ways the students of the other universities were educated in the field of information systems. Additionally, this expansion also created a competitive pressure among the lecturers because every lecturer wanted his or her teams to perform very well. This increased the motivation for a good and high-quality mentoring of the teams at every university. Therefore, the expansion of the seminar to more than one university was regarded as a good idea among the professors and lecturers of the respective universities.

Also during the different courses, the lecturers (professors and assistants) gained a valuable insight into ERP systems (some of them previously not known). Therefore, the courses also offer a chance to increase the individual ERP horizon.

5   Conclusion and Limitations

The idea of the integration of different ERP lectures and courses in the IS curriculum at TUD was to enable an insight into different ERP concepts and systems for the students. With this, a broad overview of ERP topics, functionalities, and architectural approaches is given as well as a deep practical insight into selected ERP systems. Therefore, students become familiar with using systems. Although we regard this type of course combination aiming at more diversity in ERP education as very successful, there are some limitations too. First, we are only able to handle some ERP systems and are not able to fully cover the market. However, we do not consider this a severe disadvantage. Furthermore, not all ERP systems on the market are suitable for such an ERP course. For example, older systems are often very complicated in their installation procedure. Also, ERP systems for large companies may not be very suitable for MS Dynamics Project and for the ERP Systems in Commerce as they may be too complex for unsupervised student exercises. We tried to keep the workload at the same level for all IS students especially for the groups in the "self-learning" courses. However, some groups may have to invest less work due to better ERP documentation, better usability, or more help from Internet forums.

In conclusion, for both students and lecturers/tutors, the integration of different ERP systems in the curriculum offers a good opportunity to gain a deeper insight into ERP systems and extend their knowledge about a variety of ERP systems, sharpening awareness of system differences.

Future steps are repeating the different courses in the respective semesters and varying the ERP system used in ERP Systems in Commerce in each cycle. Additionally, we are going to include the distribution game of ERP Simulation Game in the curriculum of IS students in the Bachelor Program as well as in the business studies curriculum.

References

1. Konradin Business GmbH: Konradin ERP-Studie 2009: Einsatz von ERP-Lösungen in der Industrie. Konradin Mediengruppe, Leinfelden-Echterdingen, Germany (2009)
2. Winkelmann, A.: Dynamic Reconfiguration of ERP Systems - Design of Information Systems and Information Models – Post-Doctoral Thesis. Muenster, Germany (2010)
3. Winkelmann, A., Klose, K.: Experiences while selecting, adapting and implementing ERP systems in SMEs: a case study. In: Proceedings of the 14th Americas Conference on Information Systems (AMCIS 2008), Paper 257, Toronto, Ontario, Canada, August 14-17 (2008)
4. Winkelmann, A., Matzner, M.: Teaching medium sized ERP systems – a problem-based learning approach. In: Papadopoulos, G.A., Wojtkowski, W., Wojtkowski, G., Wrycza, S., Zupancic, J. (eds.) Information Systems Development: Towards a Service Provision Society, pp. 891–901. Springer, New York (2009)
5. Barker, T., Frolick, M.N.: ERP Implementation Failure: a case study. Information Systems Management 20(4), 43–49 (2003)
6. Hsu, K., Sylvestre, J., Sayed, E.N.: Avoiding ERP Pitfalls. The Journal of Corporate Accounting & Finance 17(4), 67–74 (2006)
7. Venkatesh, V.: One-Size-Does-Not-Fit-All: Teaching MBA students different ERP implementation strategies. Journal of Information Systems Education 19(2), 141–146 (2008)
8. Seethamraju, R.: Enterprise systems software in business school curriculum – Evaluation of design and delivery. Journal of Information Systems Education 18(1), 69–83 (2007)
9. Magal, S.R., Word, J.: Essentials of Business Processes and Information Systems. Wiley Publishing, Hoboken (2009)
10. Leyh, C., Winkelmann, A., Lu, J.: Exploring the diversity of ERP systems – An empirical insight into system usage in academia. In: Proceedings of the 17th Annual Americas Conf. on Information Systems (AMCIS 2011), Detroit, USA (2011)
11. Brehm, N., Haak, L., Peters, D.: Using FERP Systems to introduce web service-based ERP Systems in higher education. In: Abramowicz, W., Flejter, D. (eds.) Business Information Systems Workshops: BIS 2009 International Workshops, Poznan, Poland, April 27-29, Springer, Berlin (2009)
12. Fedorowicz, J., Gelinas, U.J.J., Usoff, C., Hachey, G.: Twelve tips for successfully integrating enterprise systems across the curriculum. Journal of Information Systems Education 15(3), 235–244 (2004)
13. Winkelmann, A., Leyh, C.: Teaching ERP systems: A multi-perspective view on the ERP system market. Journal of Information Systems Education 21(2), 233–240 (2010)
14. Antonucci, Y.L., Corbitt, G., Stewart, G., Harris, A.L.: Enterprise systems education: Where are we? Where are we going? Journal of Information Systems Education 15(3), 227–234 (2004)
15. Boyle, T.A., Strong, S.E.: Skill requirements of ERP graduates. Journal of Information Systems Education 17(4), 403–412 (2006)
16. Hawking, P., McCarthy, B., Stein, A.: Second wave ERP education. Journal of Information Systems Education 15(3), 327–332 (2004)
17. Peslak, A.R.: A twelve-step, multiple course approach to teaching enterprise resource planning. Journal of Information Systems Education 16(2), 147–155 (2005)
18. Stewart, G., Rosemann, M., Hawking, P.: Collaborative ERP curriculum developing using industry process models. In: Proceedings of the 6th Annual Americas Conference on Information Systems (AMCIS 2000), Long Beach, CA, USA, August 10-13 (2000)

19. Noguera, J.H., Watson, E.F.: Effectiveness of using an enterprise system to teach process-centered concepts in business education. In: Proceedings of the 5th Annual Americas Conference on Information Systems (AMCIS 1999), Milwaukee, WI, USA, August 13-15 (1999)
20. Pellerin, R., Hadaya, P.: Proposing a new framework and an innovative approach to teaching reengineering and ERP implementation concepts. Journal of Information Systems Education 19(1), 65–73 (2008)
21. Leyh, C.: From teaching large-scale ERP systems to additionally teaching medium-sized systems. In: Proceedings of the 11th International Conference on Informatics Education and Research (AIS SIG-ED IAIM 2010), St. Louis, MO, USA, December 10-12 (2010)
22. Welsh, J.-A., White, J.-F.: A small business is not a little big business. Harvard Business Review 59(4), 18–32 (1981)
23. Watson, E.E., Schneider, H.: Using ERP systems in education. Communications of the AIS 1(2) (1999)
24. Neumann, G., Tomé, E.: Functional Concept for a Web-Based Knowledge Impact and IC Reporting Portal. Electronic Journal of Knowledge Management 8(1), 119–128 (2010)
25. Dreyfus, S.E., Dreyfus, H.L.: A five-stage model of the mental activities involved in directed skill acquisition. Working Paper. University of California, Berkeley (1980)
26. Schoen, D.: The Reflective Practitioner: How professionals think in action. Temple Smith, London (1983)
27. North, K., Hornung, T.: The Benefits of Knowledge Management – Results of the German Award 'Knowledge Manager 2002'. Journal of Universal Computer Science 9(3), 463–471 (2003)
28. Kolb, D.: Experiential learning: Experience as the source of learning and development. Prentice-Hall, Englewood Cliffs (1984)
29. Becker, J., Weiss, B., Winkelmann, A.: A Multi-Perspective Approach to Business Process Management in the Financial Sector. In: Proceedings of the Thirty-First International Conference on Information Systems (ICIS 2010), St. Louis, USA, December 12-15 (2010)
30. Becker, J., Uhr, W., Vering, O., Ehlers, L., Kosilek, E., Lohse, M., Neumann, S.: Retail information systems based on SAP products. Springer, Heidelberg (2001)
31. Mason, J.B., Burns, D.J.: Retailing. Cengage Custom Publishing, Houston (1998)
32. Sternquist, B.: International Retailing. Fairchild Books & Visuals, London (2007)
33. Seethamraju, R.: Enhancing Student Learning of Enterprise Integration and Business Process Orientation through an ERP Business Simulation Game. Journal of Information Systems Education 22(1), 19–30 (2011)
34. Leger, P.M.: Using a Simulation Game Approach to Teach Enterprise Resource Planning Concepts. Journal of Information Systems Education 17(4), 441–448 (2006)
35. ERPSim Lab - HEC Montreal, http://erpsim.hec.ca/
36. Saulnier, B.M., Landry, J.P., Longenecker, H.E.J., Wagner, T.A.: From teaching to learning: Learner-centered teaching and assessment in information systems education. Journal of Information Systems Education 19(2), 169–174 (2008)

Effects of Enterprise Technology on Supply Chain Collaboration and Performance

Ling Li

Department of Information Technology and Decision Sciences
Old Dominion University
Norfolk, VA, USA

Abstract. Supply chain collaboration has received increasing attention from scholars and practitioners in recent years. However, our understanding of how enterprise information technology facilitates supply chain collaboration is still very limited. This paper extends the theory established in enterprise information technology and supply chain collaboration literature.

Keywords: enterprise information technology, supply chain collaboration, supply chain performance.

1   Introduction

Enterprise Information technology integrates business functional areas and links suppliers and customers of the entire supply chain. Today, e-solutions are a must-have weapon for a supply chain to improve collaboration to compete in the global market. Equipped with integrated information technology, many manufacturing producers have adopted the collaborative strategy on production planning, demand forecasting and inventory replenishment to provide the end user what he wants, how he wants it, and when he wants it.

This study is to investigate the effects of enterprise technology on supply chain collaboration and performance. Structural equation modeling is employed to test the multi-phased conceptual model which is shown in Figure 1. Enterprise technology assimilation is indicated using two factors: enterprise technology use for exploitation (F1) and enterprise technology use for exploration (F2). Based on the theory of organizational learning [1] [2], we define enterprise technology assimilation for exploitation as the use of technology for the execution of supply china routine processes. Similarly, enterprise technology assimilation for exploration is defined as the implementation of unstructured and strategic supply chain activities. Planning collaboration (F3) and forecasting and replenishing coordination (F4) are considered as supply chain collaboration measures. Collaboration and coordination in planning is defined as jointly plan for supply chain key activities [3] [4]; while operational collaboration and coordination are defined as information sharing to achieve efficient task execution [5]. Operational benefits (F5) are defined as first-order benefits that

C. Møller and S. Chaudhry (Eds.): CONFENIS 2011, LNBIP 105, pp. 201–210, 2012.

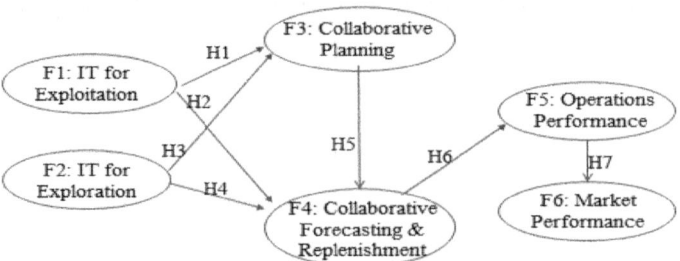

Fig. 1. Research Model

arise directly from effective supply chain collaboration. Conversely, benefits for market performance (F6) arise through better operational performance supported by supply chain collaboration [6].

2   Background

2.1   Adaptive Process Concept toward Enterprise Information Technology Assimilation

The exploitation of enterprise information technology in supply chain collaboration involves using enterprise technology to facilitate routine business practices, such as order receiving, order tracking, new accounts establishment, existing account maintenance, invoicing, material transaction, etc. These activities refine existing business patterns with benefits occurring over a short to immediate time period [7]. With enterprise technology, users are able to improve operational efficiency through measures such as increasing standardization or tightening process control. Furthermore, the exploitation approach tends to result in operational benefits such as lead time reduction and inventory accuracy [5]. Firms oriented to exploitation, use enterprise information technology for information sharing, channel collaboration, and integrated forecasting and inventory replenishment. For example, Cisco outsources more than 50% of its production capacity. Using enterprise information technology, it effectively process orders online which results in enhanced ability to rapidly respond to the demand changes in the supply chain [5].

The exploration of enterprise technology, on the other hand, diffuses beyond the organization and involves uncovering new methods to solve long-term supply chain collaboration problems. Exploration is defined by terms such as search, innovation, and discovery, with benefits occurring over a longer time horizon and beyond the organization [1] [8]. Unlike the exploitation approach that place emphasis on efficiency, consistency and process control, the exploration approach involves risk taking and experimentation. Firms oriented toward exploration of enterprise information technology develop new business models and strategies that enable them to expand new markets and develop new products [8]. For example, relied on enterprise technology to share business information with vendors and customers, Dell

Computer has gained market share by building customized computers using the Internet as an order fulfillment vehicle. Dell assembles computers but outsources most of the parts and components it needs for production. Outsourcing has made collaborative planning, forecasting, and replenishment a vital vehicle to implementing mass customization strategy in supply chain.

2.2   Enterprise Technology and Supply Chain Collaboration

A supply chain is as strong as its weakest link. The notion here focuses on strong and effective collaboration. The fundamental point that distinguishes supply chain management and traditional materials management is how the collaboration of trading partners is managed. Thus, collaboration is a most talked about issue in today's global supply chain management. In recent years, retailers have initiated collaborative agreements with their supply chain partners to establish on-going planning, forecasting, and replenishment process. This initiative is called collaborative planning, forecasting, and replenishment (CPFR). The Association for Operations Management defines CPFR as follows:

"Collaboration process whereby supply chain trading partners can jointly plan key supply chain activities from production and delivery of raw materials to production and delivery of final products to end customers" - *The Association for Operations Management*[1].

The enabler of CPFR is information technology. The earlier versions of CPFR are Electronic Data Interchange (EDI), bar coding, and vendor-managed inventory (VIM). The more current version of CPFR takes advantage of enterprise information technology. For example, Wal-Mart has engaged in CPFR with about 600 trading partners [9]. The use of enterprise technology has permitted strong supply chain coordination for production planning, demand forecasting, order fulfillment, and customer relationship management. Published studies have consistently support the effective result through association between enterprise technology use and organizational coordination [3] [5].

Supply chain collaboration has been referred to as the driving force of effective supply chain management [10] [11]. The objective of supply chain collaboration is to improve demand forecast and inventory management, with the right product delivered at right time to the right location, with reduced inventories, avoidance of stock-outs, and improved customer service. The value of supply chain collaboration lies in the broad exchange of planning, forecasting and inventory information to improve information accuracy when both the buyer and seller collaborate through joint knowledge of sales, promotions, and relevant supply and demand information.

Supply chain collaboration becomes a core competence in a global market. There are eye-opening collaborative results in forecasting and inventory management.

---

[1] The Association for Operations Management is formerly known as *American Production and Inventory Control Society (APICS)*.

Nabisco and Wegmans, for example, noted over a 50% increase in category sales. Wal-Mart and Sara Lee reported a 14% reduction in store-level inventory with a 32% increase in sales. Nevertheless, integrating disconnected planning and forecasting activities in the entire supply chain is still a challenge. It has been reported that supply chain collaboration has proved difficult to implement; it is difficult to understand when and with whom to collaborate; it has relied too much on information technology and there is a lack of trust between trading partners [10].

Given the literature and anecdotal evidence, we may conclude that supply chain collaboration has great potential in supply chain management, but further investigation is needed to understand its practical value. As such, we hypothesize the following:

Hypothesis 1: The higher the level of enterprise information technology use for exploitation the greater the supply chain perceived level of collaborative planning.

Hypothesis 2: The higher the level of enterprise information technology use for exploitation the greater the supply chain perceived level of collaborative forecasting and replenishment.

Hypothesis 3: The higher the level of enterprise information technology use for exploration the greater the supply chain perceived level of collaborative planning.

Hypothesis 4: The higher the level of enterprise information technology use for exploration the greater the supply chain perceived level of collaborative forecasting and replenishment.

The VICS Working Group conceptualized a sequential collaborative process [12]. The process has nine steps which are divided into three phases. The first is planning phase, which consists of steps 1 and 2, and creates the collaborative front-end agreement and joint business plan. The second is the forecasting phase, including steps 3-8, and the last is the replenishment phase (step 9). Specifically, a sequential process is introduced. The second and third phases execute supply chain orders which are translated from the joint business plan which is determined at the first phase [4].

The importance of collaborative has been well documented. For example, in the spring of 2001, Sears and Michelin (a French company) began discussions on collaborative planning. Later that year, their joint plan detailed a collaborative forecasting and replenishment agreement. As the result of collaboration, the combined Michelin and Sears inventory levels were reduced by 25 percent [13].   This supports our following hypothesis.

Hypothesis 5: The higher the level of collaborative planning the better the execution of collaborative forecasting and replenishment.

2.3   The Relationship between Supply Chain Collaboration and Performance

Research consistently supports the idea that collaboration in supply chain improves firm's operational performance and market competitiveness [6].   Companies that are able to establish collaborative relationship with their supply chain partners will have a significant competitive edge over their competitors. Industry practices have provided numerous examples. Mayo audio-video franchise store in Shanghai applied enterprise technology to support its collaborative planning, forecasting and replenishment activities and achieved better operational performance such as cost reduction and better market performance such as market share growth [14]. Dell Computer implements a "direct model" which builds customized computers based on customer orders. It collaborates with many of its suppliers and applies the Internet-based enterprise technology. The exploitation of enterprise technology enables Dell to implement JIT-based production system; while the exploration of enterprise technology enables Dell to develop innovative business model which opens up new markets for it. This leads us to the next two hypotheses.

Hypothesis 6: Collaborative planning, forecasting and replenishment in supply chain will directly benefit a firm's operations performance.
Hypothesis 7: Better operations performance will contribute to supply chain market performance.

3   Research Methodology

3.1   Data and Constructs

The research instrument was based upon the existing literature and pre-tested by a group of practicing managers in China, who had enterprise information technology implementation experience and supply chain collaboration knowledge. The instrument was then revised according to the suggestions from the managers. The revised questionnaire was sent in year 2006 to a group of 1000 manufacturing firms. Our effective sample size for this analysis is 177.

Six constructs based on Figure 1 are used to test the hypotheses. Among them, two constructs are used for enterprise information technology assimilation: enterprise information technology for exploitation (EIT) and enterprise information technology use for exploration (ERT). Based on March's discussion of organizational learning theory [1] and published studies on enterprise technology use [15], we define enterprise technology use for *exploitation* as the use of EIT for production scheduling, material requirement, the implementation of structured inter-firm processes such as order processing and order shipment facilitation. These items are measured on a seven-point Likert scale, ranging from not important (1) to absolutely critical (7).

Given the wide variation in definitions and usage of the concept in the literature, the collaborative activities suggested in this study are just one of many ways that can be applied to capture the overall thrust of supply chain collaboration through technology implementation. In this study, supply chain collaboration is measured by two constructs; one deals with collaborative planning (CP) and the other collaborative forecasting and replenishment (FR). We structure collaborative activities to two constructs because one is at the planning level and the other at the operational level [4]. A number of authors suggest that collaborative planning processes such as joint decision-making and planning precede operational collaboration such as demand forecasting and inventory replenishment [3]. The collaboration constructs are also assessed on a seven-point Likert scale, ranging from significantly lower (1) to significantly higher (7) as compare to their previous supply chain activities.

The operational performance construct (OP) is based on the published operations management literature [5] [15]. Inventory represents the material flow in supply chain and is the physical item that the suppliers send to its customers. The focus is placed on inventory accuracy, safety stock reduction, delivery lead time and order fulfillment lead time [15]. Operations performance items are measured from "not improved (1)" to "significantly improved (7)."

The market performance construct has empirical support. The most commonly cited financial performance indicators are market share growth, economic growth opportunity, and customer retention [13]. The performance items are measured on a 7-point Likert scale, ranging from significantly lower (1) to significantly higher (7) as compared to the firm's pre-implementation performance.

Structural equation model is employed to test the hypothesized relations among six constructs. Structural equation modeling measures multiple relationships between independent and dependent variables, thus accommodating aggregated dependent relationships simultaneously in one comprehensive model.

3.2   Construct Measure and Reliability

Our conceptual model involves relationships among six constructs. In this section, we provide evidence that the measurement of these constructs has been effective in terms of reliability and validity. All of the survey items that were used for measurement of the constructs are listed in Table 1. Empirical support for effective measurement is provided by a Cronbach Alpha. Enterprise technology for exploitation was measured using three items. The reliability for the scale is 0.81 (Table 1). Enterprise technology for exploration was measured using a three times. The reliability is 0.817 (Table 1). The reliabilities for collaborative planning and collaborative forecasting and replenishment are 0.756 and 0.868 respectively. Finally, the reliabilities for operational performance and market performance are 0.805 and 0.804 respectively.

4   Results

4.1   Structural Model Test Result

The results of the structural model tested evaluating overall model fit are shown in Fig. 2. Additionally, chisquare/df is 1.06, GFI is .916, AGFI is.890, CFI is .993, and RMSEA < .018; all meet the acceptable threshold. The standardized path coefficients are significant at p-value of $p< 0.01$ (Table 1). Combining the findings of fit indices obtained from the measurement model and the structural model, we can see that the sample data support our conceptual model. The following section presents the outcomes of hypotheses associated with the structural model.

4.2   Findings Related to Hypotheses

We further investigated the findings related to specific hypothesis and individual paths of the model.   The set of four hypotheses relate to enterprise technology and supply chain collaboration is examined first.

Hypothesis 1 is not significant.
Hypothesis 2 is supported at $p<0.10$ ($\gamma_1=0.157$).
Hypothesis 3 is supported at $p<0.01$ ($\gamma_2=0.462$).
Hypothesis 4 is supported at $p<0.01$ ($\gamma_3=0.257$).

This set of findings reveals some valuable insights on how enterprise technologies facilitate supply chain collaboration. The result suggests that applying enterprise technology for exploitation directly affects operational collaboration such as demand forecasting and inventory replenishment. However, it does not have a significant impact on collaborative planning. Furthermore, applying enterprise technology for exploration, which focuses on identifying the trends in sales and operations management and leveraging firm's expertise to create new markets and production, has direct positive effect on both collaborative planning and collaborative forecasting and replenishment. The results from this study underscore the complexity of the construct of enterprise technology exploitation and indicate that exploration may have an overarching impact on supply chain collaboration. These findings suggest that enterprise technology use creates a unique and specific value to collaborations within supply chain.

Next, we look at the hypothesis that relates the collaborative planning construct to collaborative forecasting and replenishment.

Hypothesis 5 is supported at $p<0.01$ ($\beta_1=0.3901$).

The finding provides support for the sequential process of collaborative planning and collaborative operational activities. A possible explanation is that sharing information through enterprise technology and making collaborative plans are not enough to improve operations performance. In order to achieve better inventory and lead time performance, supply chain managers have to be able to get involved with the complexity of collaborative planning with multiple echelons in a supply chain and implement the plan through demand forecast and inventory management.   This finding is consistent with the result obtained by Disney et al. [16].

Finally, we examined the hypotheses that relate supply chain collaboration to operations and market performance.

Hypothesis 6 is supported at $p<0.01$ ($\beta_2=0.2842$).

Hypothesis 7 is supported at $p<0.01$ ($\beta_3=0.6189$).

Table 1. Scales and Constructs

		Standard coefficient	t-value	Cronbach alpha
EIT1	Use ET to schedule production and plan material requirement	0.625	8.54	0.81
EIT2	Use ET to process order and invoices, and establish new accounts	1.015	14.61	
EIT3	Use ET to share delivery information and facilitate shipments	0.697	9.95	
ERT1	Understand trends in sales & operations management	0.801	11.74	0.817
ERT2	Integrate production design and manufacturing functions	0.861	12.89	
ERT3	Leverage firm's expertise to create new business opportunities	0.674	9.44	
CP1	Production planning information and data are shared with channel members	0.346	4.24	0.756
CP2	The channel managers communicate on overall business decisions	0.725	9.84	
CP3	Planning for new markets and products with channel members	0.573	7.45	
CP4	Production & capacity are jointly planned	0.799	11.03	
FR1	Sales forecasting & demand mgt are developed through supply chain coordination	0.753	11.02	0.868
FR2	Inventory level information is shared within the supply chain	0.757	11.09	
FR3	Delivery schedule and responsibilities are detailed in contracts	0.807	12.13	
FR4	Channel-wide available-to-promise system is implemented	0.710	10.17	
OP1	Inventory performance has improved, safety stock and stock out has reduced due to collaboration	0.766	10.47	0.805
OP2	Lead time has reduced due to supply chain collaboration	0.851	11.73	
MP1	Created new products and new markets	0.765	10.99	0.804
MP2	Learned new economic growth opportunity and developed new business opportunities	0.803	11.71	
MP3	Improved customer retaining and attracted new customers	0.720	10.17	

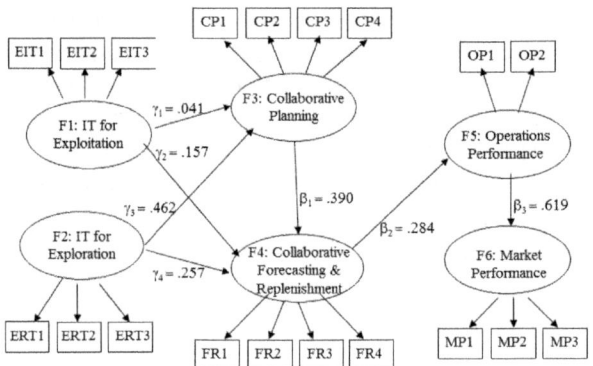

Fig. 2. Covariance Structure Model

The findings suggest that collaborative forecasting and replenishment will significantly benefit operational performance. Better operations performance is found to have a significant impact on firm's market performance.

In summary, six of seven hypotheses have been supported by the results of the statistical analysis using data from 177 Chinese firms. Examining the results, some tentative conclusions can be made. First, enterprise information technology implementation significantly affects collaborative planning, forecasting, and inventory replenishment in a supply chain. Second, supply chain collaboration benefits firm's operational performance. Finally, market competitiveness is influenced by operations performance.

5   Conclusions

The study considers how collaborative activities mediate the association between enterprise information technology assimilation and market performance in supply chain. We draw upon an empirical research from 177 companies to illustrate what collaborative activities will enable supply chain to achieve better operational and market performance, given their particular enterprise information technology implementation circumstances. We have provided three major contributions in this study: (i) uncovered importance of leveraging enterprise information technology use through supply chain collaboration; (ii) identified the relationship between enterprise ownership and enterprise technology use and supply chain collaboration; and (iii) illustrated the association between collaborative activities, operational benefits, and supply chain market performance. The result of the study indicates that assisted with advanced information technology, successful collaboration among trading partners does affect firm's operational and market performance if effective communication in the process of supply chain coordination is fostered.

There are a number of avenues this research can be extended to. For example, further research on collaboration of supply chain may include risk assessment of collaboration, optimal point of product-differentiation in a supply chain, selection of trading partners, the effects vertical collaboration, horizontal collaboration, and spatial collaboration on performance.

References

1. March, J.G.: Exploration and exploitation in organizational learning. Organization Science 2(1), 71–87 (1991)
2. Subramani, M.: How do suppliers benefit from information technology use in supply chain relationships? MIS Quarterly 28(1), 45–73 (2004)
3. VICS, CPFR Guidelines. Voluntary Inter-industry Commerce Standards (2000), http://www.cpfr.org
4. Danes, P., Romano, P., Vinelli, A.: Managing business processes across supply networks: the role of coordination mechanisms. Journal of Purchasing and Supply Management 10(4-5), 165–177 (2004)

5. Zhou, H., Benton, W.C.: Supply chain practice and information sharing. Journal of Operations Management 25, 1348–1365 (2007)
6. Li, L.: Assessing Intermediate Infrastructural Manufacturing Decisions that Affect a Firm's Market Performance. International Journal of Production Research 43(12), 2537–2552 (2005)
7. Tokman, M.: Exploration, exploitation and satisfaction in supply chain portfolio strategy. Journal of Business Logistics 28(1), 25–56 (2007)
8. Debenham, J., Wilkinson, I.: Exploitation and exploration in market competition. Industry and Innovation 13(3), 263–289 (2006)
9. Cutler, D.: CPFR: Time for the breakthrough. Supply Chain Management Review, 54–60 (May/June 2003)
10. Barratt, M.: Understanding the meaning of collaboration in the supply chain. Supply Chain Management: An International Journal 9(1), 30–42 (2004)
11. Li, L., Su, Q., Chen, X.: Ensuring Supply Chain Quality Performance through Applying SCOR Model. International Journal of Production Research 49(1), 33–57 (2011)
12. Seifert, D.(ed): Collaborative Planning, Forecasting, and Replenishment: How to Create a Supply Chain Advantage, AMACOM, pp. 27–40, 173–176. American Management Association, USA (2003)
13. Steermann, H.: A practical look at CPFR: the Sears - Michelin experience. Supply Chain Management Review, 46–53 (July/August 2003)
14. Wang, W., Guan, J., Yuan, Y., Chan, L.: CPFR and Its Application in Shanghai Maya (2004), http://www.pacis-net.org
15. Kelle, P., Akbulut, A.: The role of ERP tools in supply chain information sharing, cooperation, and cost optimization. International Journal of Production Economics 93-94, 41–52 (2005)
16. Disney, S.M., Naim, M.M., Potter, A.: Assessing the impact of e-business on supply chain dynamics. International Journal of Production Research 89, 109–118 (2004)

Changing Foundations for Global Business Systems

Dmitrij Slepniov[1], Brian Vejrum Wæhrens[1], and Ebbe Gubi[2]

[1] Center for Industrial Production, Aalborg University, Fibigerstraede 10,
9220 Aalborg, Denmark
{ds,bvw}@production.aau.dk
[2] Grundfos Management, Martin Bachs Vej 3, 8850 Bjerringbro, Denmark

Abstract. Companies are actively seeking new competitive advantages by changing the location and ownership of their manufacturing processes. This process results in increasing fragmentation and dispersion of global business systems of companies. The purpose of this paper is to identify how companies may improve the integration of such business systems. The paper draws on a case study of a Danish industrial equipment firm. The paper describes and analyzes the company's operations network configurations, which lay at the foundations of the company's global business system. It is demonstrated how the operations configurations have been changing over time and affecting the overall business system. The paper identifies the key determinants and outcomes of this change. Moreover, it proposes how the design of operations configurations can be improved through the development of a distinct systemic approach to control and coordination.

Keywords: Business system, global operations capabilities, operations network configuration, case studies.

1   Introduction

The world is changing fast. To accommodate for this change, companies are under increasing pressure to develop new adequate structures for their operations systems. Facing intense competition, companies all over the world are seeking to achieve a higher degree of efficiency and effectiveness by constantly reconfiguring their value networks and subsequently relocating discrete value-added activities to most appropriate destinations. This process may be confined only to crossing geographic borders and occur on an 'intrafirm' basis (i.e. offshoring). However, increasingly, in many industries (e.g., textile, footwear, IT services) it has also been accompanied by vertical disintegration of activities (i.e. outsourcing to external suppliers) [1], [12].

It goes without saying that the idea of global dispersion of work is not new. The existing industrial networks scholarship (e.g. [9], [16]), provides a point of departure for understanding how global operations units are configured on a global basis and consist of diverse and interdependent affiliates (linked both through ownership and non-equity relationships), which are engaged in an exchange of goods, services and information. [7] points to the essential dynamism and organizational temporality

C. Møller and S. Chaudhry (Eds.): CONFENIS 2011, LNBIP 105, pp. 211–222, 2012.

of such global operations agglomerates. With the spread of offshoring and fragmentation of operations, the networks temporality and frequent reconfiguration trends are likely to continue. We argue that the constant 'process of becoming' [17] in global operations networks poses a serious challenge for global business system management and the development of adequate systems tools and solutions. in order to avoid. Therefore, this paper investigates how changing operations configurations affect business systems of companies and how companies can establish fitness for continually evolving operations configurations.

The empirical part of the paper is based on a case study of a large Danish industrial equipment company. The offshoring process has affected most parts of its value chain activities and is no longer confined to simple or non-core activities. This process has pushed the company into the development of more elaborate operations strategy structures and infrastructures. The case testifies how Danish companies have advanced far in relocating and reconfiguring most parts of their value chain. However, this has been achieved at great initial cost of intense coordination efforts. Drawing on the experiences of the case study, the key argument of this paper is that companies need to understand the logic, factors and determinants of their global business systems and how they change over time. Such an understanding will enhance companies' ability to build and continuously upgrade organizational capabilities, support systems and knowledge supporting the integration between the lead firm and the increasingly dispersed operations network

The following section introduces the theoretical background of the study. We then proceed with the methods and the case study used in the paper. Next, the analysis and discussion are presented, before we conclude with key lessons and implications for future research.

2   Theoretical Background

2.1   Business Systems

The global business system is a rather vague concept, which has been applied at multiple levels of analysis. At one end, there is the economic concept of the national business system [20] dealing with the national institutions and conditions for conducting various business processes. At the company level, the business system has been used to describe the organisation, mode and scope of operations [15]. And at the operational level, the business system is often discussed as the specific tools supporting and or governing operations and operations development [6]. One key dimension of the latter perspective on business system is that the business system imposes its own logic on the company and the company often fails to reconcile the technical standards embedded in the system with its specific business needs [6].

In this paper, the business system is discussed as a combination of these perspectives, drawing on the idea that the business system builds on a set of structural and infrastructural means which enable the company to create, deliver and appropriate value. This does not alone include internal resources and capabilities, but also the company's ability to get access to external resources and capabilities. The paper will be working from the thesis that it is from the understanding of all the above conditions for business that we should draw our knowledge about how to configure the business system appropriately.

2.2   Organizing Principles of Global Business Systems

The business system approach [20] focuses on the effect of factors in the institutional environment on organizations. The basic dimensions of coping with these effects are: 1) coordination, i.e. the mode and extent of organisational integration through common routines, systems and management standards; and 2) control, i.e. the way the activities and resources are controlled within the organization. These two dimensions are also important for determining the degree of centralisation and decentralisation. Prior research (e.g. [14]) differentiates between three major types of organisational structures: centralized, decentralized and hybrid. Centralized structures are characterized by tight coordination and control mechanisms where decision-making authority concentrated at the top of an organisation. In decentralized structures, on the other hand, decision-making authority is pushed down to the business units level making such a structure particularly suitable for organisations with markedly different or even unique business units. In practice, however, most companies have adopted a hybrid approach that combines attributes of both centralized and decentralized form with the intention to overcome centralization-decentralization tradeoffs.

In the strategic management literature, the dimensions of control and coordination are used in defining four basic business configurations with distinctive governance forms: the multinational, the global, the international, and the transnational [4]. The transnational mode helps companies to achieve simultaneously global efficiency of the global mode, national responsiveness of the multinational mode and the ability to exploit knowledge emphasised in the international mode [4]. The transnational mode recognises the importance of decentralisation and responsiveness to cultural differences and, thus, retains national in its name. On the other hand, the transnational mentality also emphasises linking and coordinating between globally dispersed operations, as indicated by the prefix "trans". These four configurations in turn has formed the outset for addressing ERP architectures [5] dealing with the basic dilemma of balancing local responsiveness and global efficiency of the system.

Among other theories providing insights into the foundations for organizing global business systems is the resource-based view (RBV). The view adds an important dimension to this discussion. The fundamental principle of RBV is that the basis for a competitive advantage of a firm lies primarily in the application of the bundle of valuable resources at the firm's disposal [3]. These advantages are dependent on organisational trajectories, which build intrinsic organisational capabilities. The transformation of a short-run competitive advantage into a sustained competitive advantage requires that these resources are heterogeneous in nature and not perfectly transferable; in other words, they develop proprietary properties and are embedded in a specific set of context variables. Within the multinational company these resources are highly dispersed as local entities specialise. According to the RBV, the activities that enable an organisation to outperform competition should be nurtured and defended. However, the multinational company may have incentives to inject more discipline and centralized control into their dispersed operations if the costs of responsiveness significantly outweigh its benefits.

2.3   Offshoring Trends and Challenges of Continuous Reconfiguration

With the growth of offshoring, the move of competitive resources from intra-organisational base to the inter-organisational network settings is also gaining pace. In other words, the resource bases are getting stretched across locations or even organisations. The practice shows that some more mature and experienced companies are better than others equipped for dynamic, fragmented and to a large degree external set-ups of their operations. However, even these more mature companies cannot avoid challenges and costs of dealing with such complexity. Within a loosely coupled global inter-organisational network, the situation is exacerbated event further in cases of non-standard products, products with integral product architectures, and products whose output is time-sensitive [2].

However, these challenges and costs differ depending on robustness and transferability [10] of the tasks in question. An operations process is robust if its sensitivity to external factors (e.g. managerial practices, infrastructure, and government requirements) is low. Transferability here refers to how easy the process can be captured, decontextualised, transmitted and assimilated. High robustness and high transferability may be highly desired for implementing the offshoring decision. However, referring back to the arguments of the RBV, high robustness and high transferability of all processes may reduce the uniqueness of business and undermine the sustainability of competitive advantages, which in turn may push the company to choose a more integrated organizational mode.

It can be argued that few manufacturing processes possess a sufficient robustness and transferability levels to allow for perfect mobility or a standardised organizational infrastructure, which is also supported by [5] in their discussion of global ERP configuration. This raises the question of configuring business systems solutions to key contingencies. Addressing this effectively means that not only the hardware of the support system has to be changed; the process also involves building organizational capability for global operations through systems, processes, product adaptations and preparing the organization mentally. However, how this can be achieved remains a key unresolved question and therefore this paper explores the following research question: *how can companies effectively coordinate and control globally dispersed tasks which are embedded in differentiated and constantly changing organizational contexts.*

3   Methodology and Data

The primary data set for this study is derived from a case of Danish industrial equipment firm. The case was followed intensely by the authors in 2009-2011. We have interviewed COO and supply chain managers about the process, means, and strategies supporting their international operations.

The case study strategy, one of several strategies of qualitative enquiry, has been chosen for this investigation for several reasons. First, case studies can describe, enlighten and explain real-life phenomena that are too complex for other approaches requiring tightly structured designs or pre-specified data sets [18], [19]. Second, the case study strategy is well-equipped instrumentally for furthering understanding of particular issues or concepts which have not been deeply investigated so far ([8], [19]). Third, the choice of the case study strategy is based on the fit between case research and operations management (OM) [18], which is acknowledged but underexplored in the literature.

Despite having many advantages, case study research also has several pitfalls and poses significant challenges (e.g. [13]). First, there is the problem of the observer's perceptual and cognitive limitation. Second, a high probability of overlooking some key events also constitutes a threat to the quality of case studies research. Third, case studies are exposed to the challenge of generalizability. Fourth, the accuracy of some inferences can be undermined by the reliance on intuition and subjective interpretation of an investigator. To address these challenges, we followed practical guidelines and steps discussed in qualitative methodology literature (e.g. [18], [19]). The current research relied on extensive use of triangulation. Multiple sources of evidence (semi-structured interviews, documents and on-site observations) as well as triangulation of multiple data-points within each source of evidence (e.g. multiple respondents at the top and middle management levels) were used. These data combined with secondary material (annual reports, media material, presentation material to customers and stakeholders) were used to build the database for the case.

3.1   Case Study: Distributed Operations at a Danish Industrial Equipment Firm

The case company is a Danish equipment manufacturer holding a market leader position. With production in twelve countries and a global sales presence, it was working from a strong international base. The company had been acquiring approximately one production company every year since 2000 and with these new subsidiaries, it also inherited a number of business systems, processes and product configurations. By 2011, it had incorporated more than 80 companies, spanning all time zones, 90 languages and more than 100 product families. These developments were signaling a change of mindset from an early ideology of original in-house development, tight control and green-field investments.

Some of the newly acquired firms still controlled their own business agenda, while others were fully integrated under a corporate business system. The pace of acquisition had quickened recently in par with the restructuring of their main product's market characterized by increased concentration, and firms moving from component to system suppliers, adding more competencies. When referring to the business approach one of the company's executives defined it as 'centrally driven global approach with a local presence'. Such an approach inevitably resulted in a highly complex business system characterized by:

- Sales and operations location diversity: Some products were produced in one factory and sold world-wide, other products were produced in the region where they are sold,
- Components supply base diversity: Many components for local assembly were produced in one or a few factories; some components were also shared across product families
- Multiple product/solution configurations: Sales responding to local needs and standards resulting in many potential product/solutions configurations
- Multiple approaches to operations: Network consisted of all operations approaches from make-to-stock to engineered-to-order
- Diverse and dynamic operations network: The global operations network was emerging with addition of new facilities many of which had their own operation conditions

The Danish HQ had the strategic vision of establishing tighter control of foreign subsidiaries with regards to global capacity footprint, R&D and process ownership. However, each business unit had its own budget and certain latitude to select projects, allocate resources and responsibilities. Consequently, coordination efforts were organized in a corporate management function with a key focus on embedding a corporate culture, developing group standards and policies. But the entrepreneurial spirit of the individual subsidiaries remained and was seen as a key driver of development and all KPIs remained related to local operations performance, resulting in what could be termed a loosely coupled global supply chain.

The company was structured around a fundamental process perspective where the interaction between Production, Product Development and the Technology Center played a special role. With Technology Centers being responsible for technology development and establishment of production lines, a certain degree of coordination was necessary to serve their two customers, namely Production and Product Development. Although the main Production hub was still based in Denmark, parts of Production had already been widely offshored and a broad autonomy has been granted to regional hubs. With Product Development also moving out of Denmark, it made sense that Technology Centers followed its internal customers in their global expansion. Consequently, local hubs were opened in Hungary and China and a new hub was planned in Mexico/USA. Although there was a shared agenda at a higher level in relation to operations in different market segments, cooperation between foreign units was largely limited to brief collaboration on assignments and sharing of patents.

The economic downturn hit the company with a delay in 2009. The management group had just reported that the company seemed to be largely unaffected by the global crisis, when a drastic drop in turnover happened. Afterwards, it was unveiled that due to the largely decentralized reporting structure it took more than 6 months to stop component production, from the time it stopped to invoice the external customers. This experience taught the company a valuable lesson, namely that the loosely coupled operations network could not react swiftly to major changes on the market. To respond to this challenge, a strategic decision was made initiating global integration of Demand and Supply.

For implementing this decision, the company introduced a number of new technologies and processes, which challenged the decentralized approach to the global network of facilities fulfilling demand and consolidating demand planning. An overlaying federal structure was introduced to the global network consisting of a number of business system tools:

- A new process for Integrated Demand and Supply Planning
- New roles and changed responsibilities across the supply chain
- New SAP modules to support the process and decision-making
- A product segmentation according to level of demand predictability and supply chain impact

For further coordination of strategic roles and responsibilities in the global business system these measures were introduced:

- Supply Chain focus and KPIs
- ONE PLAN – transparent and visible to all
- Global decision-making with local execution

The R&D function was also in need of better coordination. The company had over 1000 R&D staff globally, indicating that even highly complex tasks are increasingly dispersed. In the coming 5 - 7 years, this dispersion of activities was expected to grow further. To illustrate, the Asian hub was planned to have the same number of engineers as Denmark. This rapid growth could also be illustrated by the more than doubling of staff in China in just a year, to more than 100 engineers. Though R&D man power in China was growing fast, they had not launched any product range on their own yet, solely supporting central development activities. It was seen, however, that future responsibilities of developing products would be decentralized to a larger extent. One key driver of this was that China had a special status as a 'second home market' with a Managing Director reporting directly to the global board. Meanwhile efforts were also taken to develop the US market as its potential had traditionally been unrealized to the full extent. To illustrate, although the company introduced some product ranges over 50 years ago, it could only claim less than 10% share in the market.

It is expected that over time, despite the introduction of measures outlined above, each regional "Network" (Technology Center/Production/R&D) will grow increasingly independent and specialized, replicating best practices, but developing own capabilities, compatible with local culture and markets. The global organization will be nurtured through a positive iterative process by gradually increasing the level of complexity of tasks overseas. The parallel activities at different hubs of the company will continue until outposts reach critical mass or until they matured enough to absorb key competencies from headquarters or other hubs of the network.

4   Discussion and Implications

4.1   Changing Operations Configurations

As a point of departure to discussing the case company and its fitness for global operations, there is a need to highlight how the operations configurations of the company have been changing over time and how the overall business system has been affected as a result of that. The long period of acquisitions and offshoring moves resulted in the creation of a complex loosely coupled network of differentiated partners and affiliates working with a variety of business systems, processes and product configurations. The belief that responsiveness to local conditions should be answered by the development of local solutions led to a number of different standards for operations and a lacking ability to compare and organize a coordinated effort across sites.

The situation is hardly can be seen as unique or just this case specific. All companies are bound to their historical legacy. The long string of strategic and operational decisions introduces a certain dependency to firms' development trajectory making it difficult, if not impossible, to design such a system from a clean slate. The case study in this paper also illustrates how the business system evolves over time and how any system development initiative need to take the changing operational realities of the fragmented system into account. This in turn means that developing solutions and capabilities related to managing the evolving global business system poses a serious challenge for multinational companies.

Factors influencing operations in the case are added incrementally as new facilities are established or acquisitions are made, new markets are opened, new technologies are added, and new suppliers seek integration. These incidences mean that the system is in constant motion and that mechanisms of coordination and control are constantly challenged by diverging standards. While the operations of sites and companies may have a clear agenda and set of stakeholders, the network of operations is not tended to; it is no-one's business. This means that the network may indeed share a common vision, but that its common focus is disintegrated by design, as each entity develops through a series of incremental moves and decisions.

In many companies, this evolution and caused by it increased complexity call for reengineering of the overall business system and its supporting tools. Like any other engineered system, the business system is designed to nurture certain capabilities, and the system is likely to be good at doing certain things, but does so at the expense of others. Ultimately, this property of the system leads to trade-offs, which have to be dealt with. The issue may, however, be solved by focusing on the possible complementarities of the system elements rather than their conflicting characteristics. We know from the field of operations management that certain complementary effects can be gained from capabilities, which are often seen as conflicting [11]. This approach has won widespread recognition as a key organizing principle for a modern business world and transnational mode of operations [4]. However, it is also recognized that governance based on these principles are difficult to operationalize in practice.

4.2   Developing Adequate Global Business System Solutions

With these conditions an increasing number of manufacturers, like the case company, are significantly reshaping their global operations configuration, including radical increases in commitments to offshore operations in scale and scope. Very often such a reconfiguration is done based on expected short term capacity and cost implications. Meanwhile, the equally important aspects of how to realise global operations and to sustain competitive positioning in the longer term get lower priority. As the example in the case shows, the company struggled to utilise global operations potential or was faced with unintended risks as it did shortly after the global economic downturn in 2009. Circumventing these negative effects requires a conscious build-up of organisational capabilities in support of global operations; which we refer to as the build-up of fitness for global operations.

When discussing the configuration of such a fragmented system configuration comprising both internal and outsourced operations, the overall system's performance should be emphasized. As systems theory suggests, any system is not just the sum of the individual parts. If an operations configuration and the relationships between units in it are not optimal, the company risks a negative synergy. The case clearly demonstrates this situation because increased performance in one factory in the network is not necessarily equal improved performance in the overall supply chain.

To tackle this, the company tried to find an optimum balance between centralization and decentralization. On the one hand, to compensate for slow response and the increased distance among their operations, the company worked on introducing a more formalized form of working. On the other hand, the company nurtured plans of upgrading its regional hubs and maintaining a high degree of responsiveness. In some instances, they compensated for the lack of direct control over the physical flow of goods by standardization and in some cases by letting go of the responsibility to suppliers. The standardization can also be observed in companies who in spite of their overall preference for direct ownership, still face the increasing distance between their HQ and subsidiaries or try to establish or utilize the economies of scale in their value chains. There is also evidence in the case to support the proposition that standardization increased the company's ability to change faster and maintain continuous improvements on a global scale.

We can conclude from this that the ownership ties that exist within the vertically integrated multinational company do not necessarily preclude the entire range of discretionary behaviors that are possible among interacting organizations that are geographically dispersed. Paradoxically, despite predominantly ownership-based relationships in the case, control was limited not only because some of the subsidiaries happen to be very physically distant and resource-rich, but also because they controlled critical linkages with key actors, such as suppliers and customers. Direct control originating from vertical integration was present in the case company, but it was limited due to its co-existence with local autonomy, inherited and diverse systems, and work cultures, which were also recognized as necessary for maintaining responsiveness to various local market demands.

In terms of explaining a particular offshoring trajectory in the case, the company specific task interdependency and the related ties between partners may be useful. For understanding why the case company experienced correlating offshoring trends across all major functions (i.e. Production, Product Development and Technology Centers), the particular relational density of a given set of activities is key. Relational density is made-up from the rate at which industries change in terms of products, processes and organizations and may be explained as the need for thickness of relational infrastructure.

It is evident that the case company has developed a high level of fitness for global operations as it advanced quite far with its global operations capability. However, the case also shows that, figuratively speaking, the company has been building the bridge while walking on it. Responding to upcoming challenges, it pushed standardization efforts, built up an integration mechanism and initiated relations building and resource pooling to build economies of scale and scope.

The case clearly demonstrated that continuous dynamics and change became inherent characteristics of the operations configurations. In this context, the old fashioned efficiency-alone-oriented global business system solutions become irrelevant. Therefore, the company faced the challenge of developing a solution which enabled it to achieve the optimum balance between local responsiveness and global efficiency. The efforts that the company instigated led to an increased systematisation of the business system and increased awareness of processes at its various levels, namely corporate management (challenging decentralisation approach e.g. through global Demand and Supply synchronization) and individual sites level (having enough autonomy for ensuring local responsiveness). The cases company carefully studied its opportunities for outsourcing parts of the operations network or otherwise extending the reach of its operations management beyond the organizational boundary as a means to focus on product development, assembly and distribution.

This systemic approach the company was developing emphasized not only short-term operational efficiency, but also increasingly longer-term strategic effectiveness.

Some of the key determinants of the system included:

- Overall system performance focus
- Limitations of direct ownership control and coordination
- Relational fitness (relational density)
  - Availability of a sourcing market driving cost opportunities and pooling of resources
  - Weak or strong ties between value chain actors
  - Types of cross-functional interdependence necessary to accomplish tasks
- Strategic reconciliation between Supply and Demand

The institutional support was also available for establishing global operations on a site-by-site basis within the organizational context as well as facilitated by the developments in the external context. However, the case also stresses how the global business system is affected beyond just the stage of establishing individual sites or contracting with an external service or manufacturing provider. It rather emerges and as an effect of this emerging process, there seems to be a clear trajectory to the internationalization of the operations system, which over time gradually changes its center of gravity to offshore destinations and absorbes new roles and responsibilities in this process. Mature offshoring decisions are characterized by their move beyond the piecemeal type decisions. They rather initiate an organizational process, which accounts for systems effects and is not just about getting something produced in a specific location, but rather about orchestrating a network of interlinked activities, which raise multiple new demands on management capabilities and management systems.

5 Conclusion

The business system evolves over time rather than is designed from a clean slate. This in turn means that developing solutions and capabilities related to managing the evolving global business system poses a serious challenge for multinational companies. Factors influencing operations are added incrementally and mean that the system is in constant motion and that mechanisms of coordination and control are constantly challenged by diverging standards. While the operations of sites and companies have a clear agenda and set of stakeholders, the network of operations is not tended to; it is no-one's business.

The purpose of the paper has been to investigate how companies can effectively coordinate and control globally dispersed tasks which are embedded in differentiated and constantly changing organizational contexts thereby establishing fitness for global operations. The findings of the investigation show that the traditional manufacturers are significantly reshaping their global operations configurations, including radical increase in offshore production. On the basis of the existing literature and the case-based example, the study identifies key determinants of the system aimed at striking a balance between seemingly irreconcilable global efficiency and local responsiveness. Moreover, it proposes how the design of operations configurations can be improved through the development of a distinct systemic approach to control and coordination.

This paper adds to the existing literature by unfolding the aspects of organisational capability required for improving the integration of globally dispersed business system and successful development of global operations. The awareness of inherent organisational capabilities often only emerges in the situation where the company fails to establish a required level of quality, gain sufficient advantages from their global scope of operations or fail to reproduce proprietary practices at a new location. As this study demonstrated, due to the integration needs and the interdependencies between globally dispersed tasks, this challenge is persistent and reveals itself even in more experienced companies.

References

1. Aron, R., Singh, J.V.: Getting Offshoring Right. Harvard Business Review 83(12), 135–143 (2005)
2. Baldwin, C.Y., Clark, K.B.: The Power of Modularity. MIT Press, Cambridge (2000)

3. Barney, J.B.: Firm Resources and Sustained Competitive Advantage. Journal of Management 17, 99–120 (1991)
4. Bartlett, C.A., Ghoshal, S.: Managing Across Borders: The Transnational Solution. Harvard Business School Press, Boston (2002)
5. Clemmons, S., Simon, S.J.: Control and Coordination in Global ERP Configuration. Business Process Management Journal 7(3), 205–215 (2001)
6. Davenport, T.H.: Putting the Enterprise into the Enterprise System. Harvard Business Review 76(4), 121–131 (1998)
7. Dicken, P.: Global shift: Mapping the Changing Contours of the World Economy. Guilford, New York (2007)
8. Eisenhardt, K.M.: Building Theories from Case Study Research. Academy of Management Review 14(4), 532–550 (1989)
9. Ferdows, K.: Made in the World: The Global Spread of Production. Production and Operations Management 6(2), 102–109 (1997)
10. Grant, E.B., Gregory, M.J.: Adapting Manufacturing Processes for International Transfer. International Journal of Operations & Production Management 17(10), 994–1005 (1997)
11. Hallgren, M., Olhager, J., Schroeder, R.G.: A Hybrid Model of Competitive Capabilities. International Journal of Operations & Production Management 31(5), 511–526 (2011)
12. Kotabe, M., Murray, J.Y.: Global Sourcing Strategy and Sustainable Competitive Advantage. Industrial Marketing Management 33, 7–14 (2004)
13. Meredith, J.: Building Operations Management Theory through Case and Field Research. Journal of Operation Management 16(4), 441–454 (1998)
14. Narasimhan, R., Carter, J.R.: Organization, Communication and Co-ordination of International Sourcing. International Marketing Review 7(2), 6–20 (1989)
15. Normann, R., Ramírez, R.: From Value Chain to Value Constellation: Designing Interactive Strategy. Harvard Business Review 71, 65–77 (1993)
16. Shi, Y., Gregory, M.: Emergence of Global Manufacturing Virtual Networks and Establishment of New Manufacturing Infrastructure for Faster Innovation and Firm Growth. Production Planning & Control 16(6), 621–631 (2005)
17. Slepniov, D., Waehrens, B.V.: Offshore Outsourcing of Production - an Exploratory Study of Process and Effects in Danish Companies. Strategic Outsourcing: An International Journal 1, 64–76 (2008)
18. Voss, C.: Case Research in Operations Management. In: Karlsson, C. (ed.) Researching Operations Management, pp. 162–196. Routledge, New York (2009)
19. Yin, R.K.: Case Study Research - Design and Methods. Sage, Thousand Oaks (2009)
20. Whitley, R.: Divergent Capitalisms: The Social Structuring and Change of Business Systems. Oxford University Press, Oxford (1999)

Author Index